THE
POPE'S
JEWS

THE
POPE'S
JEWS

THE VATICAN'S SECRET PLAN TO
SAVE JEWS FROM THE NAZIS

GORDON THOMAS

\Rᵖ\
The Robson Press

First published in Great Britain in 2013 by
The Robson Press (an imprint of Biteback Publishing Ltd)
Westminster Tower
3 Albert Embankment
London SE1 7SP
Copyright © Gordon Thomas 2012

ISBN 978-1-84954-506-8

10 9 8 7 6 5 4 3 2 1

A CIP catalogue record for this book is available from the British Library.

Originally published in the United States of America by Thomas Dunne Books, an imprint
of St. Martin's Press

Set in Dante

Printed and bound in Great Britain by
CPI Group (UK) Ltd, Croydon CR0 4YY

For Edith,
a full partner in all respects.
Her intelligence, determination, and high standards
improved this book in so many ways.

CONTENTS

RESEARCHERS

RESEARCH COORDINATOR
Edith Maria Thomas.

RESEARCHERS
The Rome Ghetto
Tina Cappelini.
Professor Marco Cavallarin. Author and historian.
Miriam Hayun. Director, Jewish Center of Culture.
Dr. Ricardo Pacifici. President of the Jewish community.
Dr. Ricardo Di Segni. Chief rabbi of Rome.
Simoneta Sacerdoti. Niece of Dr. Sacerdoti.
Luciana Tedesco. Author, cousin of Dr. Vittorio Sacerdoti.
Nando Tagliacozzo. Author and lecturer.

The Vatican
Sister Margherita Marchione. Author and pictorial archivist.
Father David-Maria Jaeger. Secretariat of state.

Israel

Meir Ben-Naftali.

Gilah Bronstein.

Alex Doran. *Ma'ariv* newspaper.

Rachel Ginsberg. Associate editor, *Mispacha* magazine.

Miro Muscati.

Itzhak Raz Rathaus.

Flora Shrit.

Einat Yaakov.

United Kingdom

Sophie Brackenbury.

Emanuelle Degli Esposti.

Greg Lewis.

Cesare Sacerdoti.

United States

William Doino.

PHOTO RESEARCH

Peter Durling.

PRINCIPAL PERSONAE

Ranks and positions are those held in 1943.

The Vatican

Pope Pius XII. Roman-born Eugenio Pacelli. When the Germans occupied Rome he held a secret meeting in the Vatican to plan how to save the city's Jews and Allied prisoners of war.

Monsignor Patrick Carroll-Abbing. Irish priest who used his ambulance to rescue Jews.

Monsignor Angelo Dell 'Acqua. Liaison with relief organizations.

Monsignor Borgongini Duca. Holy See envoy to Italy.

Monsignor Marcel Hérissé. Canon of St. Peter's Basilica.

Bishop Alois Hudal. Rector of the Pan-Germanic college in Rome for training German priests. Longtime member of the Nazi Party and informer for German intelligence. Postwar: arranged for top Nazi war criminals to flee to Latin America.

Monsignor Ludwig Kaas. In charge of St. Peter's Basilica.

Monsignor Robert Leiber. The pope's private secretary.

Sister Mary Saint Luke. American nun working in the Vatican Information Bureau. Diarist.

Cardinal Luigi Maglione. The Holy See's secretary of state and head of its global diplomatic service.

Monsignor Giovanni Battista Montini. Undersecretary for Ordinary Affairs and the future Pope Paul VI.

Monsignor Alfredo Ottaviani. Head of the Holy Office.

Father Pankratius Pfeiffer. The pope's personal liaison with the German high command.

Monsignor Angelo Giuseppe Roncalli. Papal nuncio to Turkey (later Pope John XXIII).

Colonel de Pfyffer d'Altishofen. Commander of the Swiss Guards.

Sister Pascalina. Confidante and mistress of the pope's household. Diarist.

Padre Nassalli Rocca. Pope's liaison to Regina Coeli prison.

Giovanni Stefanori. Pope's butler.

Monsignor Dominico Tardini. Assistant to secretary of state.

Count Giuseppe Dalla Torre. Editor of *L'Osservatore Romano*.

Father Anton Weber. Head of the Pallottine fathers in Rome.

Bishop Ivi Zeiger. Rector of the German college.

The Jewish Community

Dante Almansi. Deputy to Ugo Foa.

Lazzaro Anticoli. Garage mechanic.

Emma Anticoli. His wife.

Fernando Astrologo. Member of one of the oldest families in the ghetto.

Vittorio Astrologo. Jeweller.

Giuseppe Battino. Assisted peddler Mose Spizzichino.

Anselmo Colombo. Accountant.

Ugo Foa. President of Rome's Jewish community.

Elena Sonnino Finzi. Teacher at the ghetto school.

Serafino Pace. Ghetto tailor.

Italia Pace. Wife of Serafino Pace.

Aldo Pace. Son of Serafino Pace.

Graziano Perugia. Kosher butcher.

Angelo di Porto. Shopkeeper.

Mose Spizzichino. Peddler.

Grazia Spizzichino. His wife.

Settimia Spizzichino. Their daughter—the only woman survivor of the Nazi roundup.

Rosina Sorani. Foa's secretary in the ghetto synagogue and diarist.

Settimio Sorani. Brother of Rosina and chief executive of Delasem.

Umberto di Veroli. The ghetto's leading shopkeeper.

Maria Moscati/Alberto Limentani. Married in the ghetto synagogue shortly before the occupation.

Luciana Tedesco. Dr. Sacerdoti's young cousin who survived the daily struggle of living under the occupiers.

Arminio Wachsberger. Watchmaker.

Israel Zolli. Chief rabbi of Rome.

The *Fatebenefratelli*—the Jewish hospital on Tiber Island

Professor Giovanni Borromeo. Catholic director of the hospital.

Rosa Fiano. Worked as nursing aide after being chosen to hide in the hospital.

Tereza Marino. Renowned Hebrew teacher who became a nursing aid while sheltering in the hospital.

Yole Marino. A nurse's aide who later married the chief rabbi of Rome after he went to Palestine.

Dr. Vittorio Emanuele Sacerdoti. A young doctor in the ghetto hospital.

THE RELIEF WORKERS

Count de Salis. The Red Cross representative in Rome.

Renzo Levi. Jewish industrialist and president of Delasem, Jewish relief organization.

THE DIPLOMATS

Baron Diego von Bergen. German ambassador to the Holy See and doyen of the diplomatic corps. Replaced in 1943 for his anti-Nazi views.

Francois Charles-Roux. French ambassador to the Holy See. A brilliant strategist to get Pope Pius elected.

Count Galeazzo Ciano. Foreign minister to the Mussolini government.

Cordell Hull. United States secretary of state.

Albrecht von Kessel. First secretary at the German Embassy to the Holy See.

Sir Percy Loraine. British ambassador to Italy.

Sir Francis D'Arcy Osborne. British minister to the Holy See.

Myron Taylor. President Roosevelt's personal envoy to the pope.

Harold H. Tittmann. United States Charge d'Affaire in the Holy See.

Baron Ernst von Weizsäcker. German ambassador to the Holy See. He replaced von Bergen, but secretly shared his views.

Edward Wood, Lord Halifax. British foreign secretary.

THE GOSSIP MONGERS

Monsignor Enrico Pucci. Ran a news agency specializing in Vatican affairs. Worked for German intelligence.

Virgilio Scattolini. Journalist, playwright, novelist, and womanizer who became the most brazen and successful fabricator of intelligence about the Vatican. His prime client was the *Abwehr,* German secret service.

THE FASCISTS

Pietro Caruso. Chief of Rome police. Tried and executed for war crimes.

Carlo Sorza. National secretary of the Fascist Party.

Guido Buffarini Guidi. Minister of the Interiors. Described by Mussolini as the "most hated man in Italy—even more than me."

THE GERMAN OCCUPIERS

SS *Hauptsturmführer* Theodor Dannecker. Expert on the "Jewish Question."

SS *Sturmbannführer* Eugen Dollmann. *Reichsführer* Himmler's personal representative.

Obersturmbannführer Herbert Kappler. Head of the gestapo in Rome.

Field Marshal Albert Kesselring. Supreme commander of Italy.

General Kurt Mälzer. Stahel's successor.

General Rainer Stahel. Commandant of Rome.

General of the Waffen—SS Karl Friedrich Wolff. Supreme Commander
of all SS forces in Italy.

THE RESISTANCE
Ivanoe Bonomi. Head of the military council.
Rosario Bentivegna. Medical student who led the attack on Via Rasella.
Carla Capponi. Became a hunted fighter by the Germans.
Giulio Cortini. Bomb maker.
Laura Cortini. Bomb maker.
Giuseppe Morosini. Explosives expert.

THE SPIES
Admiral Wilhelm Canaris. Head of the *Abwehr*, German intelligence
service.
Claude Dansey. Deputy director of MI6.
Sefton Delmer. Journalist turned MI6 spy. Thwarted plot to kidnap the
pope.
Hans von Dohnanyi. Key member of plan to involve Pius in plot to
overthrow Hitler.
Stewart Menzies. Director general of MI6.
Josef Mueller. German lawyer who became an *Abwehr* spy and plotter to
overthrow Hitler.
Colonel Hans Oster. *Abwehr* agent. Involved in plot against Hitler.
Tony Simonds. Head of "N" section in MI9.

CRIMINAL GANGS
Pietro Koch. Head of the Banda Koch. Like the Black Panthers, was
recruited by the gestapo to hunt Jews.
Giovanni Mezzaroma. Head of the Banda Pantera Nero, the Black
Panthers.
Celeste di Porto. Jewish. Member of the Black Panthers and mistress of
Mezzaroma.

THE SECRET NETWORK

Father John Clafferty. Code name: "Eyerish."

Sam Derry. Major in the British army.

John May. Butler to Ambassador D'Arcy Osborne. Code name: "Fixer."

Monsignor O'Flaherty. Irish-born member of the Holy Office. Code name: "Golf."

Father Robert Pace. Code name: "Whitebows."

Father Thomas Ryan. Code name: "Rinso."

Father Owen Sneddon. Code name: "Horace."

Father Vincent Treacy. Code name: "Fanny."

Father Tom Tuomey. Code name: "Sailor."

Father Sean Quinlan. Code name: "Kerry."

THE BLACK NOBILITY

Princess Nina Pallavicini. A widow who was opposed to Mussolini.

Princess Enza Pignatelli Aragona Cortes. Close friend of Pope Pius XII.

Princess Virginia Agnelli. Daughter of the Fiat dynasty.

Marchesa Fulvia Ripa di Meana. Used her Vatican contacts to help Jews.

Prince Filippo Doria Pamphilj. Staunch anti-Fascist and anti-Nazi.

Princess Orietta Emily Mary Doria Pamphilj. Daughter of Prince Filippo.

FORETHOUGHTS

No crime in history has so deeply shocked mankind as did Hitler's Holocaust in World War Two. More than six million people— mostly Jews but not exclusively—were murdered and countless more still carry to this day the scars of their suffering. The horror inflicted has led to claims there are no new dimensions to explore of this unprecedented genocide. The truth is otherwise. Anti-Semitism remains the most odious of scourges, proof that little has changed from what Hitler wrote in a letter in 1919 to a comrade he had served with in the trenches of the Great War.

"Anti-Semitism on purely emotional grounds will find its final expression in the form of pogroms. However, rational anti-Semitism must lead to a carefully planned legal curbing and eradication of Jewish privileges, though its final, unalterable objective must be the removal of the Jews altogether."

In an interview in 1922 with Josef Hell for the *Institute für Zeitgeschichte* Hitler was more specific.

"If I am ever really in power, the destruction of the Jews will be my first and most important job. As soon as I have power, I shall have gallows after gallows erected, for example, in Munich on the Marienplatz—as many of them as traffic allows. Then the Jews will be hanged one after another, and they will stay hanging as long as hygienically possible. As soon as they are untied, then the next group will follow and that will continue until the last Jew in Munich is exterminated. Exactly the same procedure will be followed in other cities until Germany is cleansed of the last Jew."

Those words have formed part of a campaign against the World War Two leader of the Roman Catholic Church, Pope Pius XII. He is accused of failing to condemn Hitler for the bigotry and racial hatred with which the führer led Germany, because the pontiff feared an even greater enemy of the church: Soviet Communism.

That fear, say his critics, was fuelled by his own anti-Semitism. They have reduced this hateful allegation to a few questions: What did Pius XII do in the darkest days of World War Two to stop the horrors committed against the Jews? Why had he not excommunicated Hitler and all Nazis from the church, the greatest punishment he could have inflicted? Why had he never mentioned the word "Jews" in his wartime speeches? Had all those prewar years as a nuncio, a Vatican ambassador, in Germany made him a Nazi sympathizer? The questions have fed the slanders and prejudices which no other pope has faced. This torrent of accusations are today at the core of the opposition to Pius XII being created a saint of the Catholic Church. His critics insisted his silence over the Final Solution during the war barred him from beatification.

Thus the truth is misrepresented and buried in falsehood, leaving the historical record distorted.

Facts were cast aside, research into primary sources dismissed, and arguments about the need for balanced interpretations ignored. Pius had become another casualty of truth.

While researching my last book, *Operation Exodus,* which deals with an aspect of the Holocaust, I came across a letter written in 1943 by Chaim Weizmann, who would become Israel's first president. It offered thanks for "the support the Holy See was giving to lend its powerful help whenever it can to mitigate the fate of my coreligionists."

Three years before Weizmann offered his thanks, Albert Einstein had told *Time* magazine in its 1940 Christmas edition that "only the church stood squarely across the path of Hitler's campaign of suppressing the truth. I have never had any special interest in the church before, but now I feel a great affection and admiration because the church alone has had the courage and persistence to stand for intellectual truth and moral freedom."

From time to time items came my way with similar views about Pius XII. Monsignor John Magee, who was the English-language private secretary to Pope John Paul, spent one dinner with me dissecting what he called "the wretched calumnies against Pius." Father Lambert Greenan, an acerbic Irish Dominican priest, went back through his files at *L'Osservatore Romano* where he was one of the editors, to provide evidence of Pius's condemnation of *Kristallnacht* in 1938 and from his time as nuncio in Germany.

Of the forty-four speeches he made as a nuncio, forty denounced aspects of the emerging Nazi ideology. In 1935 he wrote an open letter to the bishop of Cologne describing "Hitler as a false prophet of Lucifer." Two years later at Notre Dame in Paris he said Germany was being led astray into "an ideology of race." Hitler ordered the Nazi press to brand him as "a Jew lover in the Vatican."

I began doing more detailed research which included tracking down new witnesses of a terrible moment in the twentieth century. Theirs is a story of fear, of an experience that still traumatizes them. Many have not spoken before, yet they gave their time to recall a story which encompasses a period somewhere between recent history and fading memory. As well as all the usual research tools for any serious investigation—official records, memoranda, a wide variety of published and private material, diaries, letters, logs, and reports—the main resource, as with my previous books, has been people. Many of the eyewitnesses for this book had not been interviewed before and often felt they could now finally speak because a decent interval had elapsed. Sometimes there can be no simple explanation for the way people behaved. But the one certainty is that theirs is the truth of honest recall.

It also became clear that the most effective way to tell the story was to focus on the relationship between the Vatican and its neighbors, the Jews of the ghetto in Rome. In all the arguments which have raged over the role of Pope Pius during World War Two little space has been given to the people living along the banks of the Tiber. Yet they not only represent the six million victims of the Holocaust but also symbolize its survivors.

As well as those who sheltered with them, the Allied soldiers who had escaped from Italian prisoner-of-war camps, those who helped them, and Pope Pius and his Vatican priests and nuns, this book is ultimately the story of the people of the Rome ghetto. Theirs is a microcosm of a cruel and unjust time.

While the tone is, of course, my own, since a writer's voice is not interchangeable, I have tried to remain faithful to the voices which have long waited to be heard.

PART I

THE POWER
AND
THE GLORY

1

A WAY TO DIE

On that cheerless winter morning, February 10, 1939, Eugenio Maria Guiseppe Pacelli stood in the bedroom doorway, watching what was happening around the brass-framed bed. The two middle-aged nuns went about their work with the gentle movements he expected. Dealing with the dead was something years of experience had given them. For Pacelli dying was a guarantee of afterlife. Long ago he had learned that promise from his mother, Virginia, a pious daughter of the Roman Catholic Church.

Her son was His Eminence, the cardinal secretary of state of the Holy See, the second most powerful figure in the church. An hour ago, following the death of the old man in the bed, Pope Pius XI, Pacelli had become the most important figure in the entire Catholic world. He was now the Camerlengo, a position which combined the role of the Vatican treasurer and chamberlain of the Holy See. He would be responsible for organizing the funeral of Pope Pius XI and the conclave to elect a new pope.

Pacelli was sixty-four years old, of medium height, and slim with a typical Roman nose—straight with narrow nostrils and a slight bump in the middle of its ridge. Behind his old-fashioned spectacles was the look of a man who understood a situation at once.

Through the closed window of the bedroom high in the Vatican's Apostolic Palace, from two hundred feet below, came the murmuring of the crowd in St. Peter's Square, praying for the soul of Pope Pius XI, the church's 261st supreme pontiff. For twenty years he had held numerous titles, offices, and power which had directly affected the lives of many millions of Catholics. For days Pius had been at death's door, barely kept alive by the drugs his doctors administered. They had left the bedroom, their work finally over. Soon Pacelli would begin his.

Pacelli continued to watch the body, still clad in its white nightshirt. A nun had removed the bed socks the pope had worn because of his poor blood circulation, one of his many medical ailments. He was eighty-one years old, his skin taut on his skull, his hair wispy gray, and the veins stood out on the back of his hands. His eyes had been closed; no longer would they look with gentle inquiry.

Only days ago they had looked at Pacelli as he had sat at the bedside and they had spoken on a familiar subject, the fate of the Jews, or, more precisely, that of Guido Mendes and his family. To the pope and Pacelli they represented what was happening to Jews in Germany and Italy, in all those countries where anti-Semitism was spreading.

Guido Mendes was the son of a Roman Jewish family whose lineage went back to Fernando Mendes, the court physician to King Charles II of England. Eugenio had sat next to Guido at school and later in college. By then they were close friends; Eugenio was a regular guest at the Mendeses' Sabbath dinners, Guido had his place at the Christmas Day Pacelli table. By the time Eugenio began to train for the priesthood and Guido had entered medical school, Eugenio's circle of Jewish friends had widened to a dozen. They came to his ordination and watched him celebrate his first Mass. He had walked with them around St. Peter's Square, pointing out the various statues of saints on top of Bernini's colonnade. They had taught him basic Hebrew.

In a lifetime of travel when Pacelli returned to Rome he always made a point of inviting his Jewish friends to meet him. Increasingly they had questioned him about the treatment of Jews and he had told them what he had seen and heard had pained him and promised he would fight anti-Semitism with all the power he had.

That authority had reached its peak when Pacelli was appointed secretary of state in 1930. He had invited Mendes and his other Jewish friends to attend the ceremony and afterward introduced them to Pius XI.

On what was to be their last conversation before the pope had died, Pacelli had told him the Mendes family was now safely in Palestine. Until a year ago Guido had been a professor of medicine at the University of Rome medical school until Mussolini's anti-Semitic racial laws had led to his dismissal. Pacelli had immediately asked the British minister to the Holy See, Sir D'Arcy Osborne, to provide the family with entry permits to Palestine, then a British mandate. Osborne's readiness to help had started a friendship with Pacelli that would last.

Afterward Pacelli had also arranged for a number of other eminent Jewish scholars, doctors, and scientists to emigrate to the United States, South America, and other countries. He arranged for those who could not leave Rome because of family reasons—a seriously ill wife or a child at a critical part of his or her education—to have posts in the Vatican. They included a world-ranking cartographer, Roberto Almagia, who produced a monograph of the Holy Land. Since the racial laws twenty-three Jewish scholars were found positions by Pacelli in the Gregorian University, the Academy of Science, and the Vatican library.

On his deathbed Pope Pius XI had spoken of the need for Pacelli to continue his campaign against anti-Semitism.

One of the attending doctors would recall that Pacelli was close to tears as the pope said he must continue to be a defender of the Jewish people.

The nuns had completed their work and murmured the traditional words: "O Lord, I raise to you my prayer . . ." Below in the square came the sound of traffic and police setting up barriers to control the growing crowd gathering to mourn the passing of the pope.

Pacelli continued to gauge the moment for him to walk over to the bed. The emotions aroused by death were already settling over the bedroom. The faces of the two nuns were mournful, their voices soft as they prayed. Beyond the window the first rays of the sun passed above the limpid Tiber to touch the cross on top of the basilica of St. Peter. From the square the sound of prayer grew louder. Pacelli walked into the bedroom pausing only for the two nuns to leave. He stood beside the bed and delivered his own prayer.

———

As dawn began to lighten the sky beyond the bedroom window, Pacelli knew that before he could begin the funeral preparations and settle a thousand matters before a new pope was chosen in conclave, he must perform his first duty as a camerlengo. He removed the Fisherman's Ring from the pope's right index finger. Later he would use silver shears to break the ring in front of the assembled College of Cardinals before they went into conclave. When a pope was elected he would receive his new ring, a further symbol of his authority.

Pacelli bent over the body and kissed the forehead and hands before leaving the bedroom, closing the door behind him.

His office was on the first floor of the Apostolic Palace. At that early hour the view from any of its windows was impressive. Stretching into the distance were the domes, spires, towers, monuments, palaces, and parks of Rome. To the right of the windows rose the basilica; long ago, when Pacelli had become a fully fledged diplomat, he had memorized its proportions: 651 feet long, 535 feet high, with 71 supporting columns, 44 altars, and 395 statues. He found the details useful in making polite talk at official functions. To the right of the windows was the roof of the Sistine Chapel, offering no clue to the splendor inside. It was there that the cardinals would elect a new pope.

Pacelli sat at a sixteenth-century desk made in the days of Paul IV. It had a hand-tooled leather writing pad, a small clock in a solid-gold frame, a gold-top roll blotter, and a letter opener. They were gifts from his family to celebrate his appointment as secretary of state. One wall was covered with shelving holding leather-bound volumes of Vatican canon law and treaties Pacelli had worked on.

Pacelli placed his first telephone call of the day through one of the nuns who manned the Vatican switchboard. In moments he was connected to Count Galeazzo Ciano, the Italian foreign minister, informing him that the pope was dead. Having expressed his condolences on behalf of the government, Ciano told Mussolini. The duce had replied, "At last the obstinate old man is gone."

Throughout the day the camerlengo had sent the same message to apostolic nuncios around the world. "Deeply regret to inform you Holy Father passed away. Inform all relevant. Yours in Christ, Pacelli, camerlengo."

Across the world the first wire-service reports of the death were appearing in newspapers. In the office of *L'Osservatore Romano* in a featureless building near the Porta Sant Anna, one of the gateways to the Vatican, the editor, Count Giuseppe Dalla Torre, was preparing the next edition which would be entirely devoted to the pope's death.

The winter sun had risen over the Vatican when the two Guardia Palatina entered the bedroom of Pope Pius XI. They moved his body off the bed, onto a trolley, and draped it in a purple cloth. The two guards wheeled the gurney to a nearby service elevator and took the body down to the basement of the Apostolic Palace and through the corridors to a room beneath the basilica. Waiting there was the undertaker appointed by Camerlengo Pacelli to prepare the body for lying-in-state in St. Peter's.

That night Pacelli sat at his desk and read the messages which had come from papal nuncios in Berlin, Warsaw, and Prague. All told the same story: Throughout the Third Reich the persecution of Jews not only continued but had increased. In the German capital Hitler had told a rally there was a need to find a solution for the "Jewish problem."

When he finished reading, Pacelli drafted a message to all the nuncios in the expanding Third Reich. He had prayed for guidance before instructing them on an issue which had been raised on behalf of the German church: What should it do about the mounting terror? Pacelli had decided that, horrific though the persecution was, there must be no public denunciation by the church. To do so would, he believed, destroy an effective strategy he had devised to protect the Jews and give them an opportunity to escape the Nazi tyranny. It was a decision he recognized was the hardest request he could expect anyone to accept in the face of what was happening in Germany. But he himself would show it must be done. The strategy was silence. Any form of denunciation in the name of the Vatican would inevitably provoke further reprisals against the Jews.

His decision, he fully realized, would be misunderstood, since the atrocities already committed by the Nazis called for protest. Yet for him to do so would cause even harsher repression against the Jews. But silence would not preclude him from working behind the scenes to help the Jews. He hoped every priest would understand that his silence was also the only way to save the lives of as many Jews as possible.

The first link in Pacelli's plan to save Jews had already been created on November 30, 1938, shortly after *Kristallnacht*, a night of terror, when across Germany Nazis had burned down synagogues, houses, and businesses of Jews.

Pacelli had sent an encoded priority message to church archbishops around the world. He instructed them to apply for visas for "non-Aryan Catholics" to enable them to leave Germany. His choice of description of the status of the applicants was deliberately intended to try and ensure that the Nazis would not learn of his initiative and make propaganda against the Vatican as an ally of the Jews.

Pacelli had asked for the visas to be obtained under the concordat he had signed with the Nazis in 1933 which specifically provided protection for Jews who converted to Christianity. Pacelli intended they should be issued to Jews who were not converts.

Pacelli had the satisfaction of knowing that already the visas his bishops had obtained were allowing thousands of Jews to leave Nazi Germany. It would not be until 2001 that the figure of successful visa applicants would be revealed to be two hundred thousand who had left Germany in the weeks following *Kristallnacht*. None suspected the role Pacelli had played in gaining their freedom.

The Vatican became the focus of the world's attention following the death of Pius XI. After the funeral there would be nine days of *Novemdiales,* the period of preparation for the start of conclave on March 1, 1939.

From dawn to late evening, soutane swishing softly in rhythm with his stride, Pacelli walked through the corridors of the Apostolic Palace. Each morning the camerlengo's first stop was the Vatican Press Office to check how its staff were dealing with the hundreds of reporters and broadcasters who had arrived in Rome. Pacelli had ignored all but one for a request for a personal interview. The exception was Camille Cianfarra of *The New York Times*.

Long experience of how the church was portrayed in the media had made him cautious. All too often newspapers used the easy simplification of polemics and the pope was described as the head of a secret monotonic institution. Pacelli knew it was far from that. The Holy See was a disparate array of departments run by cardinals not always in agreement with each other. He knew that the coming conclave would show that. But in the meantime he left speculation to reporters as they tried to penetrate a closed world over which in the coming days he had complete control.

There were appointments to be made, telephone calls returned, telegrams sent. In between apostolic nuncios had to be seen on their return for the funeral; they would remain in Rome to brief the new pope on the situations in their host countries.

Britain had appointed a permanent minister to the Holy See at the outbreak of the First World War. When the war ended in 1918 the decision was taken to keep a diplomat in Rome to maintain a close eye on the Holy See's support for Ireland's demand for independence from British rule. In 1922, when Pope Pius XI was elected, Sir Mansfield Smith-Cumming, the director general of MI6, reported "our envoy to the Vatican has still produced little of value."

However within the secretariat of state Vatican diplomacy was on the move. Ireland had become a republic and a nuncio was appointed to Dublin for the country's predominantly Catholic population. The problems of a divided Northern Ireland showed signs of deepening. In Canada, French Catholics and English Protestants were in open religious conflict. British colonies in Africa were in disagreement over denominational education. In Palestine the British mandate was in conflict over a date to be settled with the Holy See for the Easter holiday. Malta was another problem. The island's population was fiercely Roman Catholic, but was governed from London. The island also had three Anglican bishops; the conflict between the Church of England and the Vatican had been exploited by Italian residents on the island.

It was one more reason for Britain to have a seasoned minister at the Holy See. In 1936 Sir Francis D'Arcy Godolphin Osborne was moved from his post in Washington to Rome. He was sixty years old, a sprightly figure, a devout Protestant, and the son of a noble English family, the dukedom of Leeds.

The Foreign Office had found Osborne a house suitable for a minister to the Holy See on the fashionable Via Mercadante. The tall, slim, unmarried diplomat had furnished it with fine taste: Antiques, paintings, and photographs were a reminder of a career which spanned periods in Washington, Lisbon, and the Hague. The library reflected his interest in astrology, telepathy, and astronomy. Wherever he was posted Osborne had sought out the most respected fortune-teller in the area. On his watch fob chain was a charm against cosmic rays. His circle of friends included the duke and duchess of York, soon to become king and queen of England.

A live-in Italian cook and an English manservant, John May, ran the house. Osborne's private diary offered insights into the relationship between master and servant. They were on first-name terms when alone. "John told me we now have a plainclothes policeman watching the house. Intriguing and disagreeable." Weeks later Osborne diarized, "Today John lost his temper and shouted at me which is intolerable." Another incident compelled Osborne to note, "John's rudeness gave me a bad night." Among May's duties was walking Osborne's terrier, Jeremy. At night the dog slept at the foot of Osborne's bed.

Osborne's reports to the Foreign Office showed his eye for detail. "The pope is a likeable old man, very human, but a little long-winded." "The secretary of state, Pacelli, has a lot of charm and a touch of the saint about him. He really is the intellectual power behind Pius, having drafted many of those documents which we admire." "There is something sinister about Mussolini. All those Fascist students marching up and down outside my front door. And the Italian newspapers are full of gibes about Britain and Roosevelt." "Had a good briefing from Francois Charles-Roux, the French ambassador to the Holy See. No doubt he has influence in the Vatican. Regards most of his colleagues as living for their pension. He wonders when the Americans will have someone in post. All in all a sound man, though his English isn't that good." Osborne spoke fluent French and had delighted Charles-Roux with his knowledge of French literature.

———

By the eve of the funeral of Pius XI, Pacelli had spoken to all of the nuncios and most of the Vatican diplomat corps. They confirmed that ecclesiastic circles in Rome were alive with gossip and intrigue about who would be the next pope. A great deal of it emanated from Monsignor Enrico Pucci. Balding, with restless eyes and a lisp, he had no post in the Vatican and had left the diocese of Milan shortly after Mussolini assumed power. There were rumors of a scandal involving a cathedral choir boy; more certain was that Pucci was a committed Fascist and anti-Semite. In Rome he had set up a news agency and claimed friendship with Pius XI from the time the pope had been in charge of the Ambrosian Library in Milan and had arranged for him to have access to the Vatican Press Office.

For visiting journalists coming to report the funeral and the outcome of conclave, Pucci provided credible-sounding information for which he was well paid. In the news blackout which Pacelli had imposed of never confirming or denying a story Pucci became an important source when he claimed to know the voting intentions of the thirty-five Italian cardinals. If they bloc-voted, Pucci indicated, it would provide the two-thirds majority required to elect a new pope.

Over lunch served by John May, D'Arcy Osborne learned from Pucci it was likely that in the first round of voting, the electors would very probably follow tradition and show Pacelli their appreciation for his work as camerlengo. But when it came to later voting, Pucci predicted it was unlikely that the secretary of state would gain overwhelming support.

The nine French cardinals led by Cardinal Henri Baudrillart had been summoned to meet Ambassador Charles-Roux who had made it clear who the French government wanted on the throne of St. Peter's.

"Paris does not want another Pius or for that matter anyone influenced by Nazi propaganda. On the other hand Paris doesn't want a weak pope," Pucci had told Osborne.

The four cardinals from the United States, Pucci claimed, together with the five from Germany, could combine to push the candidacy of Cardinal Eugene Tisserant, the only non-Italian cardinal in the Curia. The Frenchman could also gain the votes of the Syrian cardinal and the Spanish cardinal of Tarragona who had fled to Rome from the Spanish Civil War.

Throughout the meal Pucci had worked his way through the list of potential candidates. "He was the showman I had expected, producing a name in between sips of wine, and pausing to pose a question. Should it be a religious or a political choice? It was good theatre," Osborne noted.

The minister had asked Pucci again about Pacelli's potential. From the British standpoint he would be an ideal choice, a pope who would continue to strongly challenge the Rome-Berlin axis. Pucci had sighed and spread his hands saying it was for that very reason Pacelli would not be elected. "Too close to Pius. There must be a change of policy. Conclave will go for a non-politician, a holy man."

On that note the gossiping monsignor had left to go and peddle his predictions elsewhere.

Ugo Foa, the tall, silver-haired president of the Jewish community in Rome was breakfasting with his two teenage sons and daughter in their elegant apartment in Rome's Prati district when their housekeeper announced there was a telephone call from the Vatican. A widower for the past three years, Foa had made breakfast a family occasion which could not be disturbed. Nevertheless, he could not quite hide his astonishment nor the children their excitement. In the past months there had been few calls for their father, let alone one from the Vatican.

The caller was a monsignor from the secretariat for non-Christian religions, announcing he was extending an invitation to attend the funeral of Pope Pius XI.

Foa found the request all the more welcome given his own position or, indeed, that of any Jew in Rome since the racial laws had come into force. Until then Fascism was virtually free from anti-Semitism and Jews were encouraged to join the movement. The Fascist Party was predominately middle-class and antiworker; its union-busting, strike-breaking tactics had found ready support among the professional classes the Jews increasingly occupied. But overnight Fascism became officially anti-Semitic.

Jews who held positions in the government were removed. Some had sat in the Chamber of Deputies or served as members of the Fascist Grand Council. One had been the deputy chief of Rome police, another a vice-governor of Libya. Margherita Sarfatti, Mussolini's vivacious Jewish mistress for years and the editor of the Fascist Party's ideological review, was replaced with the film starlet Clara Petacci, whose father, Dr. Francesco Petacci was the personal physician of Pope Pius XI.

Until a few months ago the fifty-three-year-old Foa would have worn his black gown and hat, symbols of his office as a magistrate of the City of Rome. He had his own courtroom in a *palazzo* where he delivered judgements on cases which violated the Fascist legal code. His clerk regularly received invitations for him to dine at top tables in the city's Fascist society. Mussolini had personally approved his appointment to be president of the country's war veterans' organization, *Nastro Azzurro*.

Decorated for valor in World War One, Foa had joined the Fascist Party in 1922 and qualified as a lawyer. His skills in prosecuting in the Tuscany courts came to the notice of the Ministry of Justice in Rome and he was offered a post in one of its departments in Rome. He was still deciding what to do—his wife preferred country life to that of the city—when she died. Foa and his motherless children moved to Rome, into the palatial apartment his legal funds in Tuscany had paid for. Within three months the minister of justice had appointed him as a magistrate. Foa's fair judgments, his refusal to be swayed by what he called "courtroom tricks" had won him growing respect. Within the Jewish community its leaders saw in Foa the man they had long hoped to find. He not only had a brilliant legal mind, but was a scholar, a scion of a family who for centuries had been either bibliophiles or doctors. There was agreement among the community to appoint him its president.

Ugo Foa was one of the last to lose his position. Colleagues asked the justice minister to allow him to remain on the bench. The minister pointed out that the racial laws were not as oppressive as those introduced by Hitler and Foa's skill as an advocate would ensure he could still make a comfortable living in private practice.

A number of Foa's Jewish friends were leaving Italy to go to the United States and others were travelling to Palestine. They had urged him and the children to come with them. But Foa insisted he must remain in Rome. His children were at a crucial stage of their education and the community depended on him for guidance. Following the "Night of Broken Glass," *Kristallnacht,* and the harsh treatment of Jews in Danzig and elsewhere in the Third Reich, he had advised them to remain in Rome because he was certain the Vatican would protect the community if the Nazis ever threat-ened them. Pius XI had always spoken up for the Jews and had shown respect for their faith.

Foa also met Cardinal Pacelli at various social functions and had found common ground when the secretary of state had revealed his own parents had been close friends with Ernesto Nathan, the first Jewish mayor of Rome. Foa had been astonished, and delighted, with Pacelli's knowledge of Hebrew and they had often spoken the language together when they met. More than once Pacelli had expressed his admiration for the Jewish way of life.

Ugo Foa was filled with hope that the next pope would continue to speak for the Jews. It would be a question he would discuss with the com-munity's new spiritual leader.

Israel Zolli, the new chief rabbi of Rome, continued to follow the advice Ugo Foa had given him to get to know the people of the ghetto. Wrapped in a black topcoat and a black hat, he walked the length of Via del Portico d'Ottavia. Already the shops were opening—fruiters, bakers, clothiers, butchers—as their ancestors had done for a thousand years since the Em-peror Augustus had dedicated the street to his sister, Octavia. A keen his-torian, Zolli saw that while the buildings dated mostly from the Middle Ages and the Renaissance there was still portions of Imperial Rome visible; decorative fragments of marble, pieces of an ancient sarcophagus, and the ruins of a portico where once the theater of Marcellus had stood. Along this street in the year A.D. 70 another emperor, Vespasian, had staged a vic-tory parade for his son, Titus, on his return from his destruction of Jeru-salem. Behind his chariots and the marching legions hundreds of Jewish slaves carried the precious artifacts Titus had stolen from the Second Temple. Zolli knew that some of those prisoners were ancestors of today's people of the ghetto.

He was sixty-two years old, stocky, with a thick neck, and wore glasses which gave his bulging eyes the look of a man who sought approval from no one. He had arrived in Rome a few weeks ago with his second wife Emma and his daughters Dora and Miriam. His first wife had died after giving birth to Dora.

Responsible for the spiritual welfare of the city's Jews, Zolli's appointment made him one of the most important figures among Italy's Jewish
population of forty-five thousand.

Zolli knew he had been selected after a period of tension between the
last chief rabbi, David Prato and the *giunta,* the Jewish committee under
the presidency of Ugo Foa. Prato was a leading authority on the medieval
Jewish manuscript, the fourteenth-century *Haggadah* and its liturgical
poems. But he had found himself uncomfortable with some of the committee members who he felt "were promoting assimilation practices under
the sway of Fascist ideology."

The clash had arisen over how Mussolini's racial laws defined who was
Jewish. There were over seven thousand foreign Jews living in Italy and
some had settled in Rome and married non-Jews. Prato insisted that children born from such unions were not "pureblood" Jews. The committee
argued they were entitled to be raised in the Jewish faith, including their
education. The racial laws banned all Jews from attending public schools.
They must only go to Jewish schools funded by the local community. Prato
insisted the Jewish school near the Tiber had no further room to expand to
accommodate the children of mixed marriages. The committee proposed
funds would be found to develop the school. The argument had continued
until Prato had resigned his post and went to live in Palestine.

Zolli's rabbinical career had been shaped by his mother, the daughter
of a long line of rabbis. He had been born in the small town of Brody, part
of Austria after the partition of Poland in 1795. His father ran a clothing
factory and Israel Zolli, the youngest of five children, had studied at the
University of Vienna and then the rabbinical college in Florence. His distinction grades include a degree in psychology and Semite philosophy.

In 1918 Zolli became rabbi of the Trieste community. Then came the
offer to come to Rome in 1938.

He had brought with him to Rome a small library of his own published
work. They included essays on Dosteyevsky and the Jews, and the role of
Chaim Weizmann in history. He had authored a book on Hebrew literature
which became a bestseller across the Diaspora.

On that February morning Zolli had cut short his walk around the
ghetto to go to St. Peter's Square. In a few days he would be a member of
the basilica congregation celebrating the funeral Mass for Pope Pius XI.

He would sit beside Ugo Foa, knowing that for the community leader it would be only a ceremonial occasion. To Zolli it would have a far greater significance—one he could not share with anyone.

From early morning crowds had filled across St. Peter's Square into the basilica where Pope Pius XI lay in state. Guardia Palatina were in constant attendance, one at each corner of the catafalque on which lay the triple coffin—the inner one of bronze, the second of cedar, and the outer coffin of cyprus to symbolize the request Pius had left in his will that his funeral should be simple, as he wanted to die *un povero,* a poor man. His other request had been that all his private correspondence should go to the Secret Archives, while his official papers were to be made available to the next pope. In between all his other duties Pacelli had supervised the collection of the documents and had them sealed in boxes.

The evening before the funeral the last of the mourners had made their way past the coffin and back down the nave, past the basilica's twenty-eight altars and the statue of St. Peter whose right foot gleamed from constant kissing by the faithful.

Only when the great doors of the basilica had been closed had Pacelli slipped through a side door into the nave and made his way to the bier. A single candle burned with a steady flame in the still air. The four Guardia Palatina stood motionless as the camerlengo knelt beside the coffin to pray in silent farewell. Close to tears, he rose and walked slowly out of the basilica.

In a side chapel near the basilica's altar a nun, disarmingly petite with luminous blue-gray eyes, rose from kneeling, her prayers over, with a movement which made her appear a full generation younger. Pascalina was Pacelli's housekeeper and confidante.

Next morning the great bells of St. Peter's stopped their mournful tolling and the requiem Mass for Pius XI began. In front of the coffin sat the red-robed cardinals, led by the dean of their Sacred College, Eugene Tisserant. The gruff voice of the bearded Frenchman's responses during the service would rise above the singing of the choir.

Behind the cardinals sat the bishops. Among them was Alfredo Ottaviani, the head of the Holy Office, the most powerful of the dozen Sacred
Congregations. Behind him sat his staff, their black soutanes relieved by
red sashes and red buttons. The tallest was a muscular, bespectacled Irishman, Monsignor Hugh O'Flaherty. His ecclesiastical career had already
made him a respected figure. Now it was his powerful baritone voice that
impressed others around him as he sang.

The guests in the section reserved for the heads of state included the
seventy-three-year-old King Vittorio Emanuele III of Italy. Alongside him
sat King Carlos of Rumania, and King Leopold of Belgium. Neaby sat
Benito Mussolini and his cabinet. The duce wore his military uniform,
the politicians black suits. General Francisco Franco, the Spanish dictator,
wore a black arm band on his uniform. Joseph Kennedy, the father of the
future president of the United States, represented the United States.

In an adjoining section were the ambassadors and ministers to the
Holy See in morning dress. Behind them was a square-jawed blond-
haired man with blue eyes and a polite smile dressed in a black suit with
a small Nazi Party emblem in his buttonhole. He was Major Herbert
Kappler, attached to the German embassy in Rome as a consultant
on security.

In the section reserved for distinguished guests sat Foa and Zolli. With
them were the leaders of Rome's business community and industrialists
who had made the journey from all over Europe. Other guests had come
from the United States, South America, and Canada.

In a cordoned area reserved for Vatican staff sat Pascalina and other
nuns chosen from convents in Rome. Among them were the Jews Pacelli
had found positions for in the Vatican. They included Professor Giorgio
Levi Della Vida, a world-ranking authority on Islam who Pacelli had placed
in charge of cataloguing the Vatican's collection of Arab manuscripts; Professor Tullio Levi-Civita, who had been Italy's top physicist before the racial
laws barred him from his research; and Professor Giorgio Del Vecchio, a
close friend of Pacelli, who had been forced to resign his position at Rome
University as its expert on international law—he now worked in the secretariat of state as a special advisor to Pacelli.

Ninety minutes after the Mass started the body of the pope was laid to
rest in his tomb in the basilica crypt. As the mourners emerged into the

great square the speculation resumed: Which of the cardinals burying Pius would take his place?

On March 1, 1939, Dalla Torre, the editor, arrived early at the office of *L'Osservatore Romano*. At his desk he removed his Roman collar and set to work. His desk was covered with paper: items clipped from the Italian press, call-back messages still to be answered, and the biographies of the sixty-two cardinals eligible to vote in conclave. He checked each one and sent them over to the Vatican Press Office to distribute to over two hundred reporters who had arrived in Rome to cover what was an event of international importance. This was the first papal election since the Lateran Treaty.

The energetic Monsignor Pucci had provided the press with his own latest analysis on the outcome. "If the electors want an intelligent pope they will favor Cardinal Luigi Maglione. If a handsome pope is required they will vote for Cardinal Federico Tedeschini. He is tall and slim with regular features, a noble air, and beautiful hands. If it is to be a 'holy man' then they might install Pacelli." It was the first time the journalist-priest had tipped the secretary of state as a potential front-runner for the throne of St. Peter's.

At four o'clock on that March afternoon four cardboard boxes were carefully loaded into a van outside 34 Via Santa Chiara, a small, nondescript square behind Rome's Pantheon. This was where the House of Gammarelli, tailors to the Vatican, had its shop. Each box contained a complete set of papal vestments: extra-large, large, medium, and small sizes of a white-silk cassock, red velvet stretch slippers, with a small cross embossed on each, a white silk sash, a rochet, a mozetta, a red stole embroidered in gold, a white skullcap, and white cotton stockings. The cassocks were left with their backs and hems held together by long looping stitches. The sleeves were also deliberately unfinished. A set of garments would be sewn to fit the chosen pope before he stepped for the first time onto the central balcony of St. Peter's to greet the world. From the time conclave began a Gammarelli tailor would remain in the Sistine Chapel side room waiting to be called to make the final adjustments.

———

At six o'clock the cardinals filed into the chapel and took their places. In a corner of the chapel stood the stove in which the results of unsuccessful ballots would be burned.

In *L'Osservatore Romano* Dalla Torre checked the different proofs of the newspaper's front page. Each contained a photograph and potted biography of one of the cardinals the editor believed could be the next pope. If all the editor's predictions proved to be wrong, he knew his carefully pre-prepared plans to obtain a scoop would ensure the nearest thing to a panic in a newspaper trying to meet a deadline.

At six-fifteen Pacelli, as master of ceremonies, called out two words. *Extra omnes.* Everyone except the cardinals must leave. The doors of the chapel were locked from the outside by the commandant of the Guardia Palatina. Conclave was under way.

In St. Peter's Square the crowd steadily grew, everyone glancing frequently toward the smokestack jutting out of the roof of the Sistine Chapel. From there would come the signal: black for an inconclusive vote, white for a successful election.

Inside the chapel the voting began. Before each cardinal was a two-inch-square card which bore the words: *"Eligo in Summum Pontificem"*—"I elect as supreme pontiff." Beneath the words was a space to write a name.

What would happen beneath the horrors of Michelangelo's version of the apocalypse—where Jesus is portrayed as judge and king, shorn of enigma, ambiguity, and mystery—was supposed to remain a closely guarded secret. But this was 1939 and the election of a new pope was of great concern to secular powers, perhaps more than at any time in history.

The French ambassador to the Holy See, Charles-Roux, had his informer, the sardonic French cardinal Henri Baudrillart. How he conveyed the voting details has remained a matter of conjecture. One suggestion is that one of the nuns, a member of a French order who prepared the meals for conclave, was slipped the results of the voting by Baudrillart to pass on to the ambassador.

In the first vote Pacelli had led with twenty-eight votes, Luigi Maglione had come second with nineteen, and Elia Dalla Costa had achieved four less. After dinner the voters retired to their cells, furnished with beds borrowed from a Rome seminary. The following morning after celebrating Mass and eating breakfast the cardinals voted for a second time. Dalla Costa's supporters had gone over to Pacelli, giving the secretary a significant lead.

At five o'clock that evening of March 2, the cardinals voted for a third time. Pacelli had the required majority of forty-nine votes to be elected. It had been the swiftest conclave in three hundred years. It was also Pacelli's sixty-third birthday.

He chose to be known as Pope Pius XII and appointed Cardinal Luigi Maglione as secretary of state. Pucci, the tireless gossip, informed reporters that "the monk in Pacelli and Maglione's liking for the good life will never make them compatible."

On March 12, Pacelli's coronation took place in St. Peter's Basilica. It was estimated that over a million people gathered in St. Peter's Square and spilled down the length of the Via della Conciliazione. It was also the anniversary of the Lateran Treaty, which Pacelli had helped to negotiate.

Among those in the basilica was Pascalina, joining in the applause as the procession made its way down the nave. First came the ambassadors and distinguished guests, then followed the Curial cardinals, the archbishops, bishops, and abbots. After a short pause, came the new pope, borne aloft on the *sedia gestatoria*, the traditional papal sadan chair. Pius XII bestowed benedictions left and right as the congregation sank to its knees as he passed. The voices of the Sistine Chapel choir filled the basilica. *"Tu es Petrus, et super hanc petram aedificabo ecclesiam meam."* Thou art Peter, and upon this rock I will build my church."

Pascalina allowed tears to run down her cheeks. The previous evening Pacelli had told her she was to become housekeeper of the papal apartment. She had reached the pinnacle of her career.

That evening, after he had met all the heads of state and distinguished guests, Pope Pius XII had invited a gathering of family and close friends, including the Jews he had found sanctuary for in the Vatican, to join him in one of the Apostolic Palace's salons. He chose as the theme for his first speech as pope a passage of the encyclical he had written for his predecessor, *Mit Brennender Sorge* (with burning anxiety).

". . . Whoever exalts race, or the people, or the state, or a particular form of state, or the depositories of power, or any other fundamental value of the human community—however necessary and honorable be their function in the worldly things—whoever raises these notions above their standard value and divinizes them to an idolatrous level, distorts and perverts an order of the world planned and created by God; he is far from the true faith in God and from the concept of life which that faith upholds. . . "

In those words Pius had declared his position as a champion of the Jews against Nazi Germany. The "silence" he had urged his nuncios and bishops to obey would now be joined by what Pius hoped was the most effective weapon he possed—his words.

He intended to demonstrate their power in his first encyclical, *Summi Pontificatus,* which he would write in the coming weeks as the dark shadow of war darkened over Europe. He would ask for peace but reject Nazism and would remind the world "there is neither Gentile nor Jew, circumcision nor uncircumcision."

Those words were seen in Berlin as a clear-cut warning that the pope would fight to save the Jews.

2

POPE PIUS XII AND THE JEWS

Like all major cities, Rome had several criminal gangs. The most notorious was the Banda Pantera Nera, the Black Panthers. Led by a veteran of the First World War, Giovanni Mezzaroma had recruited its members from discharged soldiers, corrupt policemen dismissed from the city force, and homeless teenagers. Within the Panthers Celeste di Porto had a special position. Not only was the teenager beautiful, with shiny black hair and long fingers which had made her the gang's best pickpocket, she was also Mezzaroma's mistress.

Born and raised in the ghetto, she had worked with her father as a rag collector. She was fifteen when she met Mezzaroma. He was a tall, muscular man, dressed in flashy clothes with a streetwise manner, an apartment in the city center, and a car. Still in his mid-twenties, Mezzaroma had more money than Celeste had ever seen and spent some of it on her clothes. Within the gang she became known as the Pantheress, a feared figure within the group.

In the days following the election, crowds went to St. Peter's Square to gaze up at the Apostolic Palace in the hope of seeing the new pope. In turn they were targets for the Panthers pickpockets. In her fashionable clothes Celeste would watch them working, using the techniques she had taught them. Satisfied, she would be driven by her lover to her family home in the ghetto, enjoying the envious looks she drew.

A mile and a quarter from the Vatican, the ghetto was the oldest Jewish community in the Western world. Over two thousand years ago Jews had first settled along the banks of the Tiber and on the small island on the bend of the river in what became the suburb of Trastevere. By the time Constantine the Great had converted to Christianity in A.D. 313 and proclaimed equal rights for all religions, there were eight thousand Jews living beside the river.

There had long been an acceptance between the Vatican and its ghetto neighbors that Christianity and Judaism were linked by a common creed. Both prayed to one God and based their faith on the Bible. Both shared Messianic hopes. Both faiths were born and nurtured in the land of Israel, and both had Jews as lawmakers, prophets, and apostles.

Yet Judaism had suffered from anti-Semitism in which Christian theologians and papal legislation had played their part from the time Pope Gregory the Great (A.D. 590–604) had spoken of "the treacherous Jews." Down the centuries the people of the Rome ghetto had felt the wrath of the medieval pontiffs. Despite being squeezed into a dismal and depressing corner of the city they had somehow survived the fall of the Roman Empire, the pillaging barbarians, and watched the church rise through the Dark Ages into the Renaissance, that golden age of discovery. Yet for the Jews it meant they were still isolated from society: They could not choose where they could live, what they could wear, and what work was open to them. They were held complicit in any threat to the authority of the church, punished by burning at the stake.

Persecution reached a new level in 1555 with the election of Pope Paul IV. The pinch-faced Roman had wasted no time in introducing further laws. His first papal bull, a document as binding as a Muslim fatwa, banned all Jews from prescribing medicine to Christians or employing Christian midwives. No Jew could ride in a coach or engage in anything but the lowest of occupations. He ordered a wall built around the ghetto; every Jew had to be within its confines from dusk to dawn. The pope's lasting contribution to the lexicon of hatred was the yellow badge that every

Jewish man, woman, and child had to wear. Failure to do so was severely punished. Four centuries later in the shape of a Star of David it became part of the repression of Hitler's Jews.

When Pope Pius IV occupied the throne in 1562 his first move was to introduce a theological rapprochement with Judaism, declaring the church must revise its long-held position over the death of Jesus. The Nicene Creed, the core of the church for centuries, would teach that Pontius Pilate was ultimately responsible for Christ's death sentence, and that it was the gentiles who had mocked, scourged, and crucified Jesus. Ignoring the uproar it created among the Jesuits, Dominicans, and other conservatives in the Vatican, Pius ordered the Jews of the ghetto should no longer have to wear their yellow badges and could buy land and work in other businesses beside selling rags.

The news spread across the Diaspora. In Calvinist Holland, Cromwell's England, France, Prussia, and Austria, the Jews were liberated from their segregation. In Vienna the ghetto gates were torn down and burned in the city's largest square. Finally, in 1798, the five gates of the Rome ghetto were removed.

The emancipation of Italy led to Jews having positions of importance. Three were elected to the nation's first parliament. One, Luigi Luzzatti, became the country's minister of finance and ultimately its prime minister. Soon Jews were making significant contributions in business, insurance, education, and the arts.

In January 1904, Pope Pius X received in audience Theodor Herzl, the founder of Zionism. It was also a time when Jesuit-inspired anti-Semitism had once more emerged and Herzl's passionately argued document, *Judenstaat*—for a Jewish state in the land of their ancestors—became an excuse to stoke the fires of racism. *Civilta Cattolica*, the organ of the Jesuits, resurrected the ritual-murder myth against Jews. "The practice of killing children for the Paschal feast is now very rare in the more cultivated part of Europe, more frequent in Eastern Europe and, all too common, in the East where every year the Hebrews crucify a child. In order that the blood is effective, the child must die in torment." It published its blood libel under its masthead bearing the legend: "Happy is the nation whose Lord is God."

It was not only to enlist the pope's support to end such vile propaganda which had brought Herzl to the Vatican. He wanted the Holy See
to endorse the idea of a Jewish state. Several countries, he told Pius, had
already expressed support for the idea; for the Vatican to do so would be
a tremendous boost. The pope's response was damning. "The soil of Jerusalem, if it was not always, has been sanctified by the life of Jesus Christ.
But the Jews do not recognize our Lord, therefore we cannot support the
Jews in the acquisition of the Holy Place."

Chief Rabbi Israel Zolli found getting to know ghetto people was not
easy; their language consisted of Hebrew, Romany, and Italian, a dialect
which had come down through the centuries. Intermarriage had also kept
family names to less than fifty. After consulting synagogue records, Zolli
discovered often a dozen families with the same names living on the
same street.

Initially he sensed their distrust toward him; he was an outsider from
the north. But his social skills had won them over and they began to tell
him about life in the ghetto, especially their pride that young people were
leaving the community to be educated in Rome's colleges as lawyers, den-
tists, and doctors and were working in the city.

Nevertheless life in the ghetto remained as before. Women still sat on
stools outside their homes, darning and knitting, and their men pushed
handcarts through the streets of Rome, hawking goods in the high nasal
tone of their ghetto voices. While it was still a life of poverty and malnu-
trition it was also one where people helped a sick neighbor, assisted at
childbirth, and laid out a body for burial.

Zolli liked to stop and talk: to a woman hanging out her washing on a
line which stretched from one side of the street to the other; to an old man
stuffing hunks of wool into an old mattress before it was ready to sell. He
learned that in Via dei Funari there used to be a woman who brewed love
potions while on Via Catalana there were once no fewer than five fortune-
tellers—now there was only one, living in a room at the top of a steep
stone staircase. He found that some of the young people, who could trace
their families back over centuries of living in the same house, having married, had decided to move, carrying their belongings across Ponte Garibaldi

to the other side of the Tiber where the government had built working-class houses to rent.

The majority who remained in the ghetto could not imagine, or want, any other life than they had. They had heard that in Turin, Milan, and the port city of Venice, Jews nowadays often paid only lip service to their religion. But it was their faith which bound the people of the ghetto. Zolli respected that. He had his own belief, but it wasn't theirs.

Mose Spizzichino's ancestors were itinerant peddlers in Sicily until Jews were expelled from the island in 1497 and had eventually reached Rome to continue their business of selling secondhand clothes. They had managed to save sufficient *scudi,* the currency of the time, to begin to build a home on what became the ghetto's first street, Via della Reginella.

Down the centuries Spizzichinos had hammered and chiselled and dug a drain to carry away the frequent floodwaters from the Tiber. By 1939 oil lamps had given way to electric lights and the front door, the only exit from the house, had been strengthened. The rooms were small, plastered, but left unpainted. There were a few hangings on the walls; cheap paintings which Mose had picked up on his rounds and some photos of a past generation preserved behind glass, their faces reminders of a hard life.

Mose had been born in the house and his wife, Grazia, was delivered in her family home at the end of the street. He had been twenty when they married; she a small young woman just turned seventeen. Grazia had shown herself a good homemaker and made the house more comfortable than it had ever been. There were rugs on the floor made from pieces of rags she had washed and sewn on old sacking. Mose and the children learned to wipe their feet before going upstairs to bed. The parents slept on the third floor, under the roof. Settimia, and her sister Giuditta, a chubby-cheeked seventeen-year-old, occupied one of the bedrooms on the second floor. Settimia was black-haired, with sparkling eyes and a friendly laugh. At nineteen years old, unusual at her age, she had yet to marry. Her elder sisters, Ada and Gentile, and their husbands, slept in the other adjoining bedrooms. The children helped in the family business: The girls repaired clothes for Mose and his sons-in-law to sell from handcarts they trundled through the streets of Rome.

Mose was a large man, long across the shoulders and people recalled him as endearing in the way strong men are.

In 1927 he joined the Fascist Party: Throughout the ghetto many men were doing the same, not from political conviction but because they felt it would be easier to work with a party card. Mose was largely indifferent to the world of politics; his life revolved around family, work, and synagogue. Grazia always kept a pot of broth on the stove in case any of the children became ill or a neighbor knocked on the door and said someone was unwell and needed soup, the panacea for all illness in the ghetto. On Friday nights she lit the candles for the Sabbath and Mose said the blessing. On Saturday Mose did not light a cigarette so as not to break Mosaic Law.

He had led his family into a packed synagogue to hear Zolli and Ugo Foa pay homage to the pope's memory, reminding the congregants he had been a true friend of them. Foa had added that he was certain, from his own contacts with the new pope that Pius XII would continue to behave in the same way.

On his regular round of the ghetto Zolli crossed Ponte Cestio to visit the hospital on Tiber Island. Most patients came from the ghetto. The hospital's doctors were graduates from Rome's medical schools and their reputations were respected throughout the Jewish community. The nurses, some of them nuns, had been trained at the city's teaching hospital. The doctors and nurses lived outside the ghetto; the nuns had their own quarters attached to the hospital. There was a modern operating theater and separate wards for women and children. Patients who could not afford the modest fees were treated for free.

Originally built in 1584 by the Order of Saint John as a monastery, it dominated the Roman galley-shaped island. Over the centuries it had expanded to become Rome's hospital for the management of tuberculosis and other bronchial infections. The mortality rate was high, but gradually improved as new treatments became available.

By the turn of the twentieth century the hospital had established itself as one of the best in the Order of St. John and was known as the *Fatebenefratelli*. To the ghetto Jews it was simply "our Jewish hospital."

Since 1930 the hospital was run by professor Giovanni Borromeo, a stylishly dressed Catholic physician with a high forehead and brown eyes and a gentle voice. In Rome's medical community he was known as an anti-Fascist who selected his own staff from doctors working in hospitals and clinics in and around the city. He told them their pay would be less than they presently earned and their hours longer. But he promised that under his guidance they would have a chance to develop their skills—and give the Jewish community medical service no other Rome hospital provided.

It was where Dr. Vittorio Emanuele Sacerdoti had decided to work. The first family photographs of Vittorio show a child with deep-set eyes that would never lose their curiosity. He did well at school and at nineteen had been accepted as a student at the Bologna medical school, one of the best in Italy. After graduating as a general physician he joined the staff of a hospital in Ancona in the north of Italy. He was dismissed under the racial law banning Jews to be employed. However Professor Borromeo had offered him a position. Under the Lateran Treaty the hospital was listed as one of the properties the Vatican owned in Rome and was exempt from the racial laws. Vittorio was given a room in the basement where other students lived. He soon became a popular figure with his ready smile and reassuring words to patients. He always carried sweets to give to the children and let them play with his stethoscope while he discussed his diagnosis with their parents.

After the synagogue service of homage, Foa had asked his personal assistant, Rosina Sorani, to bring to the Vatican a letter he had written expressing the community's congratulations to Pope Pius on his election.

The tall, fine-boned, twenty-six-year-old Rosina had flawless olive skin, a bright smile, and an exuberant manner. Her brother, Settimio, was a young lawyer in the Jewish community who, since the enactment of racial laws had been preparing paperwork for families to travel to the United States and other countries. His contacts with foreign diplomats in Rome had also enabled him to obtain visas. Increasingly they were needed for Jews from Germany and Poland who had arrived in Rome, fearful of the Nazi tyranny.

In his small office near the Spanish Steps Settimio had listened to their grim stories and over dinner he recounted them to Rosina. Next morning she had repeated them to Foa. In turn he had passed the details on to two trusted friends, Count de Salis, the Rome representative of the International Red Cross and Renzo Levi, a Jewish industrialist. He immediately agreed to finance visas and Settimio's work.

Approaching St. Peter's Square, Rosina saw that a growing number of ghetto dwellers were in the crowd. The coronation of a new pope had provided the souvenir sellers with a ready market for their items.

Sister Pascalina's appointment as the mistress of the papal apartment came in her twenty-sixth year as his housekeeper. The daughter of George and Maria Lehnert, farmers in Ebersberg, Bavaria, they christened her Josefina.

She was seventeen when she became a postulant in the Order of the Teaching Sisters of the Holy Cross. Four years later she took her final vows of poverty, chastity, and obedience and donned the black robe of a professed sister.

A new crucifix hung over her heart and a heavily starched headpiece with a gleaming white inner lining covered her head. Across her forehead and eyebrows she wore a stiff white coif which emphasized her rosy cheeks and lips. Before Mass to celebrate her induction into the order she had said her farewells to her parents, explaining that in future she would be called only by her religious name, Sister Pascalina. She had chosen it after the Paschal, the Easter candle, symbolizing the Resurrection and her new life.

Trained as a nurse in the order's hospital, she was sent to work in its rest home in the Swiss Alps where Vatican clergy went to recuperate. On an August morning in 1917 another priest arrived. In her diary she wrote: "He is pale with all signs of being delicate. He has piercing dark eyes. When I was introduced he only nodded. I could see that even the prioress is in awe of him."

It was Archbishop Eugenio Pacelli.

Pascalina was assigned as his nurse. She took him on walks along the alpine slopes, encouraging him to deeply inhale the mountain air.

Day by day the color returned to Pacelli's face and his clothes no lon-ger hung on him. Soon, she knew, he would be able to return to the Vati-can. She wrote in her diary, "He is someone who has not been used to having a woman tell him what to do. Even with other patients he has little contact. His mind is always on his work."

Pacelli had left without a word of good-bye. Though she had been trained in humility and obedience, she confided to her diary she was "be-wildered and hurt by the way he left."

Three months later she was summoned to the office of the prioress and told she was being transferred to act as housekeeper at the nunciature in Munich for the new apostolic nuncio, Archbishop Pacelli. She was twenty-three years old.

Carrying her suitcase through the first snow of winter, she arrived in Munich on December 17, 1917. The nunciature was in the city center. The three-story building had seventeen high-ceilinged rooms and a domestic staff of a butler, valet, a cook, a chauffeur, and two nuns to clean. Pacelli had a priest-secretary, Robert Leiber, a German Jesuit, who slept in a room adjoining the nuncio's suite. Pascalina's bedroom was next door. The rest of the staff slept in servants' quarters on the top floor. Pascalina was the youngest employee and in her diary she noted: "The other staff think I am too young to be in charge."

In January 1922, Pope Benedict XV died. Pacelli travelled to Rome to attend the funeral and remained for the coronation of Pius XI. He was told he was to move to Berlin, one of the most important diplomatic postings in the Holy See.

The Vatican had provided Pacelli with an impressive mansion in the Tiergarten district of the city and Pascalina found herself in charge of an even larger domestic staff than in Munich. "It was a world of splendor I could never have imagined," she wrote in her diary.

Pacelli hosted lavish dinner parties and glittering balls where an orches-tra played into the small hours for Berlin's high society. More than once she confided to her diary how fortunate she was to be close to a man of increasing power. Father Leiber had told her that soon Pacelli would be called back to the Vatican. She was certain she would go with him, to look after his personal quarters, his clothing, and liturgical vestments, and con-tinue to serve his meals. More than once she had shown him her ability to dissolve some anxiety of the moment and when he wanted to be alone, she ensured no one disturbed him, not even Father Leiber. He called her, not always amused, "Pacelli's guardian angel."

In the winter of 1929 Pascalina persuaded Pacelli to take a break from the pressure of work. He had gone to the rest home where they had first met.

It was there he received a telephone call to return to the Vatican. When he took the train to Rome, she remained in Berlin, wondering and waiting, sharing her thoughts with only her diary. She sensed "something important is to happen."

A week after Pacelli had taken up his appointment as cardinal secretary of state on February 7, 1930, Sister Pascalina arrived in Rome. She had spent her last days in Berlin packing his belongings in the nunciature, including hand-carved pieces of medieval furniture which the German bishops had given Pacelli to commemorate his time among them.

On a Saturday morning a Vatican-registered automobile, gleaming black, had collected her from Rome's main train station to drive her to her new home. As the car swept up Via della Conciliazione, Pascalina had her first view of St. Peter's in its setting of flanking colonnades and pillars topped by Bernini's statues of the saints. To her surprise she saw that the piazza was not a square but an oval shape with an obelisk marking the spot where Peter had been hung upside down on his cross. Priests were everywhere, coming and going from the square and in and out of the basilica. Tourists pointed their cameras at the Apostolic Palace. Somewhere in there was the pope, she reminded herself. Soon as Pacelli's housekeeper she would be part of his world. That night Pascalina confided in her diary, "To live and work here is my lifelong ambition."

Reality soon set in. She spoke almost no Italian and was a stranger to the Vatican's atmosphere and culture. She quickly saw that careerism was the mainstay of the male-dominated Holy See.

She was given a room in the nun's quarters in the Apostolic Palace and assigned a nun to help clean the cardinal's apartment. When the housework was completed, the other nun would go to buy food while Pascalina ironed

Pacelli's vestments; it was a duty she insisted on doing herself. By early afternoon she resumed exploring Rome.

She spent little time among the tourists walking around the Coliseum and the Pantheon, preferring to visit the city's old churches on side streets. Pacelli had told her there were hundreds of them. Unlike Saint Peter's and the basilicas of Saint John Lateran and Saint Paul Outside-the-Walls, huge imposing edifices, the churches she sought were small and dusty, filled with the devout smell of incense. Sometimes as she approached one, she would hear the murmuring of the litanies, the rigid dialogue between a priest and his congregation. They were mostly old women; their heads covered as they knelt on the stone floor. Pascalina would stand inside the door joining in the service. At other times she would find herself alone in a church and would light a candle and place it on a holder before the statue of a saint.

One early autumn afternoon after visiting a church near the Trevi Fountain, into which tourists threw coins to bring them good luck, Pascalina had walked along the Via del Portico d'Ottavia, that led to the ghetto. She saw that its people were unlike those in the slums in other parts of the city.

They were darker skinned than Romans and looked at her curiously then started to smile as she stopped to examine some of the items for sale in their stalls. When she didn't buy they shrugged. A few days later she returned again, this time to walk deeper into the ghetto, drawn to learn more about its people. She had done the same in Munich and Berlin, visiting the slum quarters, learning about the life of the people there and their struggle to make a living. On her visits to the ghetto she learned it was no different. Gradually, she came to know some of the women and found that what mattered most to them was their Jewish faith, and the high point of their week was the visit to the synagogue. In that way Pascalina had learned her first phrase of their language, the words the faithful spoke as they entered the synagogue. *Leba, dodi, richra, cala.* It was the call to greet the Sabbath.

As the years passed she found that despite her position as housekeeper to the Vatican's most important cardinal most prelates still pointedly ignored her; there was rarely a friendly smile or greeting when they passed her in the corridors of the Apostolic Palace. Finally she had told Pacelli of her unhappiness. He had reassured her that many people found it difficult to settle into Vatican life. That night she had written in her diary, "I should have realized that his life left him little time to deal with my personal problems."

It made her determined to find a solution by herself.

Priests from the Sacred Congregation regularly requested meetings with Pacelli on matters not directly linked to his busy schedule. Father Leiber turned many away. Finally several of the supplicants started to approach Pascalina. When she felt a request was reasonable she would ask Pacelli to find time to see a monsignor or bishop. News of her intercession spread. When Father Leiber protested, Pacelli told him what she was doing was no more than she did in Berlin: ensuring nothing important escaped his attention. In the Vatican Pascalina increasingly came to be regarded with new respect.

Pacelli arranged for her to move into a small comfortable suite close to his spacious apartment. She had become friendly with his family, especially his widowed sister, Elisabetta, and as a birthday gift she gave her a small altar for her bedroom.

Early in October 1936, Pacelli told Pascalina she was to accompany him on his visit to the United States, the first time a papal secretary of state had travelled to that country. The trip was to last a month and cover over sixty-five hundred miles visiting Catholic colleges, convents, monasteries, and parish churches.

The prospect of her first sea voyage and the trip across America had filled Pascalina with excitement. During the last day before leaving she had ironed Pacelli's robes and vestments and carefully packed them into the cabin trunks the Vatican had provided. Her own garments went into a suitcase. On board the Italian liner *Conte di Savoia*, Pacelli had been assigned the owner's suite, while Pascalina had a cabin belowdecks.

She spent most of the seven-day voyage in her cabin, reading and praying, taking her meals in a corner of the steerage-class dining room. From the ship's library she had collected U.S. magazines and had clipped items she knew could interest Pacelli. They would arrive in New York during the 1936 World Series, when the New York Yankees and the Giants would play.

Every evening Pascalina had a ship's steward carry the clippings to Pacelli's suite.

When the liner docked in New York she was led down to the quayside into one of the waiting limousines. On the upper deck the New York press was welcoming Pacelli in a blaze of flashing lights.

The American tour was a cavalcade of limousines sweeping in and out of airports into cities and towns for a succession of breakfast meetings, lunches, and dinners; speeches and lectures; and presentations to Pacelli of honorary degrees. In turn he delivered blessings at the Grand Canyon, Niagara Falls, the San Francisco Bay Bridge, and on a Hollywood film set.

The tour had also been an opportunity to deal with Detroit's notorious Father Coughlin who not only hosted an anti–New Deal radio program but used it to promote anti-Semitism. In one short meeting Pacelli "silenced" the priest and CBS lost an audience of thirty million every Sunday afternoon.

In his own speeches Pacelli denounced anti-Semitism and made a point of praising the contributions Jews had made to the United States. Privately he was even more ascerbic about the Nazis. He told Joseph P. Kennedy, soon to become the ambassador to Great Britain who met Pacelli in Washington, that he had "a strong antipathy to the whole Nazi regime."

The headlines for President Roosevelt's landslide victory in winning forty-six of the forty-eight states for a second term were matched by glowing accounts of Pacelli's trip. He sent his congratulations to the president who responded by inviting him for lunch at Roosevelt's country home at Hyde Park.

The next day Pacelli was driven to Hyde Park. That evening after they had boarded the ship for the voyage back to Europe Pascalina wrote in her diary, "His Eminence told me he had enjoyed lunching with a typical American family. The White House recognition of the Vatican is assured."

The physical strain of the American trip had left Pacelli with the appearance of a figure in an El Greco painting. He was thin, his skin almost translucent. In New York he had purchased new spectacles which gave his eyes an even more forbidding look.

The president's promise of diplomatic recognition, his success in winning over the American bishops, and attracting unprecedented crowds had given Pacelli a sense of increased power. He was not only the foreign minister of a vast medieval organization but he had learned how it could be presented on the international stage. His meetings with America's power brokers had also shown him how secular diplomacy and politics worked and how a president governed.

In the thirty-one days Pacelli had crisscrossed America he had learned much and had responded in kind. His lectures at the country's leading universities in which he condemned Nazism and Communism had brought standing ovations. Back in the Vatican he was once more confronted by events in Germany. The apostolic nuncios were reporting that anti-Semitism was spreading.

A week after Pius XII was elected Mose Spizzichino had parked his cart outside the new store which had opened that morning opposite the synagogue. The rotund owner, Umberto di Veroli had waddled forward to greet the peddler with a bearlike hug. The two were old friends from the day Umberto had been a pushcart peddler who had once walked the streets with Mose selling his combs.

Umberto was among the wealthiest men in the ghetto. Only money, Mose had mused, could have paid for the high-quality goods on sale: suits and racks of shoes up front in the store and, farther back, rails of overalls and boots for workmen. The shop was filling with people inspecting the merchandise. For them all Umberto had a smile and a word.

Usually they would talk about their times on the road. But on that March day in 1939 shoppers gathered around Mose when he started to speak. He had chosen to return to the ghetto by going past the Vatican when he heard a great cheer. Standing in the window of the Apostolic Palace waving to the crowd was the pope. It was the first time anyone from the ghetto had seen Pius XII.

In the first weeks of his papacy Pius had remained preoccupied with the fate of the Jews in the Third Reich. He had summoned the German cardinals to tell them that Hitler's totalitarianism was proof he had "abandoned the Christ's cross for the swastika." While the Catholic Church was not a political institute and could not ally itself with any nation, he must condemn Nazism for crimes against the Jews: "the church will be belligerent as to its moral position." He authorized the cardinals to channel money to those Jews in need and issue baptismal certificates for their protection. He read them a resolution which had been adopted at the latest meeting of the Jewish Congress in Geneva. "We record the Jewish people's deep appreciation of the stand taken by the Vatican against the advance of resurgent paganism, as well as inalienable human rights upon which alone enduring civilization can be found. The congress salutes the supreme pontiff, symbol of the spiritual forces which under many names are fighting the reestablishment of the rule of moral law in human society."

He handed each cardinal a copy of the resolution to take back to Germany, saying it should be "your beacon to light your way through the darkness."

3

THE CODE BREAKERS

The election of Pope Pius XII saw a new arrival in the marketing of real or spurious Vatican intelligence. Dressed in a velvet jacket and black trousers and chain smoking through a slim holder like one of the characters in the films he reviewed for *L'Osservatore Romano*, Virgilio Scattolini was also a novelist and playwright; his talents had made him a popular figure at Rome's society dinner parties. His visits to the newspaper gave him access to a confidential document: the papal audience schedule. It contained the time and length of each meeting and who had been present. Secretary of State Cardinal Maglione always attended those meetings with foreign ministers and members of the Holy See diplomatic corps. Each schedule also contained a concise summary of what was discussed.

Scattolini immediately saw how the document could improve his income. Melding the summaries with dinner party gossip, he began to provide the papal audiences with a life of their own. With the same skill with which he gave his stage actors persuasive dialogue he provided Pope Pius XII with imaginary views on such diverse subjects as how he intended to use international law to shape his policies or how Britain's empire was so vast and expensive to rule it could never afford to enter European war. Éamon de Valera, Ireland's prime minister, was said to have described Winston Churchill as having "a warlike attitude." In another summery, Count

Ciano, Mussolini's son-in-law, was credited with telling Pius Italy would never go to war to support German aspirations.

Scattolini's *Notiziario,* news bulletins, were immediately seen as the work of a Vatican insider. Diego von Bergen, the German ambassador to the Holy See, became one of the first subscribers to Scattolini's concoctions.

Soon his version of papal audiences had a growing subscription list of diplomats, journalists, and intelligence officers, all eager for any information on the pope's views as the war clouds darkened over Europe. The Rome offices of the Associated Press and United Press, engaged in intense rivalry, rushed to circulate Scattolini's fantasies. *The New York Times* and *The Times* of London published accounts from *Notiziario.* The very authority of those newspapers gave credibility to the bogus reports. Soon every embassy in Rome subscribed. Messengers would arrive at Scattolini's apartment with an envelope of money to collect a copy of the latest bulletin. In the United States the Bank of America ordered its traders to read *Notiziario* before trading. In London it was studied in the Bank of England as carefully as the market.

In Berlin, Foreign Minister Joachim von Ribbentrop had formed a *Buero Ribbentrop,* a highly secret office designed to check on usually rather pedestrian diplomatic reports from Reich embassies. The *Buero* was staffed by handpicked analysts from the foreign ministry intelligence department and its political office.

Pope Pius XII, with his years spent in Germany, his admiration for its culture, who spoke its language fluently and had surrounded himself with German staff, had become a target for the *Buero.* Von Ribbentrop ordered it to find out more about papal policies. He appointed an old classmate, Rudolf Likus, to do so. Given the rank of an SS major, the moon-faced Likus had a habit of finger snapping to show his delight and did so when he read a copy of Scattolini's work. He flew to Rome and offered Scattolini double what he was charging if he would send his reports to Berlin before they were published.

Scattolini continued to excel himself with fictitious summaries of papal audiences. Likus presented them to von Ribbentrop with confidence and authority, pointing out he had personally met Scattolini in his apartment and concluded he was *"der am Vatikan taetige Gewahrsmann"*—"our man in the Vatican."

Reassured, the foreign minister began to send the reports to Hitler. On his next visit to Rome Likus informed Scattolini who was reading his work. The forger told Likus that, for a further substantial increase in his fee, he would arrange for material to be passed on exclusively to Berlin and never published elsewhere. An elated Likus agreed. Hitler's fantasist in the Vatican continued to allow his imagination to flow freely.

Traditionally the first encyclical of a new pope sets the agenda for his immediate concerns. In the summer of 1939 Pascalina saw that Pope Pius had once more added to his *Summi Pontificatus*, this time to take into account what was happening to the Jews in Poland. Not for the first time she sat in his study as he read her a passage of writing he had taken an hour to compose. This time, she sensed, he pondered every word, knowing it would be the first time he had been specific.

"The blood of countless human beings, even noncombatants, raises a piteous dirge over a nation such as our dear Poland, which, for its fidelity to the church, for its services in the defense of Christian civilization, written in indelible characters in the annals of history, has a right to the generous and brotherly sympathy of the whole world, while it awaits, relying on the powerful intercession of Mary, help of Christians, the hour of a resurrection in harmony with the principles of justice and true peace."

Throughout the summer he had arranged for several more Jewish academics banished from Italian universities to hold posts at Vatican-controlled universities, both in Italy and abroad. From hospitals and medical research centers in Berlin, Hamburg, Frankfurt, and Munich where Jewish doctors had held positions, he had ordered his cardinals to arrange for them to either come to Rome or to be sent to safety in the United States, Canada, or England.

Britain's secret intelligence service, MI6, had opened a station in Rome in 1917. However, post–Great War cutbacks had reduced the Rome SIS station to a minor role.

The emergence of Hitler led to the resurgence of the station. In 1931, Claude Dansey, a veteran MI6 officer, was appointed Rome's station chief. He ran his spying from an office overlooking the Piazza Navona posing as an antique exporter. His purchases were shipped to London and sold from a shop in the Old Kings Road which was a front for MI6. The money helped to pay for running the Rome station. Dansey's handpicked agents were scattered across Italy and into Austria. One spy posed as a film company location finder and was sent to Vienna to discover the German order of battle. With war looming Dansey was recalled to London in 1938 to work alongside MI6's next chief, Stewart Menzies.

In July 1939, Menzies learned from an MI6 officer in Munich that two *Abwehr* officers had travelled to Rome. They were Colonel Hans Oster, the head of the *Abwehr*'s central division and his deputy Major Hans von Dohnanyi, a lawyer who was responsible for gathering intelligence about foreign diplomats in Berlin. On MI6 files both men were described as "very possibly anti-Hitler."

The MI6 Rome station established that both men had come to see Father Robert Leiber, the pope's German secretary. The meeting was to see if Pius XII would become involved in a plot to remove Hitler.

The plan was the creation of Admiral Wilhelm Canaris, the head of the *Abwehr*, Germany's foreign intelligence service. He had come to see that Hitler was leading Germany to both physical and moral destruction. Imbued with courage and nerve Canaris was determined the führer must be stopped.

Canaris had met Pius XII during his time as a nuncio in Berlin and had found common ground in discussing history. Traditionally popes as temporal leaders down the centuries had often performed the role of adjudicator in disputes between states; the treaties which divided the borders between Spain and Portugal were an example. Now, a decade after their Berlin meeting, Canaris had pondered whether Pope Pius XII would be prepared to help depose Hitler. While it could expose Pius XII to danger for himself, like every spy chief, Canaris was long used to putting aside such matters as the safety of an asset.

Canaris had sent the two *Abwehr* officers to Rome to explore his idea with Father Leiber, another contact the spymaster had made in Germany.

Oster explained to the pope's secretary how a growing underground opposition to Hitler—members of the German high command—were committed to returning Germany to democracy by dismantling the Third Reich and creating a federation which would include Austria. But before doing anything the opposition wanted an assurance from the British and French governments that neither would exploit what would undoubtedly be Germany's vulnerability at the time. They had come to Rome to see if the pope would be ready to obtain that guarantee. It called for D'Arcy Osborne to act as the intermediary between Pius and Britain's prime minister, Neville Chamberlain, to obtain it.

Von Dohnanyi added that to show they believed the pope was the ideal person to help and be ready to challenge Hitler, they were aware that on April 4, 1933, only days after the new Nazi government had taken office, the then Secretary of State Pacelli had ordered the apostolic nuncio in Berlin, Cesare Orsenigo, to warn the führer against persecuting the Jews after his government had announced a national boycott of all Jewish businesses. The two envoys said it was proof to Canaris that the pope had shown courage in his first initiative to intervene on behalf of the Jews.

Father Leiber had thanked them but made no other comment. It was not until 1962 that he chose to reveal this early aspect of the pope's determination to defend Hitler's Jews.

Chief Rabbi Zolli had established a daily routine. After breakfast with his wife, Emma, and their daughters, Dora and Miriam, he went to his study to write or read. His scholarly output since coming to Rome continued to be impressive as he discussed numerous aspects of Judaism. His style was fluid, his arguments carefully constructed.

There was also an intriguing aspect to his work. He often liked to publish under various first names. In some articles he chose to be called "Italo." In other pieces he identified himself as "Ignazio," the baptismal name of Loyola, the founder of the Jesuits. Other times he selected "Antonio," a name he first chose for his tribute to the Catholic saint of Padua,

Saint Anthony. Later he wanted to be bylined as "Anton Zoller" in two comment pieces he wrote for *The New York Times*. Critics suggested he was like Proteus, the sea god of Greek mythology who changed his shape to suit the occasion.

It was midmorning when Zolli usually began to telephone some of the other chief rabbis around the country.

By late summer in 1939, his telephone conversations had been about the growing persecution of the Jews in Germany. What would it mean for Italy's Jews? Zolli continued to be reassuring. The pope would never allow that to happen in Italy.

Umberto di Veroli's shop had become a meeting place for people after a Sabbath service in the synagogue. While the leaders of the Jewish community—Ugo Foa, Dante Almansi, Renzo Levi, and members of the *giunta*—the Jewish council—had their own meeting room in the synagogue, the congregation preferred to gather in Umberto's store to discuss the latest sermon of Rabbi Zolli.

When he had first come to Rome Zolli had assured them, "You are all held in my heart and I promise to include you in my prayers as long as I live." He had exalted them to be faithful to God, Israel, and their faith. But increasingly he had made references that the Catholic faith had allowed him to better understand his own. He had also started to read passages from his book, *The Nazarene*. For a people who had cleaved closely to their religion down the centuries Zolli's behavior was a radical departure from what they had expected from a chief rabbi. However, impressed by his intellectual stature they knew they could not challenge him on his pronouncements.

As the likelihood of war increased Pascalina had ensured that the domestic running of the papal apartment would be disturbed as little as possible. Since arriving in the apartment she had introduced changes. The pope's living quarters were refurbished. A shower stall was installed in his bathroom and the bedroom repainted a pastel shade. On a bedside table was a framed photograph of his mother and a wireless tuned to Radio Vatican.

She had arranged for Pius's own bed to be installed. Throughout the apartment there were new drapes and carpets on which stood his favorite pieces of furniture which he had been given by the German bishops. Fresh flowers were delivered every day.

Pascalina had made changes among the domestic staff. Nuns who only spoke Italian were replaced by German-speaking nuns. She gave each a month's trial before an appointment was confirmed. Those who failed to live up to her standards were sent back to their former posts. Failure included not completing their daily duties on time whether it was in the kitchen and bringing dishes to the pope's table for Pascalina to serve, or cleaning and dusting the apartment. Pascalina reserved for herself making the pope's bed and placing fresh towels in the bathroom.

Those who remained were governed by strict rules. There was a midnight curfew and a ban on pets. The exception was Pius and Pascalina. The pope had a caged bird which he released every lunchtime while he dined and the canary was fed crumbs from the table. Pascalina kept two neutered cats in the storerooms in the basement of the Apostolic Palace where all the supplies for the apartment were kept. Pius had given her permission to do so and Giovanni Antinori, Pius's valet, later claimed he had heard her frequently talking to the cats as she stroked them. It was a piece of gossip that eventually found its way into *The New York Times*.

Like all the apartment's staff, Antinori knew not to cross Pascalina who had been nicknamed throughout the Vatican as *la papessa*. A sign of authority was her selection of participants for Mass in the apartment's private chapel with its pews for forty-six worshippers. She would also suggest to the pope guests to be invited for lunch.

Curia officials who had ignored the nun in her first year at the Vatican came to realize that access to Pius depended on being in her good graces. Visitors from Germany who Pascalina remembered favorably from her time in Munich and Berlin could count on an audience with the pope. Others she felt had shown her a lack of respect were curtly told the pontiff's schedule was full for the foreseeable future. Even cardinals came to realize they were wise to cultivate relationships with the nun or risk being kept waiting to see Pius. When she spoke to him it was in her native tongue and princes of the church found it important to have some understanding of German if they hoped to impress Pascalina.

There was always space for Cardinal Francis Spellman, the powerful archbishop of New York. Pascalina had met him during her visit to America and a mutual respect had developed; on his regular visits to Rome Spellman would bring her a gift of a book or a religious picture which became prized possessions in her suite. The cardinal would usually stay for dinner with the pope, an opportunity for Pascalina to cook and serve the pasta dish both men liked.

Within the papal apartment there had developed another tension, this time between Pascalina and the most senior of the cardinals, Eugene Tisserant, the dean of the Sacred College of Cardinals. From the outset he had resented the increasing power of Pascalina, especially the way she controlled access to the pope. Pascalina had firmly told him he must first make an appointment through her. When he protested Tisserant was told that Father Leiber would ensure the cardinal could always see His Holiness on any urgent matter. The proud prince of the church was not mollified.

By the summer of 1939 others in the papal entourage found they had lost favour with Pascalina. A nun was upbraided for preparing a bowl for the pope's study that did not contain fresh fruit. The luckless sister was ordered to go to the market and collect fresh produce. Incidents like that were small but they added to the feeling that Pascalina had too much power. Yet no one could deny her energy. She awoke a full hour before the pope rose at six-thirty, and listened to Radio Vatican's early morning news broadcast.

After shaving and taking a cold shower Pius went to the apartment's private chapel. Pascalina was already in her pew in the front row with the household nuns she had chosen to partake in the Mass. Afterward she served Pius his usual breakfast, a cup of warm milk and a slice of black bread. For them both another day was under way.

Vaticanologist Paul Hofman described her relationship with Pius XII as "that like many devoted wives who have been married for a long time. Pascalina appeared to feel that the otherworldly pope couldn't do without her."

Three floors below the pope's chapel where the early morning Mass was being celebrated a specialist team of priests were at work. They included

Franciscan monks with skills in ancient languages and Jesuits with degrees in advanced mathematics. Between them they spoke the languages
of Europe, the Middle East, and Asia and shared a common skill: the ability to use random groups of letters and figures to create unbreakable
codes or decipher others. They were the cryptologists of the Holy See.

Their average age was twenty-eight years and in the late summer of
1939, they numbered twenty-four. As well as the vows all priests took—
charity, obedience, and poverty—the cryptologists had all sworn an oath
of secrecy. Only Pope Pius XII and his secretary of state, Luigi Maglione,
were fully aware of their duties and in the center of the room were two
large tables with wicker trays, each either marked "outgoing" or "incoming." Outgoing trays were filled with messages which had been encrypted
and were ready to be sent to the dispatch room for transmission to apostolic
nuncios; incoming trays contained cables from the nunciatures which had
been decoded and would be taken to the secretary of state in a sealed box.
Those for the pope were brought to him in a separate box.

When Pacelli became secretary of state in 1930 he ordered an overhaul
of the Holy See codes, especially those used to communicate with nuncios
in Berlin, Washington, Paris, and London. Each diplomat in those cities
was given his own system consisting of a group of numbers interspersed
with letters selected from medieval alphabets, often going back to languages at the time of Christ. The code for the Berlin nuncio was known as
RED cipher; Washington as YELLOW cipher, London and Paris had BLUE
and SILVER. The most secret of all was the GREEN code and only used
by the pope to convey his most urgent instructions.

Other codes were assembled around twelve thousand groups of letters.
For extra security the groups were further encrypted by using cipher tables
consisting of alternating letters and numbers.

By July 1939, the probability of war in Europe became closer in the
messages from the nuncios. The diplomat in Washington summarized his
meeting with Undersecretary Sumner Welles. "He made clear he wants
a military program to defend U.S. interests." From Munich came the report that "the German press has launched a campaign against Poland for
its war agitation."

———

In August the pope had asked nuncios in Germany and Poland to keep him informed of how many Jews they had helped to emigrate. With documents that identified them as Catholics they travelled along a chain of convents and monasteries eventually into France and the Netherlands. Others had made their way to northern Italy where they were sheltered in Jewish communities. Once more, the pope ordered local bishops to use church funds to support the emigrants.

In the meantime he and Secretary of State Maglione met with the ambassadors to the Holy See to ask them to consult with their governments to provide entry visas to the emigrants. On the whole, the request was coolly received. Determined to press the matter the pope had sent on August 24 the text of a speech to all his nuncios he intended to deliver over Vatican Radio that evening.

Its opening words set the tone. "The danger is imminent, but there is still time. Nothing is lost with peace. All can be lost with war. Let men return to mutual understanding. Let them begin negotiations anew, conferring with goodwill and with respect for reciprocal rights."

Within the Vatican's foreign diplomatic corps the sunny days of late summer did little to ease a sense of failure many envoys felt in trying to establish the position of the Holy See.

In the view of British Minister D'Arcy Osborne, any hope Pius had of brokering peace was over since the day he had spoken a sentence rich in metaphor after his coronation. "We grasp the tiller of Saint Peter's ship with the intention of steering it to the port of peace across many waves." That mythical ship had sunk on what the French ambassador, Charles-Roux, called "the rocks of appeasement" after Hitler dismembered Czechoslovakia on May 13, 1939.

In Berlin *Reichsmarschall* Hermann Goering had completed his inspection of a new department inside the massive Luftwaffe Air Ministry building. The *Forschungsamt* was an intelligence communication unit, equipped with the full range of intelligence-gathering equipment and a team of cryptanalysts. Their task included monitoring every nunciature within the

Third Reich; all mail was to be intercepted and Vatican Radio broadcasts transcribed in search for codes. The German post office was to copy all telegraph messages between the Holy See and its nunciatures.

On September 1, 1939, Hitler invaded Poland.

In the early hours of that first day in the month, his bedside telephone awoke Luigi Maglione. The caller was Archbishop Giulio Pacini, the papal nuncio in Warsaw to report German forces had begun invading Poland by land and air. Maglione ordered the nuncio to prepare to destroy confidential papers and to "look after the code book and seek a place less immediately threatened by the advancing German armies." The cardinal ended with the benediction, "May the Lord protect you."

Maglione dialed the Vatican switchboard and the night-duty nun connected him to the pope's bedroom. When Pius heard the news he went to his chapel to pray. Meanwhile, Pascalina had aroused the other nuns in their rooms on the floor below to join her in the apartment's kitchen and told them "our world, the whole world, is changing" and asked them to pray.

Father Leiber was the first to arrive in the apartment having heard the Vatican Radio announcement that war had broken out. He joined the pope at prayer in the chapel. Maglione appeared shortly afterward. He had already sent his aides, Tardini and Montini, to their offices in the secretariat of state to begin telephoning members of the diplomatic corps with the news.

The secretary of state went with the pope and Father Leiber to the dining room where Pascalina served them breakfast. While the pope sipped his warm milk he began to issue his first orders. Maglione was to send a GREEN code message to Pacini to start organizing Poland's Jews into hiding in every available shelter. A second similarly encoded order was to go to the Istanbul nuncio, Monsignor Angelo Giuseppe Roncalli (the future Pope John XXIII) to "prepare thousands of baptismal certificates to give to Jews which will allow them passage through Turkey to the Holy Land."

Other messages were to be sent to all other nuncios and bishops in neutral countries ordering them to increase "all pressure you can" on their host governments to provide visas for Polish Jews.

Pope Pius had also asked Father Leiber to contact the head of the Pallottine fathers in Rome, Father Anton Weber. The religious order was founded in Rome in 1835 by Vincent Pallotti, an Italian priest, to send missionaries across the world to set up schools and clinics. A month ago Father Weber had telephoned from the order's General House on Rome's Pettinari Street and asked Pascalina to arrange an audience. When he explained the reason she had quickly found a place for him on the pope's daily schedule. Pius had asked Father Leiber to attend.

The pope's secretary recalled, "Weber asked His Holiness to approve the Pallottines be allowed to set up a network to bring German Jews to Rome where they would be safe." On that September morning Father Leiber had been ordered to tell Weber he should start his clandestine network.

Two days later Britain and France declared war on Germany.

In his office in midtown Rome the representative of the Red Cross, Count Alexander de Salis, held a meeting to discuss events with Ugo Foa. With them was a slim elegantly dressed woman, Princess Enza Pignatelli Cortes, the daughter of one of Rome's Black Nobility families, aristocrats who had supported the Vatican following the seizure of the papal states. She was respected for organizing fund-raising events for Catholic charities and her friendship with Pius XII dated since he was secretary of state and she had invited him to address the girls' private school where she once was a pupil. Since then Pius had been a regular guest at her palace near the Arch of Constantine.

Seated beside Princess Cortes was Dante Almansi. The barrel-chested forty-year-old came from modest origins in Trastevere and was the only Jew appointed deputy chief of the Rome police force. He had been dismissed under the racial laws and Foa had made him his deputy on the Jewish community committee. Both were very different personalities. Almansi had not quite lost his streetwise stare that suggested he often did not believe what he heard. Foa had the self-control of a judge.

Beside Almansi sat Renzo Levi, a short, stocky man who was a wealthy Jewish industrialist. The group was completed by lawyer Settimio Sorani. Where Levi was forceful and decisive, Sorani was gentle and persuasive and Foa had appointed him as legal counsel to the community's committee. He lived with his sister, Rosina, who was Foa's secretary.

His minutes of the meeting included Foa's figures for 3.5 million Jews living in the Soviet Union; 3 million in Poland; 360,000 in Germany; 500,000 in Hungary; 300,000 in Czechoslovakia; over 250,000 in France; almost 200,000 in the Netherlands; and 100,000 in Belgium. Including Spain and Portugal and smaller nations like Sweden and Switzerland, Foa said close to 10 million Jews lived on the European continent. All were now at risk.

Almansi asked his first question: What could the Red Cross do to help them? De Salis explained it would use its influence with all governments to help the Jews. But the organization must respect the Vatican's neutrality. The day after the invasion of Poland de Salis said he was telephoned by D'Arcy Osborne. The diplomat had told him that both himself and Charles-Roux, the French ambassador, had made a joint approach to Cardinal Maglione to get the pope to condemn the invasion. The secretary of state had refused, saying that "the whole world will condemn the Germans without the Vatican's intervention."

Princess Cortes said she was certain that "Italy does not want to be in this war. But His Holiness cannot say much, if anything at all. Yet his silence must not be misunderstood. I know he will do everything to help the Jews."

By November the heat of summer had lifted and dampness drifted off the Tiber and clung to the walls of the *Fatebenefratelli* hospital on the island. At night the traffic headlights on Via Lungotevere, the road which ran beside the river, were no more than yellow blurs in the mist.

In the surgical wards patients waited for operations or lay in the recovery room. On a separate floor was the children's ward, long and narrow, its windows overlooking the Tiber and its shutters closed at dusk to keep out the night cold. On another floor was the maternity ward and its delivery rooms. Everywhere there were nuns in the long white robes of their nursing order and secular nurses in starched uniforms, white stockings, and caps. In a separate part of the hospital was the isolation area for tuberculosis patients, identified by their persistent coughing.

Every morning Professor Giovanni Borromeo and his doctors conducted their rounds. The children's ward was their first visit. Parents were always waiting to be reassured. Among them were Antonio and Giogina Ajo, cousins of Dr. Vittorio Sacerdoti. Pierluigi, their first son, was seven months old and a patient, with a chest infection. His father was a successful stockbroker and the family lived in the fashionable Viale Parioli district of the city.

When Pierluigi was born on July 26, 1939, the event was celebrated by a party under the benign eyes of the family's grandmother, Clotilde Almagia. A table near the baby's crib was stacked with gifts which Luciana Tedesco, a pretty six-year-old watched over, telling the other children to guess what was inside the wrapped packages. Dr. Sacerdoti had loaned her his stethoscope and she had ordered them to line up so she could listen to their heartbeats. "She'll be a doctor one day," the young doctor laughed. "Better yet a teacher," replied Luciana's mother.

That November day when Professor Borromeo completed his examination of Pierluigi he told his parents they could take him home. He assured them there was nothing to worry about. Sensing their concern he added the war was a long way from Rome.

Its outbreak was a matter of discussion within the ghetto. Many families had relatives scattered across the countries of northern Europe. Among them was the Polacci family who had an apartment on Via Pagoda Bianca. Already crowded with three elderly uncles and grandparents, Pietro Polacci decided there was still room for his wife's Polish cousin and had written to him in Warsaw. There had been no reply. A similar lack of response followed the letter Graziano Perugia, the ghetto kosher butcher, sent to his widowed sister-in-law in Krakov inviting her and her three children to come and live with them. But weeks had passed and there was still no news.

As he pushed his cart through the ghetto Mose Spizzichino had found an unexpected market for his old garments. People were buying them in anticipation of their relatives arriving and needing clothes. Selecting jackets, coats, and shirts, they had taken them to Serafino Pace's tailor shop to have them repaired. His son, Aldo, would recall, "Most of the fixing was on suits and overcoats. My mother would repair the shirts. Customers said they wanted everything to look good when a relative arrived."

Serafino had been a bus driver until the racial laws banned all Jews from working in the public sector. He had studied tailoring and opened a shop in his front room, his shears cutting bolts of cloth well into the night while his wife, Italia, mended worn collars. The business had thrived sufficiently to move out of the ghetto to a house on the bank of the Tiber in Trastevere.

In October the first refugees appeared in the ghetto. They had been smuggled out of Germany by the Pallottine network, moving from one safe house to another across Austria and over the border into Italy before finally coming south to Rome. Among them was Giuseppe Battino, a distant cousin of the Sabatello family who lived on the same street as Mose Spizzichino. Mose had offered Giuseppe a job and as they made their rounds around Rome the refugee had begun to describe the start of industrialized mass killing in the Third Reich.

Pope Pius XII met with Maglione to discuss the aftermath of the conquest of Poland; half the country had been captured by the Red Army and given Germany and Russia a common frontier. Pius had expressed the view it was not only a huge loss to Catholicism, but the death of an untold number of Jews. He feared it would also be the precursor of Communism spreading across Europe. The secretary of state was pragmatic: The alliance between Moscow and Berlin "may only be a temporary one as they have so little in common." Pius had not been reassured and asked Maglione to arrange an audience with Italy's King Vittorio Emanuele III so he could urge the monarch to use his influence to keep Italy out of the war and at the same time the pope would call for a truce between the warring countries on Christmas Eve and Christmas Day.

Maglione asked D'Arcy Osborne to send the proposal to London and Charles-Roux to inform his government. A similar request was made to the German ambassador, Diego von Bergen. France was the first to regret the cease-fire as "unpractical." Hours later Osborne refused *dolentissimo*, very sadly. Von Bergen informed the secretary of state, "Germany has been left with no alternative but to reject the pope's proposal."

4

DECISION ON PIAZZA VENEZIA

On December 21, 1939, another morning came to an end in the papal apartment and after lunch Pascalina had told the pope's chauffeur, Mario Stoppa, to bring the pope's limousine to San Damaso courtyard. It was time for the pope's afternoon walk in the Vatican gardens.

When the car reached them the chauffeur helped the pope out of the limousine, and Pascalina walked beside him.

Years ago, when she had first walked with him in the Swiss foothills while he recovered his health, she would pluck an alpine flower and hand it to him. Now, on that winter's late afternoon she picked a rose, his favorite flower, and gave it to Pius. After an hour they stood in silence looking out over the Christmas lights of Rome starting to twinkle in the dusk before walking back to the car.

Standing beside the Cadillac Pius had looked out toward where the Tiber ran on down past the ghetto. That night in her diary Pascalina had noted what the pope had said.

Rabbi Zolli's office was on the second floor of the synagogue. The first thing Zolli had done was to fix on the right-hand doorpost a *mezuzah*, containing the words of the Shema prayer. No one knew that in a locked drawer Zolli kept a notebook which contained another and altogether different record. It was his confession that he had become a "Catholic in my heart." He had chartered his steps from that first day in Trieste when he had written about professing a new faith.

"Jews do not become Christian lightheartedly. Nor do they do so without powerful help from God. Experience has shown that a convert will always face severe boycotts from his family and friends and all Jewish associates. He must expect his own father to turn against him and put him out of his home and blot his name from his will."

Zolli had taken care that Ugo Foa or members of the Jewish community committee did not know his secret. "I knew I would be expelled from office for what I had done and word would spread throughout the Diaspora of what they would call my religious crime."

His notebook was filled with descriptions of "the mysterious attraction" he felt for Christ; how, the first time he touched a crucifix, it had loosened the "hold of the faith of my people"; that secretly reading the New Testament after his family had gone to bed reinforced his belief in Christianity.

Zolli was convinced that "Judaism and Christianity meet in my very soul. Judaism is a promise of the Messiah to come. Christianity is that the Messiah has arrived."

Zolli believed he could still be a righteous Jew when conducting the funeral of one of his congregation. After leading the pallbearers to the open grave and, as the body in its shroud was lowered into the ground, he chanted the appropriate Hebrew words. But on returning to his office he recited the Lord's Prayer. In his notebook he had promised God that he would publicly announce his conversion once the war was over.

Once a week Zolli lectured at the ghetto's Jewish school. There were classrooms on its four floors and a large hall where he spoke to the senior pupils. He was a gifted speaker and he brought alive the stories of the prophets, holy places, ancient fortresses, and Jewish heroes. He mixed his talks with the Scriptures, Mishnah, Tosefta, Talmud, and Midrash. Teachers would often come to stand at the back of the hall and listen to his mesmeric performance.

When he finished he walked around St. Peter's Square and stared at the Apostolic Palace, wondering if the day would ever come when he would meet the pope and tell him of his conversion.

On February 20, 1940, Harold H. Tittmann walked into the Excelsior Hotel, one of the finest in Rome. He was the United States consul general in
Geneva, Switzerland, and now the first member to arrive of the American
mission to the Holy See. It was the latest move in the career of a diplomat
whose ancestors came from the Saxon city of Dresden.

Tittmann had been a pilot in the Great War, a member of the famous
ninety-fourth pursuit squadron and was shot down near the French line.
He spent two years in a hospital and was reputed to be the most seriously
wounded American in the war. In 1920 he joined the U.S. foreign service.
After a spell as third secretary in Paris in 1925 he was posted to Rome. In the
eleven years he remained there he had met and married Eleanor Barclay,
a Texas belle and became the State Department's expert on Fascist Italy.
A year after receiving his Geneva appointment he was now back in Rome,
this time to prepare the way for the new U.S. ambassador to the Holy See,
Myron Taylor.

His first task was to ensure that the best suite in the Excelsior would
serve as the base for the mission, and where Taylor could host return visits
from key Vatican officials and members of the foreign diplomatic corps.
Days later the ambassador, a muscular sixty-year-old millionaire, swept
through the hotel suite, with its office and living quarters for him, and
additional rooms for his staff and announced, "Mr. Tittmann you've done
just fine."

Taylor had been a banker and president of the United States Steel Cor-
poration. He remained an Episcopalian, a humanitarian, a friend of President Roosevelt, and had hosted the pope, when as Cardinal Pacelli, he had
visited New York in 1936. He owned sizeable estates near Florence and
spoke Italian. Tittmann had told D'Arcy Osborne that Taylor was "a real
fit for the Vatican."

Taylor had presented his credentials to the pope as President Roosevelt's personal envoy and explained his prime duty was to encourage Mussolini to remain neutral.

Taylor had shown he was master of his brief. He told Pius that while
Roosevelt was prepared to do anything to achieve peace, he expected
that soon Hitler would invade France and Mussolini would see it as an

opportunity to join in the war. The successful conquest of France, which Roosevelt felt was very likely, would enable the duce to claim his share of the spoils of victory from the French. He had long coveted Corsica and Tunisia.

In his first cable to the State Department Taylor had said the pope had told him the Holy See would do all possible to keep Italy out of the war.

That first audience was the first of seven Pope Pius XII accorded Taylor between February 27 and May 23, 1940. It was the largest number of audiences Pius had with any foreign envoy in such a short period.

None can have been more dramatic than the audience in late April, when the pope informed Taylor that in the event of Italy entering the war, the Holy See would provide sanctuary to all Allied members of the diplomatic corps. Pius then made a request which could only have startled Taylor. Could Vatican Bank transfer the gold ingots in its vaults to the United States and have them stored in the Fort Knox repository where America's gold reserves were kept? The pope had described the matter as "very urgent."

On May 21, U.S. Secretary of State Cordell Hull telegraphed Taylor. "Agreed. Need value." The value of the gold was placed at U.S. $7,665,000, nearly all of the Vatican's gold reserves. The transfer was organized by Cardinal Spellman, the archbishop of New York. To this day the details of how the shipment was carried out has remained in the Secret Archives of the Vatican.

In early June 1940, Monsignor Enrico Pucci had a new story to peddle. The past months had been lean for the gossip monger. There were few foreign reporters left in Rome who trusted him and while the embassies of neutral countries still bought his information his fees had dropped since the halcyon days before conclave. In his last call to D'Arcy Osborne Pucci had been firmly told that unless he had "something really interesting, there was no point in knocking on the door."

Pucci believed that moment had come. One of his mysterious sources in the Vatican had told him that the pope was planning to move to the United States if Italy entered the war. Taylor's arrival in Rome and his past relationship with the pope as his New York host during his prewar visit, was to prepare for Pius's move to the United States. Cardinal Spellman was identified as being in charge of the American end of the operation to establish the Vatican in Boston.

In the Vatican two other senior priests according to Pucci's story were also involved in the secret plan. They were Borgongini Duca, the nuncio to Italy, and Father Tacchi Venturi, a Jesuit priest who was close to Mussolini. Other names were woven into the story. Maglione was said to have discussed the matter with Count Ciano, Italy's foreign minister who was said to be still "very much against the war." Polished and honed to fit with the Vatican's mentality of secrecy, the story was ready to be marketed.

He had found Osborne receptive, listening carefully to what Pucci said. In the past weeks the minister had himself noted the atmosphere had become "very electric" in the secretariat of state. Officials were increasingly difficult to meet and it was clear the pope had started to come under pressure. It had also become hard to pin down Taylor if he had another purpose in coming to Rome. The ambassador had merely confined himself to saying he was there as Roosevelt's personal envoy. Osborne increasingly wondered if Pucci's story might just be plausible. In his diary the minister had already written he had started to burn all sensitive documents in preparation for war. "In these blitzkrieg days I do not wish to run the risk of telegrams or dispatches being found which could be used either against the Vatican or other sources of information." Osborne paid Pucci for his information and sent it to the Foreign Office inside the daily diplomatic bag. The following day Sir Percy Loraine, the British ambassador to Italy, asked to see Osborne. Loraine's own reports to London had remained optimistic that Italy would remain neutral. "The terrible events in Poland have made Italians loathe the Nazis and it is most doubtful that Italy, the most Catholic minded of nations will ally itself with an anti-Semitic and anti-Christian and murderous government."

Pucci's account of the pope fleeing to America had created consternation at the Foreign Office; its two diplomatic sources of information in Rome were clearly out of kilter. At Loraine's meeting with Osborne was the local MI6 station chief. He told Osborne Pucci was a German informer and his story was "totally untrue and created in Berlin for its man in the Vatican to pass on to Pucci." The intelligence officer had asked to see any further information Pucci offered. A dismayed Osborne had agreed.

Admiral Wilhelm Canaris, the director of the *Abwehr*, had spent another weekend in his office at 76/78 Tirpitzufer, two former town houses, overlooking the beautiful chestnut and lime trees in Berlin's Tiergarten. Since dawn he had read the reports that came from his chiefs of intelligence throughout the world. That afternoon he had gone for a stroll in the Tiergarten with his deputy, Colonel Hans Oster, walking along the bridle paths where they passed several members of the German general staff taking afternoon rides. Canaris let his dachshund, Seppel, off its lead, watching the dog run in and out of the bushes, as he told Oster that the *Abwehr* must do nothing to prolong the war by a day, that while a defeat for Germany would be a disaster, a victory for Hitler would be a catastrophe.

Therefore he was ready to make a new move to once more try and involve Pope Pius XII in the plot to overthrow the führer. He was sending to Rome Josef Mueller, a Bavarian lawyer, who had joined the *Abwehr* at the outset of war. His well-tanned face, reddish-brown hair, and customized black suit was a familiar sight around the Munich Palace of Justice. A devout Catholic, he represented the Munich diocese in the building's courtrooms. Mueller's success had given him connections in the Vatican where he was respected in the Holy Office and the secretariat of state for winning cases for the church.

Canaris had told Mueller that the first visit to Rome by Colonel Oster and his co-conspirators had failed because they had asked "too much too soon" in their meeting with the pope's secretary, Robert Leiber.

Mueller's own brief in Rome would be to try and once more persuade Father Leiber to get the pope to support "negogiations with Britain and a new and honorable government in Berlin after Hitler had been overthrown." Once contact had been made with Father Leiber and he agreed to present the proposal to Pius, the pope should send for D'Arcy Osborne who would act in the initial stage as the go-between with the Holy See and the British government. If the discussion continued to move forward more senior diplomats would be called in to carry the plan to conclusion—the removal of Hitler.

His legal skills had taught Mueller to take his time in preparing a brief. He had studied the *Abwehr* file on Pope Pius XII and read his speeches. He concluded that the pope shared his own pro-Jewish sentiments. When the time came he would use that as part of his argument that a new German government would guarantee that Jews would no longer be persecuted. He had also decided he would not go to Leiber at once, but approach him through another German in a powerful position in the Vatican. Monsignor Ludwig Kaas had been a contact of Pius since his days as a nuncio in Germany and Kaas had represented the Catholic Center Party in the Reichstag. When Hitler came to power Kaas had moved to Rome to become secretary of the congregation in charge of St. Peter's Basilica. On May 10, 1940—the day Neville Chamberlain resigned and Winston Churchill became Britain's prime minister—Mueller arranged to meet Leiber. While no record exists of their meeting, later the widow of one of the principal conspirators, Hans von Dohnanyi, revealed that her husband, a lawyer, had drafted articles of peace terms for the pope to review. According to Frau Dohnanyi, Leiber had taken them to Pope Pius XII, who had told the secretary to inform Osborne that the German opposition to Hitler continued to gather momentum.

Two days after meeting the pope's secretary, Mueller had flown to Berlin to brief Canaris. The spymaster doubted the peace initiative would succeed with Churchill now in office.

On Monday afternoon, June 10, 1940, Rosina Sorani was typing letters Ugo Foa had dictated to her before he left to visit a friend in the hospital when her telephone rang in the synagogue. The caller was Settimio. Her brother rarely phoned her at work and she had never heard him so excited. Radio Rome had announced Mussolini was to address the nation at six o'clock that evening. Romans should go to Piazza Venezia; the rest of Italy should listen to the wireless. Settimio reminded her the last time Mussolini had made such a broadcast had been on the eve of Italy invading Ethiopia in October, 1935.

During the afternoon Maglione had made several attempts to speak to Count Ciano. Each time the secretary of state was told Ciano was in a meeting with Mussolini and could not be disturbed. Maglione had gone to the pope. Pius had told him to alert the heads of the Sacred Congregations to listen to Mussolini's broadcast and to inform the nuncios to provide the reactions in their host countries.

Myron Taylor and Monsignor Joseph Hurley, an American priest in the secretariat of state, had spent the afternoon discussing the portents of the coming broadcast. The splendor of Taylor's office did nothing to lift his mood. He felt he had failed, he had said more than once.

Over the past weeks he had conferred with Maglione, Osborne, Charles-Roux, and others in the diplomatic corps. All had been certain Mussolini would keep Italy out of the war.

Now, he told Hurley, it "is too late. Mussolini has been watching, waiting, jackal and vulture-like for the order from Hitler. Meantime he has made a fool of us. You, me, the president, the whole shooting match."

Taylor had already asked President Roosevelt to make a direct appeal to Mussolini to remain neutral. Roosevelt had done so. The response had been polite but noncommittal. On April 18, Lord Halifax, Britain's foreign secretary, had sent a message to Taylor urging him one more time to ask Roosevelt to intervene and convince him the Allies "are in friendly relations with many countries which are governed by an authoritarian regime and that the kind of regime prevailing in other countries is no business of ours."

The response to Roosevelt was blunt. "Peace is not possible until the fundamental protection of Italy's liberty is settled with other parties."

Taylor pondered who those "other parties" could be and what "protection" Mussolini was speaking about. Now, as the office mantle clock approached six P.M., he was increasingly certain what the answer would be.

Giovanni Mezzaroma and Celeste di Porto had sent the Black Panthers pickpockets to Piazza Venezia. A crowd of that size was a target not to be ignored. The couple had taken up their positions at the edge of the tight-packed crowd. The pickpockets would remain among them until people began to disperse. That was when the police would try and arrest those they recognized as members of the Black Panthers or other gangs.

Celeste had devised a way to outsmart the police. With each Panther was a child, some no more than six or seven years old. As the thieves worked their way through the crowd they would slip their pickings to the children to carry out of the square. At an arranged spot Celeste would collect the stolen items. For the children it was their induction into the gang.

Ugo Foa and Dante Almansi had been invited to Renzo Levi's office to listen to the broadcast. After the meeting with Count de Salis the millionaire had set up Delasem, *Delegazione per l'Assistenza degli Emigranti Ebrei*. The organization was to help the emigration of Jews who had arrived in Rome through the Pallottine fathers network. So far over five hundred Jews were registered with the organization. Levi had gone to New York and arranged for funds from Jewish organizations to pay for visas and sailing tickets to the United States and other countries. He had also set up a bank account in Rome with the approval of the Fascist government eager to receive an influx of foreign currency. By the first week of June twenty thousand dollars a month was being transferred.

Princess Enza Pignatelli Cortes had invited an old friend, the Marchesa Fulvia Ripa di Meana, another member of a Black Nobility family, to join her to listen to the broadcast. The princess had telephoned Count Ciano's wife, Edda, who was Mussolini's daughter, to ask her if she knew what her father was going to say. She said she didn't know.

Professor Borromeo had invited some of his doctors to join him in the staff lounge to listen to the broadcast. He had installed its wireless after the start of the war. Several of the off-duty nurses had gone to the square. A priest was standing near the entrance to the square.

Six feet two inches tall, dressed in his distinctive red-and-black vestments, forty-three-year-old Monsignor Hugh Joseph O'Flaherty was a *scrittore*, a writer on the staff of the Holy Office, one of the most important of the Sacred Congregations. His duties had included stamping out all kinds of heresies and banning books which contained what canon law called "dangerous affirmations," including fundamental errors in sex education for Catholics. Several times a year he had recommended a priest to be defrocked for immoral behavior. His assessments were important enough for Monsignor Alfredo Ottaviani, the head of the Holy Office, to pass on to the pope. Pius had finally sent for O'Flaherty to congratulate him on his theological judgements.

O'Flaherty's fund of jokes had made him a popular figure among the younger priests in the Vatican. Senior priests said he could become an archbishop or finally even a cardinal. But there were also older prelates in the Curia, the Vatican civil service, who said he was too ready to challenge the *Regolamento Generale della Curia Romana*—160 pages of rules which governed the life of everyone in the city-state. But his critics knew there was little they could do. O'Flaherty had the support of Ottaviani. He was one of the closest officials to the pope.

It was an open secret in the Apostolic Palace that Hugh O'Flaherty had an active social life in Rome. He dined and danced in its high society, regaling guests with his stories. But what he called his "nights on the town" had another function. The gossip he picked up he relayed to Ottaviani who, in turn, passed details on to the pope.

As the church bells of Rome tolled the hour, six o'clock, on that evening of June 10, 1940, the huge balcony door was flung open from inside Mussolini's office.

Flanked by the twin symbols of Fascism carved into the stone wall behind him, the axe and the lector, stood Mussolini in his gray uniform, Sam Browne belt, jodhpurs with red stripes, and his black boots. He placed both his hands on the balcony railing, his body ramped straight, staring out over the crowd, his broad chin thrust out, his brown eyes sweeping over the crowd, his face set in a familiar scowl.

He waited, as he always did, for the applause. When it came he raised his hands in the Fascist salute. He silenced the cheering with a downward chopping move of the hand. His words began to thunder around the square.

"Fellow Italians. From midnight this nation is at war with Great Britain and France." Rosina Sorani remembered how she did what so many others were doing around her: She gasped and, in her case, clung to Settimio's arm as Mussolini continued to speak.

"War has been declared under the Pact of Steel I signed on your behalf on May 20th of this year which commits this nation to be enjoined to our ally, the Third Reich, which has already achieved huge victories against our decadent enemies."

In her salon Princess Enza stared in openmouthed disbelief at the Marchesa di Meana. Over the wireless came the voice of Mussolini.

"The great Italian people are resolved to meet the risks and sacrifices of war because our honor, interests, and future demand it."

In his office Myron Taylor shook his head at Monsignor Hurley.

"He is mad. Stark raving mad," said the ambassador.

"Worse, he thinks he is sane," said Hurley. "He is ready to sacrifice his people to show Hitler how powerful he is."

Settimia Spizzichino would recall how her father had shook his head in fury and motioned for his family to follow him out of the square. "He kept saying, 'enough, enough.' My father was always a man who could control his feelings. But not this time."

Mussolini's voice rolled across the square.

"To win must be our aim! It will give us a long period of peace and justice. We shall take up arms with courage and tenacity. We have done so before! We will do so now!"

In Renzo Levi's office, Ugo Foa and Dante Almansi looked at each other. Finally the millionaire broke the silence. "Now we know the truth, we all have work to do."

———

In Maglione's office the secretary of state and his two assistants, Monsignor Tardini and Monsignor Montini listened intently as the broadcast continued. Mussolini's voice had risen.

"We will fight with valor! Victory will be ours!"

The broadcast was over. The pope had listened to the speech on his bedroom wireless set. When it ended he went to the chapel. Shortly afterward Pascalina and the other nuns in the apartment joined Pius in prayer.

Later that evening the pope asked Maglione to inform Count Ciano that the Vatican, under the Lateran Treaty, had prepared accommodation for diplomats of nations at war with Italy, who were accredited to the Holy See, to be housed inside Vatican City. Only two families for each Allied embassy or legation would be accommodated. All others must be given safe passage home.

Harold Tittmann had already returned to his post as consul-general in Geneva. Myron Taylor would not be moving into the Vatican. His mission as President Roosevelt's official representative had failed to bring about peace. In his final audience with Pius he told the pope he would remain in Rome "for the moment to dedicate myself to the humanization of the new order." The pope had expressed his concern over the future of Great Britain, "which seems black indeed." Taylor had offered a vision of American military and economic aid, only for Pius to respond that aid would "turn out to be too little and too late."

Taylor had invited Ugo Foa to visit him in the Excelsior Hotel to discuss the situation of the ghetto Jews. He had served as Roosevelt's nominee on the Inter-Governmental Committee on the Political Refugees before coming to Rome. Its main role was to facilitate the emigration of Jews from the Third Reich. Foa had told him about Delasem and the Pallottine priests which had by now brought over six hundred Jews to Rome. When Taylor asked if they were sheltered by Jewish families who had no blood relationship with them, Foa had said "it is enough they are Jews."

The day after Mussolini delivered his declaration of war the pope asked Father Leiber to find space in his audience schedule for him to see Ugo

Foa. He told his secretary he would meet the Jewish community leader in the papal apartment "as an old friend." It was the signal that Pius wanted no note taker present to keep a record of the meeting.

It was late afternoon when Foa was escorted into the pope's study. It would be their first meeting since Mussolini had introduced the Nazi-inspired racial laws. Since then Rome's Fascist press had continued its attacks on the pope for his criticism of the anti-Semitic legislation. Foa had brought with him a letter from Dr. Nahum Goldmann, the president of the World Zionist Organization thanking the pope for his "unflinching support of the Jews."

There were now over four thousand Italian Jews—army officers, civil servants, academics, and journalists—who were still unemployed as a result of the racial laws.

The pope began by saying that as well as helping them, he had not forgotten his "near neighbors," the Jews of Rome's ghetto. If any were experiencing problems he had arranged for the papal nuncio to Italy, Monsignor Borgongini Duca to deal with the matter "loud and clearly" with the Fascist authorities.

Foa would recall how the pope had spoken with "quiet passion as he said he would lay to rest any thought he would follow a plan more conciliatory to the totalitarian states than his predecessor. He made it clear that the safety of the Jews was growing more intense and was one of the gravest of the many other serious problems he now faced."

Pius had said he would employ all the weapons in his power: prayer, liturgy, and international law to confront the Nazis, who for all their technical skill were filled with a spiritual emptiness, in what the pope defined as the "Age of Agnostism driven by anti-Semitism."

In the meantime if any member of the Jewish community wished to leave Rome he had arranged with the Pallottine fathers to assist them in obtaining foreign visas. It may take a little while to obtain the documents but they would be forthcoming.

Finally Pius had said he wanted to assure the community that he would continue to attack anti-Semitism and protect the Jews. He handed Foa a bound copy of *Summi Pontificatus*, with the words "where there is a question of saving souls, we feel the courage to deal with the Devil in person."

Foa had responded with a Hebrew saying. "A man is compared to the stars in Heaven and to the dust of the earth. He can soar to heights."

The accredited diplomats of the United Kingdom, France, Belgium, and Holland, with their families, had been assigned accommodation in a hospice which formed part of the Vatican's Santa Maria compound of the Order of the Sisters of Saint Vincent de Paul. On the far side of the compound was the convent. Its nuns in their steel-blue habits and wide-winged coifs would carry out the domestic duties in the hospice.

D'Arcy Osborne was the last to arrive. The days following Italy entering the war had been spent selecting what to take with him into the Vatican. Finally he had taken down the British coat of arms over the front door. He had then sent John May and his English secretary, the spinsterish Edna Tindall, ahead to prepare their future home.

After a final walk through the streets of Rome and with his cairn terrier, Jeremy, sitting beside him in the passenger seat, he drove into the Vatican. With Jeremy at his heels, the minister strolled into the hospice. When a Guardia Palatina looked at the dog, Osborne said, "It's okay. He's got diplomatic immunity. So you'll have to get used to him sniffing around."

Osborne's apartment was on the top floor of the hospice. His neighbor was the Belgium ambassador, Adrien Nieuwenhuys, who developed neurasthenia from the ringing of the bells of nearby St. Peter's. Close to a mental breakdown, he was allowed to return to his Rome residence and Osborne had taken over the Belgian's apartment, giving him twice the space than any other diplomat. He had enjoyed telling the Foreign Office of his success.

In January 1942, Josef Mueller was back in Rome to see Father Leiber. He told the pope's secretary that Amt VI, the department of the RSHA intelligence organization monitoring papal nunciatures, had broken a code used by the Vatican. It was not only sufficiently serious to lead to the certain death of the anti-Hitler plotters in Germany, but would compromise the pope if the code had been used to convey sensitive information.

Leiber was reassuring: The Holy See's codes were unbreakable.

Whatever the German code breakers had done they simply could not have had access to any of the Vatican codes.

Mueller produced a sheet of folded paper, smoothed it open, and handed it to Father Leiber. The secretary stared at it in disbelief. It was a decoded copy of a telegram the pope had sent to the nuncio in Portugal two days before, confirming he was to stay in post for another year. The priest had said he must show the document to Pius. Mueller had agreed. That night when they met again, Father Leiber confirmed the pope had not used the code to convey any sensitive information but had ordered it to be discontinued.

By late 1942 the Italian code breakers of its intelligence service had also started reading encoded messages sent from and received by the Holy See. The discovery came when Foreign Secretary Count Ciano—with characteristic indiscretion—informed Maglione. He immediately ordered a new cryptographic system to be created. It took weeks to develop the new system which contained twenty-five thousand groups, each one encrypted with twenty-five digital keys. Each key had its own digraphic table and a random mixed alphabet. Built into each code was a key capable of switching an encryption as many as eight times within a single transmitted message. While the Vatican would neither confirm nor deny, the evidence points to the codes having remained unbreakable to this day.

Settimia Spizzichino knew something was wrong when her father came home. Usually as he came down the street he would be singing as he pushed the cart, and calling out for the family to come and help him unload. Instead he had come into the house empty-handed and told Grazia to bring the family to the kitchen.

Sitting around the table Mose told them the Mussolini government had reduced the vending licences of ghetto peddlers to one person per family. He had heard the news on Radio Rome.

In the shocked silence Settimia remembered how her mother had pointed to the pot of soup she kept on the stove for sick neighbors. Grazia said she could no longer share it with them, a custom she had maintained

from her first day as a housewife. Soon she would not be in a position to
feed her own family, she said through her tears.

Settimia saw her father put his arm around his wife and say that would
not happen. He would see to that; they would all see there would still be
food on the table.

There was a determination in his voice that Settimia had not heard
before as Mose said that as well as old clothes he would peddle sewing
needles, buttons, and thimbles, the items he had started out selling as a
boy. His daughters would find work as seamstresses; their husbands could
become market porters or road sweepers. Between them they would earn
enough to survive.

He reminded them there would be other families who would be worse
off and with no money saved to fall back on. Every day, he said, he had put
aside money for an emergency. It was something his own father had done.

Settimia would remember how Mose had looked at them. "If there
was one thing my father taught me it was to be always ready for a problem. 'I'm ready and so will you be,' he said."

Mose told them after dinner the children would all go out and find
whatever work was available.

December 16, 1942 was the start of Harold Tittmann's second year as the
State Department's chargé d'affaires, the senior United States diplomat
accredited to the Holy See. His apartment was a floor below where D'Arcy
Osborne lived in splendid comfort and the family had adjusted to life in
the Vatican. Tittmann had hired a butler and a maid/cook paid out of his
monthly budget. The State Department transferred funds into the Mor-
gan Bank in New York where Vatican Bank had its account. After it had
been exchanged into 28,500 lire it was sent to Rome and paid over to Tittmann to maintain the mission.

Diplomats paid no rent as they were classified as "guests of the Holy
Father." Each mission paid one hundred lire every month for a telephone,
though no calls could be made outside the Vatican. Garage space for a car
was fifty lire a month. Every three months each mission would pay one
thousand lire to the Order of St. Vincent de Paul to cover the costs of maintaining the apartments, including weekly changes of laundry. Food brought

from the pope's farm at Castel Gandolfo by the Vatican's railway train could be bought from the market stalls inside the Vatican.

Between 2 P.M. and 6 P.M., the Vatican gardens were out of bounds when the pope walked there. Osborne had noticed it took the pope ten minutes to make a complete lap of the garden. Some days he did eight laps, other days ten. Osborne had started to bet with May how many laps Pius would do on a given day. Another bet was to guess whether the pope would be reading a book on one of his laps.

While there were regular meetings with members of the secretariat of state to discuss a wide range of events connected with the war, by nature Osborne was not cut out for the monkish life of the Vatican. "Miss Tindall was no compensation for the sight of the pretty women in Rome," he observed. It often took him hours to prepare or decipher an encoded report to or from London. A diary note captured the mood of depression which afflicted him from time to time. "I have reached the grave conclusion that I am nothing but a pencilled note in the margin of the Book of Life."

As 1942 drew to an end he noticed that physically and mentally he was changing. His rheumatism had grown worse and he needed his sword stick to help him walk. He was sleeping badly and his hair had started to fall out and his eyes seemed to be sinking into their sockets. He had told May, "If I go on like this I could lose my sanity."

May had reminded Osborne that he would not be in post unless London appreciated his reports. The relationship between the minister and his manservant had grown close, a friendship of mutual respect.

May continued to ensure that Osborne's daily needs were met. He had arranged with a Vatican gardener to supply cigarettes and whisky, bought on the growing black market. He encouraged Osborne to hold regular dinner parties, taking care to sit the minister always next to Tittmann's wife, Eleanor. Osborne had confided to May he found her "the most vivacious and witty woman in this place."

On sunny afternoons, when the gardens were reserved for the pope, Osborne went up to the flat roof above his apartment to sunbathe in his shorts. On those occasions May would carry up a watering can of cold water into which he had emptied salt and poured it over Osborne. "It heightened my sense of being in the sea. To avert sunburn I used shaving cream," recalled Osborne.

In his office the minister had a rowing machine and he visualized he was in the Oxford crew for its annual boat race against Cambridge as sweat ran down his domed brow. Other times he would close his eyes and imagine the machine was a rowboat and he was fishing on a loch in the south of Ireland. When he walked in the garden with Jeremy at his heels, he would toss the terrier into one of the fountains and watch him paddling among the fish. At sunset May would sometimes go to one of the fountains and catch a trout which he would serve for dinner for a special occasion: Miss Tindall's birthday or the anniversary of another year spent in the Vatican. But the table talk of war was never far away.

A few months ago the pope had reluctantly received Joachim von Ribbentrop, Hitler's foreign minister, with one purpose. He was determined to express his condemnation of Nazi atrocities and its anti-Semitic policies. When von Ribbentrop had tried to dismiss the charges as "Allied propaganda," Pius had quoted from a file of reports sent by nuncios and bishops across Europe detailing evidence of atrocities. *The New York Times* reported that the foreign minister had left the Vatican looking crestfallen.

Since then the pope had ordered Vatican Radio to broadcast the evidence and *L'Osservatore Romano* to continue to publish it. *The New York Times* had editorialized, "The Vatican has spoken with authority that cannot be questioned and has confirmed the worst intimidation on Jews."

But the reports of atrocities had increased along with the attacks by Goebbels's propaganda machine on Pius as "the Jew lover." The pope had countered by asking all Catholic bishops in Nazi Germany to sign a protest against the Nazi Party plan to extend the wearing of the Star of David to include the offspring of mixed marriages. The Nazi response was to seize convents, Catholic hospitals, and other church property throughout Germany; Catholic organizations were closed down and religious images removed from schools.

PART II

THE GATHERING STORM

5

EYES WHICH HAVE WEPT

The clock on the bell tower told Dr. Vittorio Sacerdoti it was five o'clock on that morning in January 1943 as he made his way through the corridors of the *Fatebenefratelli*, the hospital on Tiber Island where he had become Professor Borromeo's deputy.

It was the third year of a war and Allied ground forces were preparing to invade Italy. Aircraft had already begun bombing the country's industrial heart in the north. In Rome people wondered when it would be their turn. Meanwhile, Jewish refugees continued to seek shelter. They included the family waiting in the hospital courtyard for Vittorio. He saw the man and woman and the two children had the same haunted faces as all the other refugees who had waited for him in the courtyard over this past year.

He smiled reassuringly at them, knowing what they must have gone through to reach Rome, moving across Italy, through a world which continually cracked with lethal violence from the air and on the ground. They had come to collect documents which they hoped would allow them to escape the war.

Settimio Sorani had brought the family to the courtyard at this early hour to avoid the Fascist police who would soon start their day of hunting refugees. For each one they caught they received a bonus.

Though Delasem had already provided the family with Panamanian

passports and sailing tickets to Panama, they still needed medical certificates confirming they were in good health. Vittorio would provide them.

He had signed hundreds of certificates allowing Jews to enter not only
Panama but the United States, Argentina, Cuba, Tangier, and Shanghai.
The risk for him was considerable. Under the racial laws he could be imprisoned for helping other Jews. But he had not hesitated to do so when first
approached by Settimio Sorani. His sister, Rosina, had found shelter for the
family waiting in the courtyard while the documents were prepared.

Vittorio had again been moved by their tearful gratitude as he handed
over the certificates and watched them leave with Sorani. Walking back
into the hospital he felt as he did at those moments: They made his life as
a doctor worthwhile.

"You can only feel as you do with eyes which have wept," Professor
Borromeo told him.

Both doctors knew medical supplies were scarce. Disinfection equipment and drugs were increasingly in short supply. Sterile bandages, operating gloves, and anesthesia were rationed. Conditions were even worse
in other Rome hospitals. At the San Giovanni, there was not only a lack
of bedding but an infestation of ants. One of its doctors had described
to Professor Borromeo how "they come in from the walls and the cracks
in the floor. When I am operating they try to climb the table and get into
a patient."

Vittorio knew that cases of tuberculosis had increased; he had been told
that in some areas of Rome one in five people had contracted the illness.
Malaria had also staged a comeback. Day by day medicines and foods for
infants were running low. The black market continued to spread. That
morning a patient in the outpatient clinic had tried to sell a bottle of olive
oil for fifty lire, which the day before had cost far less. When Professor
Borromeo had remonstrated with her, the woman had said, "Tomorrow it
will be more expensive." He had told Vittorio, "Her attitude adds to the
breakdown in our society."

In February 1943, Delasem moved into a new office in the same building
as the headquarters of the Union of Italian-Jewish Communities. Using
their contacts in the Rome Fascist administration Ugo Foa and Dante

Almansi had enabled the organization to continue to operate unhampered. Both had grown up in a society where, Foa would recall, "Mussolini encouraged that a deal was always possible." Almansi remembered, "Our deal was that we would keep Delasem low-key." To do that, they had appointed Settimio Sorani to run the organization. In turn he had enlisted the support of Count de Salis, Princess Enza Cortes, and Marchesa di Meana. Between them they organized donations to augment those from Jewish relief organizations in the United States. The extra money bought food, medicine, and clothes for the ever-increasing number of Jews being smuggled along the network of safe houses the Pallottine fathers had established at the pope's request.

On that Sabbath morning in the first week of March 1943, Mose Spizzichino, his hair neatly combed, sat beside his wife, their four daughters, and two sons-in-law, each with a child on their knee in the synagogue. The adults had all found work. Behind sat the Astrologo family, who claimed its ancestors had smuggled out of Jerusalem priceless artifacts before the Roman emperor Titus had ransacked the Second Temple. Nearby were the Muscati family, including one of its daughters, Maria, and her new husband, Albert.

The Marino family was another family whose ancestors had arrived in Rome at the height of the Roman Empire. Down the centuries they had passed on stories of their forefathers mourning the assassination of Julius Caesar and bearing witness to the senate appointing Herod as King of Judea. In their accustomed places sat the ghetto tailor, Serafino Pace, and his wife, Italia, and their nine sons and daughters. Sitting behind a pillar were Celeste di Porto and her parents. Despite her chosen way of life the Black Pantheress never failed to attend the Sabbath morning service. She had arrived in the latest fashionable dress, her arm linked to her mother's, smiling at the stares she attracted.

That Sabbath morning not only Celeste was a figure of attention. From the moment Rabbi Zolli had made his way to the bema, the step from which he would address the gathering, they had stared at him, absorbing the tension he exuded.

In the past Rosina Sorani had heard him expound on subjects she suspected were not easily understood by many of his congregation. She knew an increasing number had come to see him as icy and distant. There had been times when she herself found him haughty and unapproachable. While she still respected him as "Zolli the scholar, Zolli the rabbi lacked rapport with his congregation, many of whom were poor and uneducated."

Zolli stared into their faces, his fleshy lips pursed, hands clasped over a potbelly under his broad-sleeved black robe, black hat squarely on his head. Rosina had seen him adopt this posture many times. But now there was a difference: The tension on his face was after he had deliberately ignored Ugo Foa and the members of the *giunta*, the council responsible for running the synagogue.

Earlier that morning Rosina had been in her outer office in the synagogue when Zolli had arrived to see Ugo Foa. Usually it was to discuss his sermon.

But from inside Foa's office Rosina had heard the president warn Zolli that he was not to make public the controversy which had threatened to tarnish his position as the spiritual leader of Rome's Jews.

In Trieste, after a series of complaints about his behavior from the city's Jewish community, the city prefect, who had widespread powers, had stripped Zolli of his Italian nationality and registered him as a Polish Jew. At his interview for the post of chief rabbi of Rome, Zolli had convinced Foa he had been the victim of an unappreciative Jewish community and any doubts in the president's mind were overcome by Zolli's scholarship which undoubtedly would reflect glory on Rome's community. Foa had assured the chief rabbi that his registration as a Polish national because of his birthplace did not matter. But it became an issue for Zolli when Italy entered the war. Germany was rounding up Polish Jews by the trainload and sending them to concentration camps. He wanted his Italian nationality reinstated. Anxious to please the chief rabbi, Foa had asked the *giunta*, the synagogue council, to employ Rome's leading law firm to handle the matter.

The finance officer of the *giunta* was a sharp-eyed accountant, Anselmo Colombo. The legal billings for the reinstatement of Zolli's citizenship had stunned Colombo; the charges included substantial sums for entertaining members of the Fascist government and Rome's business community. The costs had been approved by Zolli on the grounds he needed "substantial referees." Colombo had said these charges should be met by the chief rabbi. He had refused and told Foa that the accountant was *"malvagio,"* wicked. When Foa asked to review the legal costs, Colombo had also sent along a file of other allegations from members of the community about Zolli.

Foa had been aware of the accusations for some time and concluded a number were made by troublemakers. But when he had read in the file that Zolli had told Colombo that "I consider it an honor for the community of Rome to have me as chief rabbi but I do not consider it an honor for me to be chief rabbi of the community," the president had decided he must act. That morning he had sent for Zolli and read out the contents of the file. The chief rabbi stormed out.

In the synagogue Rosina watched Zolli gather himself. His voice had an edge as he said he wanted to lead them back to "the true meaning of Judaism." From what he had seen, the way they expressed their faith was often tainted by superstition.

All around Rosina heard stunned gasps. Foa sat stony-faced among members of the *giunta*. Zolli spoke again as his eyes swept the congregation.

"Many of you doing *yahrzeit*, go to the grave at the anniversary of the death of a parent, a relative, or a friend, and sacrifice a chicken on the grave. I have told you this must stop; you still do it. The anniversary of a loved one's passing does not need that sacrifice. Judaism does not need it. Your chief rabbi does not need it."

He waited for the whispers to subside. Rosina knew many of the older families in the ghetto felt such customs were embedded in their religious life and would be deeply offended by his demand to end a ritual which had come down through the centuries.

There was a coldness in his voice as he told them he had been made aware of accusations against him. They were false. He would not repeat them in the sanctity of the synagogue. But those who had made them knew they were falsehoods. *"Malvagio."* Wicked lies.

Rosina watched his eyes sweep the congregation, stopping for a moment then moving on. "It was an intimidating performance," she recalled.

Zolli looked into their faces, his voice vibrant. In the beginning he had found many of them hard to get to know and in many ways he still felt an outsider. But his belief in what he was doing had guided him. He had tried to share with them what he had learned from a lifetime of reading Scripture. If they did not always understand the meaning of what he said they should tell him. But there was one matter they must understand.

Zolli had placed his hands inside the sleeves of his robes. His next words had a new certainty.

"I have spoken to enough refugees in Rome to know the peril of Nazi persecution. Friends of mine, rabbis in Germany and other occupied countries had been beaten, tortured, and sent to their deaths. I prayed for them. I believe my own faith will protect me. It will also protect those of you who share it with me."

The chief rabbi stepped off the bema and walked out of the silent synagogue.

That evening, wearing the dark lounge suit he wore at the coronation of Pius XII, Zolli had joined evening Mass in St. Peter's Basilica.

Monsignor Hugh O'Flaherty's living quarters overlooked the inner courtyard of the German college where he had lived since coming to Rome.

With his Irish nationality he could have resided in the Irish college. But the German college was closer to the Holy Office. Several other priests lived there. Like him they worked irregular hours and usually only met going to and from the college chapel to celebrate the daily Mass. Monsignor Ottaviani had told O'Flaherty one of them was a cryptographer and another worked in the secretariat of state. They never spoke to him about their duties and O'Flaherty had never explained his sudden absences from the college.

Since 1941 he had been the pope's rapporteur to investigate conditions in the Allied prisoner-of-war camps in the north of Italy. There were thousands of prisoners often held in poor conditions. On each visit his first task was to check the camp records for new internees. When he was back in Rome he would hand over the names to Count de Salis so he could arrange for the new prisoners to receive Red Cross parcels. O'Flaherty would also ask for Radio Vatican to broadcast their names so relatives would know their loved ones were safe.

By 1943 there were seventy camps holding seventy-five thousand Allied officers and men. The majority came from Britain and its Commonwealth countries who had been captured by the German Afrika Korps over two years of desert warfare. Fifteen hundred were Americans, mostly shot down U.S. Army air force pilots and their crews.

O'Flaherty's relationship with de Salis had grown to a friendship which led to his meeting Princess Enza Cortes and the Marchesa di Meana. They had used their influence to support O'Flaherty's campaign for more doctors and chaplains to be assigned to the camps.

At one of the dinner parties Princess Enza gave, he had been introduced to an attractive young widow, Princess Nina Pallavicini. Her husband, an Italian air force pilot, had been shot down over Sicily during a dogfight with an American fighter. Her loss had deepened her opposition to the Fascist government. After dinner as he walked her back home to her palazzo near the Quirinale, Nina told him she had a radio which picked up BBC and other banned broadcasts. When he asked if she was in danger of being arrested, Nina smilingly replied that she would count on him to help her. He promised she could always depend on that. As they arrived at the palazzo doorway she impulsively reached up and kissed him on either cheek.

For two years O'Flaherty continued regular visits to the camps, bringing news of further Allied successes and distributing copies of a prayer book he had compiled and arranged for *L'Osservatore Romano* to print. At each camp he had celebrated Mass and heard confession. He brought with him a mouth organ and tin whistle and led the prisoners in singing; his rendition of "Danny Boy" and "Its a Long Way to Tipperary" were favorites.

Back in Rome he had often worked late at night in his room typing up reports on an old typewriter and left them with the night-duty priest at the secretariat of state to hand over to Cardinal Maglione in the morning. After a short sleep O'Flaherty walked the streets around the Vatican where the day began early with the market stalls being set up, shop shutters raised, and the first cafes open.

As usual he breakfasted in one down a side street, sitting at a plain wooden table, sipping hot chocolate and eating a freshly baked cake, enjoying the early morning company of Romans. They looked at him with respect, always asking for his views on the war. He told them he hoped that Mussolini was realistic enough to know that the Axis were irrevocably losing it; the duce had failed the Italian nation but, unlike Hitler, he was surely not willing to allow Rome to be bombed. He knew it was what they wanted to hear, words of reassurance from inside the Vatican.

The mood in the city was daily becoming more hopeful with news of further disasters for the Axis: the Russians had recaptured Stalingrad and the British were chasing the Afrika Korps out of North Africa.

O'Flaherty's reports on his visits to the camps reflected a growing mood of gloom among the Italian guards, often no more than conscripts. In contrast, optimism filled the majority of the prisoners. He suspected the number of tunnel diggers had increased.

On more than one occasion when he arrived at a camp after a successful escape the commandant had accused him of helping. Matters came to a head when one of the mail censors discovered in a prisoner's letter to his family in London how "our monsignor brings us news that Mussolini is a dead duck. Our priest says he'll soon get his comeuppance."

The letter was passed to military headquarters in Rome where it was sent to the foreign ministry department which liaised with the Holy See. The letter was given to Monsignor Montini, undersecretary for Ordinary Affairs, to deal with.

He had sent for O'Flaherty and said while the pope recognized his work was valuable, the Italian government was being pressed by its "Nazi partners"—Montini never refered to them as anything else—to find any means to compromise the Holy See's neutrality and that it would be best if the camp visits stopped.

In his note of the conversation Montini wrote, "There are always the Jews who need our help."

O'Flaherty wondered what his next task would be.

Foa had decided to wait a full week before sending for Zolli to discuss the incident in the synagogue. The chief rabbi said he had not only come to

apologize for any misunderstanding he had caused to the congregation—
he was there to discuss something far more important. From his brief-
case he produced a bundle of letters, explaining they were written to
him before he came to Rome.

After he had read out loud several of the letters, Zolli had said the writers were dead, caught by the Nazis.

Foa sat silent in his high-backed chair as Zolli selected another letter.
The writer said it was a relief to stay in the ghetto and not have someone
in the street pointing him out as a Jew or have a *Hitler Jugend* spit on him.
Zolli had placed the letter back in the bundle.

"His ghetto was in Lodz. Now it is no more. The Nazis have taken all
its people," said Zolli. There was a different tone to his voice as he told Foa
that until now he had believed the Jews of Rome were safe in their ghetto.
But no longer.

"The Nazis will come," he repeated. "As the Scripture says, 'No one
knows the day or the hour'. But they will come and we must prepare ourselves. We must leave Rome."

The chief rabbi described what had happened to other Jewish communities in Europe. He had spoken to refugees who had reached Rome and told
him how they had managed to escape from a bloodbath. All asked him the
same question: How long would Rome be spared?

Foa had finally spoken. To even contemplate what Zolli proposed, a
mass emigration of the community, would unnerve its people even more.
There was enough talk already. Zolli's duty was not to shock his congregation but to reassure them.

Foa told him about his visit to the pope and the reassurances he had
received. The chief rabbi looked astonished: How had Foa managed to see
the pope? Foa explained they had known each other for years. Zolli shook
his head in wonder.

Kosher butcher Graziano Perugia was putting the last of his meat away in
the cold storage in the back of his shop when a car parked outside. People
stopped and stared; it was unusual to see a motorized vehicle in the street
as goods were delivered by carts, including Graziano's meat.

The smartly dressed man who emerged from behind the wheel was also a stranger among the men in their workday overalls and women and children in well-worn garments. They stopped and stared as he checked the name over the butcher's shop and entered.

Count de Salis had come to deliver news that the Red Cross headquarters in Geneva had learned from its representative in Krakow that Graziano's widowed sister-in-law and her three children had been taken away by one of the *Einsatzgruppen,* or action squads, in a roundup of Jews some weeks before.

At 7 A.M. on Monday morning, July 19, 1943, municipal police in their white summer uniform patrolling the city side of St. Peter's Square watched the refuse collectors sweep up leaflets which the Allied bombers had dropped overnight once more, urging Romans to "separate yourselves from the doomed Mussolini dictator." The previous evening the raucous voice of the national secretary of the Fascist Party, Carlo Scorza, had demanded over Radio Rome for "Italians everywhere to resist. Resist. Resist!" The paper tumbling from the sky had mocked his words and sent a further shiver through the regime, proof that Allied airpower controlled the Italian skies.

Ten days ago the Allies had landed on Sicily and the Mediterranean island was suddenly no more than a stepping stone to the mainland of Italy.

Not only did Scorza's cries have a hollow ring but there already was a Resistance.

Rome's six anti-Fascist political groups had secretly met at the turn of the year to form a clandestine movement to overthrow Mussolini. Communists entered into an uneasy alliance with Monarchists; Socialists joined Liberals. Out of this coalition came the National Liberation Committtee, the CLN. Under its umbrella would be a number of underground units including the powerful Trotskyite-anarchist movement, the *Bandiera Rossa*, the Red Flag. Collectively they were the Resistance.

Soon they would include students, rail workers, journalists, housewives, artists, writers, lawyers, university professors, teachers, shopkeepers, doctors, and nurses. Few had fired a gun in anger; they would be taught how to do so with weapons which were old. Some came from upper-class families, many were members of the working class, others were disenchanted Fascists, disgusted by its vulgar rituals. All loved their country and above all Rome. It was a city with no trade unions, no right of assembly outside the Fascist parades, and a press which largely followed the Fascist Party line. By word of mouth the Resistance had come together, meeting in secret, avoiding the police and its informers, knowing if caught they faced prison or death. Dr. Vittorio Sacerdoti spoke for many when he said he had joined the Resistance because he wanted to make Rome a better place.

On that morning they began by gathering the leaflets the planes had dropped and pushed them through the letter boxes of government buildings and daubed on their walls one message: THE RESISTANCE IS READY.

The leaflets were picked up from St. Peter's Square by nuns and priests and taken back into the Vatican where gardeners were gathering those which had fallen on the flower beds, lawns, roads, and pathways.

In the papal apartment Pascalina had read a copy before continuing with her preparations. Once a week she visited in turn one of the hospitals the Vatican was responsible for under the Lateran Treaty to establish what medicines and other supplies were needed. Food came from its farm at Castel Gandolfo, the summer residence of the pope. Drugs were becoming harder to obtain due to strict government contracts. Though it was never mentioned by hospital administrators, Pascalina suspected that essential medicines were bought on the black market.

On May 23, 1943, Secretary of State Maglione had sought reassurance from Count Ciano that Rome could become an "open city."

Under the international laws of war the city could be declared "open" if a belligerent said it would not defend it or use it for military purposes. In 1940 the French government had evacuated Paris to go to Bordeaux and declared Paris to be an open city. In theory Mussolini could do the same and move his entire government and military headquarters to Milan or Turin just as Hitler had established his Wolf's Lair as his command center.

But in Rome the situation was more difficult. It had the Vatican in its suburb. Italy's transport system meant that Rome could not be avoided for any military movement into the southern part of the country. Mussolini had also allowed the Germans to have headquarters at Frascati in the Alban Hills, and in Rome at a hotel in the Piazza del Popolo, as well as the Ministry of Marine and a number of buildings on the Piazza del Oca. The city was the strategic key city for the Germans to funnel supplies south to fight the Allied forces.

After one of his meetings with the pope, D'Arcy Osborne had conveyed to London that Pius "is in a state of faith over the matter and seems to feel he has a mission from God to save the city as holy as Jerusalem." However it was not a view shared by Maglione. The secretary of state feared that the British and Americans would have no alternative but to "at least bomb Rome's marshalling yards."

For the Allied high command, preparing for the invasion of Italy, the decision had been made that Rome's marshalling yards and railway station as well as nearby airfields, could all be bombed.

6

NOTHING SACRED

It was a clear morning and the crews of the first wave of B-17 Flying Fortresses and B-24 Liberators of the U.S. Nineteenth Air Force could see the dome of St. Peter's Basilica glittering in the sun. There were 521 planes, each carrying eight five-hundred-pound bombs, a total of one thousand tons of explosives. In the lead aircraft the bomb bays began to open. It was a little after 8 A.M. on that Monday morning of July 19, 1943.

Rosina Sorani and her brother, Settimio, left the cafe where they usually breakfasted and began to walk to work alongside the Tiber when the air-raid sirens began to wail. As they saw the first wave of bombers approaching, Rosina shouted, "More leaflets!" Settimio shook his head: The planes were too high for a pamphlet drop. In the past months he had become an expert on the drops. He told his sister they were probably heading north to bomb targets. "They're flying toward the Vatican," insisted Rosina.

"They always do. It helps them to navigate," explained her older brother.

She smiled; Settimio was a know-it-all. They continued walking.

Suddenly there was a loud explosion from the direction of the University of Rome Medical School near the railway station. Then came another thunderous bang, quickly followed by a string of huge explosions, like gigantic Chinese firecrackers. An ever-spreading cloud of smoke rose into the air. All around them people started to scream and run—anywhere but toward the rising smoke. The bombs continued to drop. Clutching his sister's hand, Settimio ran toward the building where Delasem had its offices.

Princess Virginia Agnelli, the daughter of the Fiat family, was driving one of the latest cars produced by the dynasty's automobile company along the Appian Way toward Rome. She had spent the weekend with friends in the country and the talk had been about the war.

She was still miles away from the city when she saw the sky over the San Lorenzo district was turning black. "Black tinged with red," she remembered. From her vantage point on the ceremonious route along which victorious Roman legions had marched into the city two thousand years ago, she saw bombs were falling near its ancient walls.

Mose Spizzichino and other still-licensed peddlers were near the main railway station when the first bombs fell. The explosions were accompanied by billowing clouds of dense smoke. People were coming toward them shouting and bleeding from their wounds. The peddlers began to use rags to bind the injuries and those unable to walk were placed on their carts which they began to push back into the city to the nearest hospital. Behind them the bombs continued to fall.

In his office, Count de Salis was monitoring events for the report he would prepare for the International Red Cross headquarters in Geneva. Rome Radio was broadcasting a continuous appeal for all able-bodied men to go to the San Lorenzo district to help with rescue work. Off-duty nurses were to report to their hospitals. Doctors not attached to hospitals were to go to San Lorenzo. Princess Enza Pignatelli had already called de Salis to say she was contacting convents in the city to send nuns to help. Shortly afterward the radio reported bombs had fallen on Rome's main cemetery, Campo Verano. Later it was discovered that among the graves damaged was the Pacelli family tomb where Pope Pius's parents and brothers were interred.

Secretary of State Maglione had joined the growing group on the Apostolic Palace roof terrace watching the bombs falling. A month ago America's envoy Harold Tittmann had delivered a response from President Roosevelt to the pope's request that Rome "be spared from attack." Roosevelt had written, "Attacks against Italy are limited, to the extent humanly possible, to military objectives. We have not and will not make warfare on civilians or against non-military objectives. In the event it should be found necessary for Allied planes to operate over Rome, our aviators are thoroughly informed as to the location of the Vatican and have been specifically instructed to prevent bombs from falling within Vatican City."

On the flat roof of his apartment at Santa Marta, D'Arcy Osborne watched the raid with May and Jeremy, the minister's dog. From their vantage point they saw the medieval basilica of San Lorenzo was engulfed in flames. Osborne would later record that "there happened to be several trams outside the church. The dead would be included in the official figure of 717 killed and 1,599 injured in the air raid."

The moment he heard the crump of the first explosion, Professor Borromeo had activated the hospital's emergency plans. Patients began to be moved to the basements while porters closed window shutters against bomb blasts. Nonessential operations were postponed and surgical teams prepared to stand by for casualties. A triage team was positioned in the hospital's entrance to receive casualties and establish the seriousness of injuries. Dr. Vittorio Sacerdoti was in command. Similar procedures were being implemented in other city hospitals.

Harold Tittmann was with Monsignor Montini in the Apostolic Palace when an usher rushed in, shouting Rome was being bombed.

"The planes were wonderful to see. Flying in perfect formation of three, they swept toward their objectives, gleaming in the bright sunlight. The antiaircraft defenses made a lot of noise but were completely ineffective. They always seemed to be shooting behind the planes. When we saw huge clouds of smoke rising in the direction of the railway station we knew it was Rome's turn to suffer the horrors of war," recalled the Great War fighter pilot.

The freight yards and steel factory in the San Lorenzo district were well alight, so were several buildings at the Rome university medical school.

Ugo Foa and Dante Almansi had organized every available man in the ghetto to go to the San Lorenzo district to help. Equipped with picks and shovels they had commandeered trams and trucks to take them to the bomb-stricken area.

Among them was Settimio Sorani. When he arrived he found a friend, Asmelo Ricci, who lived on one of the bombed streets.

"Asmelo was shouting his wife and daughter were buried under the rubble where their house had stood. He was digging like a madman with his hands. We started to help. Flames were everywhere and there was little water to fight them. The pipes were broken and stonework was falling all around us. We pulled the daughter out first, and then we found her mother. Both were dead. We loaded them on an ambulance," recalled Settimio.

On the terrace of Villa Savoia less than a mile from San Lorenzo the seventy-three-year-old King Vittorio Emanuele and the queen watched the bombers wheeling over the target. Through his binoculars he was trying to count the aircraft and distinguish the Flying Fortresses from the Liberators. The king's aide-de-camp, General Paolo Puntoni, a veteran of the Abyssinia war, arrived with the news that the runway at Ciampino was pockmarked with craters and its hangars were gutted with planes still inside. Rome's air defense had gone up in flames.

————

The pope had stood at his office window with Pascalina watching the raid until it finally came to an end with the sounding of the all-clear siren. She saw the tears in his eyes had turned to anger. He told her to arrange for Stoppa, his chauffeur, to ready his car. For the first time since the war had started Pius was leaving the Vatican.

The sound of its powerful engine announced the arrival of the pope's car, displaying the white-and-yellow Vatican City pennants on its front fenders. It stopped before the bombed basilica of San Lorenzo. Pius emerged in his white soutane and skullcap and knelt on the ground, his face pale with grief as he intoned the words of the *De Profundis*, the psalm for the dead.

Nearby, ambulances were taking away the bodies. Crackling flames were destroying scores of passenger and freight cars in the rail sidings. Smoke poured from houses and warehouses. The basilica continued to shed its stonework as flames roared away inside where the tomb of Pope Pius IX rested.

Monsignor Montini who had accompanied the pope had brought with him a supply of money for the Capuchin monks in charge of the basilica to distribute to local families.

Montini would recall how Pius had moved among the wounded and the dead, blessing them equally, as doctors and nurses went about their duties. Among them were students from the nearby bombed medical school. One was Rosario Bentivegna, a third-year student hoping to qualify as a surgeon who had joined the Resistance. He was twenty-one years old but a lifetime later he would still remember the terror.

"Within a short time we were working up to our ankles in rubble and blood. It was the turning point of my life. I had seen the most hideous side of a lost war. It was the slaughter of innocents."

The evening before the raid Benito Mussolini had flown out of Ciampino to the Venetian town of Feltre to meet Hitler—their thirteenth summit since they had joined forces. On the flight north his military and political advisors had urged the duce to convince Hitler to release Italy from mutual agreements, a move which would benefit Berlin as well as Rome. Instead he had assured Hitler Italy would fight on.

That decision was the turning point in the plot to overthrow Mussolini which King Victor Emmanuel had secretly approved. The plot was masterminded by Stewart Menzies, the head of MI6, who the king had met on a prewar visit to London accompanied by a senior member of the royal household, Duke Pietro d'Acquarone, who became the conduit between London and the plotters. They were led by General Vittorio Ambrosio, the armed forces chief of staff.

Osborne also had a role in the plot, after Menzies asked him whether Count Ciano should be sounded out: He was no longer Italy's foreign minister and was now Italy's ambassador to the Holy See. Osborne urged no approach should be made to Ciano: Within the Vatican his appointment was regarded as a calculated insult to have an ambassador so identified with Mussolini and Fascism.

After the Italian air force transporter had returned from the summit at Feltre, General Ambrosio drove to see the king. They had met in the library of the Villa Savoia where the general revealed Mussolini's decision to continue with the war, adding that the Germans would not have the military resources to launch a counter coup against the plotters. Ambrosio recalled he said, " 'Your Majesty, it is now time to make the decision to liquidate Mussolini.' The king nodded. The date was set for Sunday, July 25, six days away."

Menzies decided to bring Osborne to London to brief him as the plotters moved their plan along. It was vital to know which of the Italian generals could be trusted when the time came. Osborne was instructed to consult the Vatican doctor "about my health." The physician recommended that Osborne should be given permission by the Italian government to fly to Switzerland to consult a specialist. Maglione had informed the Italian foreign ministry, that under the Lateran Treaty, Osborne's medical condition permitted him to travel to a neutral country on the understanding he would return.

Inside a week Osborne was in London. He briefed Menzies who gave him a letter from a Swiss doctor confirming he had examined Osborne and was treating him for stress. The doctor was an MI6 contact in Geneva. Osborne was then driven to Buckingham Palace and privately knighted by King George VI. He would become the Duke of Leeds, a title he could not use until after the war. Before he returned to Rome he had spent a day with an instructor at the MI6 Cipher School to learn how to use the latest codes.

Over dinner with Menzies, Osborne had told him about Hugh O'Flaherty and his visits to see Allied prisoners.

"An useful-sounding chap—even if he is a little anti-British," Menzies said.

In the wake of the bombing the cryptographers of the Holy See worked tirelessly handling communications to and from the pope. Pius had ordered his message to the nuncios to be made public. "What we feared so much as a result of bombing is now a sad reality. One of the most important basilicas, San Lorenzo Outside-the-Wall is now for the most part destroyed."

When Osborne read the message in the next issue of *L'Osservatore Romano,* he told Tittmann he regretted that Pius had failed to raise his voice against the destruction of English churches by German bombers earlier in the war.

Chief Rabbi Zolli visited San Lorenzo to see the extent of the damage. Among the rescue workers were some of his students at the rabbinical college. Covered in dirt, their faces stained with sweat, they picked their way through the rubble to pull out bodies.

During the night slogans had been daubed on the walls of buildings. The two most common were WE WANT PEACE and DOWN WITH FASCISM. One of the students told Zolli that Mussolini had come to the area around midnight and an old woman, searching for her grandchildren, had screamed at the duce. He had ordered one of his aides to give her a handful of lire. She had spat on the money and turned away.

The bombing had convinced Zolli that it was no longer safe for his family to remain in their home; now that the Americans had bombed Rome it could only be a matter of time before they did so again. Inevitably the Germans would come to the aid of Mussolini to defend the city and its Jews would be rounded up. He had not told his wife, Emma, of his fears, not wishing to alarm her and their daughters. He wondered whether he should discuss the situation with Father Weber. He had met the Pallottine priest when he brought refugees to the ghetto. Weber had told Zolli that if he ever needed help he would provide it, explaining he had received fifteen hundred immigration visas from the Brazilian government for Jews to go there. Zolli had thanked him. But going to Latin America, he later admitted, had little appeal.

Baron Ernst von Weizsäcker, a former German naval officer, had replaced Diego von Bergen as ambassador to the Holy See. He had finally been recalled to Berlin by the foreign minister Joachim von Ribbentrop for "poor quality of reports." Weizsäcker had spent five years at the foreign ministry, and risen to be undersecretary.

His journey to the upper echelon of the ministry had included reading the daily reports from the *Einsatzgruppen,* the special SS units systematically murdering Polish and Russian Jews. He had attended the Wannsee Conference in Berlin to finalize "the Final Solution of the Jewish Question" and had signed a copy of the minutes. On his desk came the railway schedules from Adolf Eichmann's office for deportations to the death camps. At some point, he later insisted, "I became sickened of what was being done in the name of the German people."

He had persuaded Ribbentrop to allow him to take charge of a less odorous task—analyzing the intercepted traffic by the *Forschungsamt,* the German code-breaking unit. It included messages between the Holy See and its nunciatures. By 1943 the German cryptologists had managed to break some of the Vatican codes, but the success did little to add to Germany's war effort. Nevertheless, Weizsäcker had to present his analysis to Admiral Canaris.

At first their meetings were no more than briefing the spy chief in his office and answering a few questions. But gradually Canaris had begun to explore Weizsäcker's attitude to the war. Though he realized the risk he was taking, Ribbentrop's deputy had said its continuation could only result in Germany's defeat and dismemberment. A negotiated settlement was the only hope. Weizsäcker would recall how Canaris had "sat perfectly still, his eyes fixed on me. When he spoke his question was simple. Did I believe that the Vatican could act as a mediator? I replied that Hitler would only accept papal mediation if he was satisfied of the pope's sympathy for Germany."

There were further meetings in which Weizsäcker was encouraged to criticize von Bergen's reports to Ribbentrop. In the meantime Canaris had told the foreign minister of the importance of having Weizsäcker in Rome. In a memo dated May 8, 1943, which would surface at the Nuremberg Trials, Canaris wrote to Ribbentrop:

"Weizsäcker is one of the most interesting phenomena of the time, a type brought to light and perfected through disinterested idealism and shrewdness, such as is particularly rare in Germany. I strongly urge he should be posted to Rome where he can most usefully serve our nation."

On July 10 Weizsäcker presented his credentials to Pope Pius XII. Canaris had briefed the new ambassador on what he expected from him.

It was customary for both the pope and a new ambassador to be alone after the accreditation ceremony. It was a time when an envoy would outline his government's current policy toward the Holy See and express the hope of mutual cooperation. Weizsäcker had begun by saying he had been instructed to say that Germany would never bomb "or in any way damage" the Vatican. The only record of what followed would be Weizsäcker's account: The pope had thanked him and "I had gone on to discuss the prospect of peace. His Holiness said he wished for nothing more and I had carefully suggested that the Vatican could have an important role in bringing that about."

There had, recalled Weizsäcker in his subsequent telegram to Berlin, "been a silence. The pope's answer was, 'At present there seems no lead on which to base any practical work for peace.'"

The audience was over. Canaris's plan to use Weizsäcker to persuade the pope to become involved in the plot to overthrow Hitler had met its first obstacle.

———

It would be years before the pope's response would emerge in the Nuremberg War Crimes Trial which Weizsäcker faced in 1946. He would be sentenced to seven years imprisonment. The only other reference to his role in Rome as Admiral Canaris's collaborator to use the pope came in 1950 when the ambassador wrote in his autobiography, "To anyone who could not of himself understand what I was doing I really have nothing more to say." He died in 1951, his silence unbroken.

In a box file of affidavits—those dealing with Weizsäcker listed as Case Eleven on the Nuremberg list of trials of lesser war criminals—is a document which might explain those words. It refers to the most controversial priest in the Vatican in 1943, Bishop Alois Hudal.

The German mission to the Holy See was housed in the Villa Napoleon and consisted of Weizsäcker, First Secretary Albrecht von Kessel—a scion of a land-owning family in Bavaria, a couple of secretaries, a cook, a chauffeur, and gardener. In contrast the Reich embassy to Italy was housed in the sumptuous Villa Wolkonsky, whose ambassador Rudolf Rahn commanded several attaches and five secretaries. Its domestic staff included four maids and a butler, two chefs, three gardeners, and two chauffeurs.

Kessel had described to Weizsäcker the key German priests in the Vatican: Father Leiber "is a dedicated anti-Nazi"; Monsignor Johannes Schonhoffer "runs Propaganda Fide and can be trusted"; Ivi Zeiger is the rector of *Collegium Germanicum,* the German college, and "is outstanding in his teaching and dislikes Hitler"; Father Augustine Maier is a professor at the Benedictine university in the city and "a delightful dinner guest."

When he came to Bishop Alois Hudal, the young diplomat had delivered a different portrait.

Hudal was the rector of the pan-Germanic college of Santa Maria dell'Anima, the main training center in Rome for German priests. He had become a member of the Nazi Party after Hitler had thanked him for a telegram supporting the annexation of Austria. But reports of his membership are not confirmed in Vatican records. In 1937 Hudal had sent a copy of his book *The Foundations of National Socialism* to Hitler and with a letter of thanks from the führer came a golden Nazi Party membership badge. The book was published in the same year that the papal encyclical *Mit Brennender Sorge* openly attacked National Socialism. While Hudal continued in his post, his steady rise in the Vatican had stopped as his pro-Nazi views became known.

By 1943 Hudal had found a new outlet. He became an informer for the RSHA—*Reichssicherheitshauptamt*—Reich Security Main Office. Its chief Ernst Kaltenbrunner saw Hudal's recruitment as an intelligence triumph at a time when Germany was trying to establish a rapproachement between the Holy See and the Third Reich.

Hudal regarded himself as providing important information. His RSHA controller, Waldemar Meyer, who regularly travelled secretly to Rome, saw Hudal as the éminence grise of the Vatican. "He knows everybody and everybody respects him."

Hudal had also aligned himself with Giovanni Preziosi, a rabidly anti-Semitic former priest who edited *La Vita Italiana*, the Jew-baiting Rome newspaper patterned on *Der Sturmer*. He was also in touch with a Benedictine monk, Prior Hermann Keller, who Kessel called "an agent of the gestapo." Kessel described them to Weizsäcker as "our pro-Nazis in the Vatican."

Weizsäcker was nevertheless startled at his first meeting with Hudal. The bishop's opening words were he saw Hitler as "a latter-day Charlemagne, the guarantor for creating a modern replica of the Holy Roman Empire."

The ambassador was still wondering how to respond, when the bishop assured him that the air raid on Rome had been arranged by Stalin. "He hopes it will break up the alliance between Mussolini and Hitler."

Bemused, "wishing I had not come to listen to this nonsense," Weizsäcker later recalled, he asked Hudal how he knew that Stalin had been involved in the attack. Hudal stared at his guest. "You may not be aware, but I have my well-placed sources."

He had gone to one of his bookshelves and removed a copy of *The Foundations of National Socialism*. He signed it and handed the book to Weizsäcker, adding that Hitler kept a copy in his office.

———

On Sunday, July 25, 1943, Benito Mussolini sat down for lunch with his wife, Rachele, dressed in his morning suit, winged collar, spats, and gleaming black shoes. It was the clothes he always wore when meeting the king. He told Rachele he was confident the monarch would support him and get rid of "those bastards."

The night before, the Grand Council, the supreme body of the Fascist Party, had asked him to attend an emergency meeting. He assumed it was connected with repairing the bomb damage. Instead he had been confronted with a demand that he should resign. Sitting at the head of the conference table, his face puce, veins in his neck throbbing, he demanded a vote. Nineteen of the twenty-six council members raised hands in favor of his resignation.

He had stormed out of the building knowing he needed the approval of King Victor Emmanuel III to dismiss the council. He had telephoned the monarch's secretary, General Puntoni. The aide-de-camp said the king would not be available until late Sunday afternoon. In the meantime he would contact General Vittorio Ambrosi to provide a military guard over Mussolini's residence, where he must remain until it was time to be driven to see the king. Instead of his usual police escort he would have a military one. Reassured, the duce had relaxed.

Shortly before five o'clock his Fiat limousine had driven through the gates of the royal residence. Mussolini got out of his car to greet the king standing in the palace entrance. Parked out of sight was a military ambulance.

The king escorted the duce into the building. Walking behind them, Puntoni heard the king say: "You are the most hated man in Italy and you have only one friend left—me." Mussolini had stared at him and said, "Then this is my complete collapse."

Puntoni had showed them into the king's study, closed the door behind them, and pressed his ear against it. He heard the king saying, "I am sorry, but there is no other way."

Puntoni stepped away from the door as he heard footsteps from inside the study. The king emerged, followed by Mussolini. Puntoni took his place behind them as they walked back down the corridor to the entrance. In the driveway the ambulance was surrounded by soldiers each carrying a rifle. One opened its rear door. Mussolini turned to the king and asked for his car. The monarch said, "The ambulance will hide you from the anger of my people." Mussolini visibly sagged and then climbed into the ambulance. The door was closed and the vehicle immediately drove off.

Shortly after the vehicle had passed through the gates of the royal residence, Radio Rome announced the king had accepted Mussolini's resignation and a new government had been sworn in under His Excellency Army Marshal Pietro Badoglio.

Tittmann's message to the State Department stated: "The Fascist Party has voted itself out of office. Throughout the city people are joyfully taking part in the liquidation of all Fascist organizations. The attitude of the Germans is an unknown factor. Cardinal Maglione expressed his hope that the Allies would show patience and understanding toward the new Italian government."

On September 8, 1943, as British invading forces increased their foothold on the southern tip of the mainland and American forces prepared to land at Salerno, Marshal Badoglio, the conqueror of Ethiopia in 1936, and King Victor Emmanuel fled south to negotiate an unconditional surrender with the Allies. That night Radio Rome broadcast the terms of the armistice.

"To all the forces on land, at sea, and in the air. The Italian government recognizing the overwhelming power of the enemy has requested an armistice from General Eisenhower. This request has been granted. The Italian forces will, therefore, cease all acts of hostility against the Anglo-American forces wherever they may meet. They will however, oppose any attacks from other quarters."

In Rome and elsewhere the celebrations over Mussolini's abduction were matched by the anticipation that the Allied armies would advance up the leg of Italy in a matter of weeks.

In Berlin, already facing military reverses in Russia, when Hitler heard the news his first move was to order two German armies to enter Italy and begin advancing down the peninsula. With equal speed an SS force would accompany them to occupy Rome. In a broadcast of an Order of the Day Hitler said he would "clear out that gang of swine in the Vatican and deal with the Jews they are protecting."

Throughout the summer of 1943 Pope Pius had continued to express his horror over the fate of the Jews. On June 2 he had used Vatican Radio to warn that "any man who makes a distinction between Jews and other men is unfaithful to God." In a direct warning to Hitler Pius said: "He who guides the fate of nations should not forget that he who bears the sword is not the master over life and death." Seven days later, after Goebbels boasted that Berlin "was now free of Jews," the pope had written a long text in German on the rights of Jews which Vatican Radio broadcast. In July the pope broadcast to Yugoslav Jews that he would continue to pray for them because "every man has the stamp of God."

In between he had written letters to nuncios and bishops asking them to urge their host countries to do everything possible to save the Jews and "replace the hatred with charity." In his speeches and sermons Pius constantly called for help "for the hundreds of thousands who because of their race are condemned to die." More than once he had quoted the Apostle Saint Paul—"there is neither Gentile nor Jew"—adding he used the word *Jew* as a call to reject racial ideology. He had gone so far as to say he was "ready to let himself be deported to a concentration camp rather than do anything against his conscience," Pascalina would recall.

He had also turned Vatican Radio into a powerful weapon which, despite attempts to jam it had become a success in attacking the Nazis.

Through her illegal wireless Princess Nina Pallavicini followed the war as it came closer. She learned that Sicily had been captured by the Allies with a loss of sixty-five thousand German troops, either killed or captured. A powerful Allied task force had crossed the Tyrrhenian Sea to land its armies—one British, one American—on the crescent of beaches south of Naples at Salerno. The princess's summer house was there and until then she had never heard the area mentioned on the wireless. Now it was spoken of in every BBC bulletin as German defenses crumbled and the U.S. Fifth Army under General Mark Clark began to move inland.

Every evening Princess Nina sat at her desk in her palazzo and wrote down the BBC news from London and brought it to Hugh O'Flaherty in the German college.

Serafino Pace, the ghetto tailor, had never been so busy. Mothers bought their children's clothes to be altered: boys trousers were changed; girls had their dresses lengthened. Men's clothing also underwent Serafino's skilled tailoring. Rationing and the rising cost of food were the cause of the alterations.

The Spizzichino family were among those who had found a way to add to their income. In the past Mose had saved old shoes and boots from which he could use the leather to mend other footwear he had bought on his rounds. Now he repaired the old footwear and sent Grazia to sell them to a shoe shop.

The growing black market had criminalized large sections of previously law-abiding citizens. In the ghetto, as elsewhere in Rome, they had their "sources": a marketeer on a street corner with his or her sack of food or a peddler carrying essential household goods under his rags. Most of the market was controlled by the Black Panthers. The gang stole chickens and eggs from farms around Rome, slaughtered, and sold them. Robbery had also increased as the gang broke into homes looking for items to sell.

Queuing had become a way of life and no one was too proud to stand in line. Zolli's wife, Emma, was among those who lined up outside a neighborhood baker for the family's ration of bread before she joined customers down the street waiting to be served by kosher butcher Graziano Perugia.

Even the usually well-stocked shops on the Via del Portico d'Ottavia had increasingly empty shelves. Rosina Sorani had asked her brother how much worse it would become when the Germans came. He had reassured her that the Allies would soon arrive and drive back the Nazis.

———

Late at night Dr. Vittorio Sacerdoti led Monsignor Patrick Carroll-Abbing down the dimly lit hospital corridor and past the small reading lamps and tables where the ward nurses could read their patients' files. The stocky Irish priest was a chaplain in the ancient order of the Knights of Malta, a medieval religious order, which, like the founders of the *Fatebenefratelli*, had a long tradition of nursing. Father Patrick had brought wounded Resistance fighters in one of the order's ambulances to the hospital from the battle being fought in the nearby Alban Hills to defend the city from the German forces now in sight of Rome's ancient gateways.

Since dawn Flying Fortresses had bombed Kesselring's own headquarters in the town of Frascati. He had managed to crawl out of the wreckage unharmed and ordered his troops to show no mercy as they continued their advance. Facing them were units of the Italian army from the city's garrison, and thousands of Romans—veterans of the Great War and members of the Resistance. They were armed with rifles, hunting guns, pistols, and machine guns whose ammunition belts were salvaged from a 1918 battlefield.

With the advantage of knowing the countryside the Italians fought a guerrilla battle against an altogether more powerful enemy. But their casualties were high and the dead and wounded were brought to a first-aid station near the Pyramid of Cestius, the ancient monument where Saint Paul was reported to have paused to pray on the way to his crucifixion on the Ostian Road. The dead were laid out in rows by women who ran the makeshift post. Father Patrick had been assigned to take a number of the wounded to the *Fatebenefratelli*. Among them was a seriously wounded youth whose leg was shattered by shrapnel. He told Father Patrick his name was Cesare. Around his neck hung a Star of David.

Father Patrick remembered how Cesare had asked for a rabbi and was told none was at the hospital. "He looked at me and his deep brown eyes were filled with pain and he asked if I could stay with him until his operation started. I said I would be there when he awoke." Vittorio had told him that night and day the surgeons operated and arms and legs were often amputated in a last desperate attempt to save lives. Now, in the early hours of that September morning the air in the hospital was filled with the stench of anesthetic and rotting blood, as he walked down the corridor with Vittorio who explained Cesare had not only lost his leg but was suffering from terminal tuberculosis.

"There is no hope. He knows and understands. He has so much courage," the doctor said.

Father Patrick had seen the approach of death many times. Standing at Cesare's bedside, he saw a look of inner peace had taken possession of the youth.

In his hand Cesare held his Star of David. He motioned Father Patrick to come closer and placed the emblem in his hand and asked him to keep it safe until after his surgery.

Pascalina sensed the mood change in the city. In her diary she noted: "The Germans are closer to Rome than we thought. What will they do?"

The question also preoccupied another nun. Jessica Lynch was the daughter of an Irish family in Brooklyn, New York, and when she took her vows she chose to be known as Sister Luke. After training she had been sent to France and then Italy to teach in a Catholic school before moving to Rome in 1932. She was given a room in the order's convent off the Via Veneto and with her linguistic skills—she spoke Italian, French, and German—she was assigned to run the Vatican Information Bureau. It was one of the busiest in the Apostolic Palace, answering the letters every day addressed to the pope seeking his intercession in a wide variety of matters. With a small staff of nuns Sister Luke decided how to answer; each response was handwritten and imbued with her own faith and humanity.

A common interest in the historical role of women in the church had brought the two nuns together. They had met in the Vatican library. Pascalina was researching the subject for a sermon Pius was preparing. Sister Luke wanted details to answer one of the letters she would respond to.

They sat together in the library's reading room studying the leather-bound volumes they had asked for and making notes.

Sister Pascalina and Sister Luke had agreed the subject of women in the church was a fascinating topic. For Pascalina the most important was the life of Sister Catherine of Siena, the visionary who Pope Pius XII had proclaimed a saint on the eve of World War Two. She told Sister Luke how

Catherine had found a special place in her own daily diary and asked if Sister Luke kept such a record. On hearing not, Pascalina had urged her to do so. Sister Luke began her diary on Wednesday, September 8, 1943. That morning she wrote: "I had awoken with a stab of anxiety. What would the day bring forth?"

7

PIUS GOES TO WAR

It was a question which also troubled Ugo Foa after he made several telephone calls to officials in government offices. They rang out. Earlier that morning he had walked through the ghetto. All the shops were closed and peddlers' carts were parked outside houses with windows shuttered. The synagogue's doors were locked, and the caretaker had not responded to the doorbell. A telephone call to Zolli's home had gone unanswered. The ghetto was like "a place of the dead," Foa told his children.

Every hour the sinister thud of artillery shells came closer, falling at Ponte Milvio and Piazza San Giovanni in the suburb of La Ferno, places were Foa had walked all his life. At noon his telephone rang. It was Rosina to say her brother, Settimio, was down near the Gate of Saint Paul. "He says German armored cars are coming down Via Marco Polo into the city. People are running everywhere. Some are looking for places to hide. Others are shooting, but they are running out of bullets. Bodies are everywhere my brother told me," she said.

Foa told Rosina to call him with any further news. In the meantime he tried again to reach Zolli. There was no reply.

———

Outside their home on Via Reginelle, Mose Spizzichino unfurled the Italian flag he had once carried during Fascist parades in the early days of Mussolini's rule. Now he called him *"Porco! Carogna fascista!"*—Pig! Fascist scum! He told his daughters' husbands, Umberto and Marco, they would bring pride back to the flag for what they were about to do—join the Resistance. Each had a hunting rifle slung over his shoulder and an ammunition bag attached to his belt. In the summer they would have gone hunting in the hills. Now they were going to defend their home.

Settimia and her younger sister, Giuditta, stood with their mother, Grazia, taking their turn to kiss the flag before Mose handed it to Umberto. Struggling to hold back their tears the women watched Umberto and Marco march down the street, the flag held high. Settimia would recall they never looked back.

Chief Rabbi Zolli ordered Emma not to answer the phone and to remain inside with the children while he went to see what was happening. He had not told her he planned to go to St. Peter's Basilica for the midday Mass he regularly attended.

In the city the sound of gunfire was louder and flames were coming from the direction of the Hotel Continental where Resistance fighters were throwing petrol bombs into the building at the trapped Fascist police. Around the Ministry of the Interior—where Zolli had gone to collect his Italian passport after his nationality was reinstated—a street battle raged near a blazing German armored car. The flash of exploding hand grenades and the rattle of machine guns came from nearby Circus Maximus.

He hurried through side streets toward the Vatican. St. Peter's Square was a sight he had never before seen. Guardia Palatina stood at the edge of the piazza facing out into the city. In place of their usual medieval pikes they held rifles with fixed bayonets. People standing in front of them were being told that the pope had ordered the basilica closed. So were the Porta Santa Anna, the Arco delle Campane, and the Bronze Door, the gates which led into the Vatican.

Zolli turned away and headed home. "I knew I should have convinced Foa that I had been right to say we Jews should have left when there was

time. Now it would be everyone for himself," his daughter Miriam recalled her father saying.

Ignoring the sound of battle in the city and the sealing of the Vatican,
O'Flaherty continued to spend the morning in the Holy Office dealing
with the case of an Argentinean married couple. The wife wanted an annul-
ment because her husband had committed adultery after refusing to have
children. During the years O'Flaherty had worked in the Holy Office he
had dealt with several such cases. None had been easy for him to judge
and he knew he had been given this case because of its unusual sensitivity.
The couple came from wealthy Catholic families, generous supporters of
the church and had endowed a number of Catholic hospitals and convents
in Argentina.

O'Flaherty had read legal submissions, aide-memoirs, and letters,
some of them intimate exchanges between the couple, which helped him
chart their relationship. It had taken him weeks to evaluate the submissions. In between O'Flaherty had put the case aside to visit the prisoner-
of-war camps.

When he arrived for work that morning as the rumble of explosions
came from the Alban Hills, on his desk was a memo from Monsignor Montini. When he had first joined the Holy Office, Monsignor Ottaviani had
told him that Montini managed all the legacies, trusts, mortgages, and
properties donated to the Holy See. "Never forget what Montini wants,
Montini gets."

What Montini that morning wanted was a judgement on the annul-
ment case, one which took into account that the family of the petitioner
had just made a further substantial donation to the diocese of Buenos
Aires.

The Irishman put aside the memo and resumed reviewing the case.
The sounds of battle drew closer.

On Friday afternoon, September 10, D'Arcy Osborne stood on the flat roof
of Santa Marta, where he usually sunbathed, watching the fighting in the
city. He had been there for most of the day, pausing only to sit at a small

table and chair which John May had set up for him to eat the sandwiches and swallow the tea the manservant served him.

May had stood beside the minister taking turns to use Osborne's binoculars to follow the battle. Osborne reminded May that when the Porta San Sebastiano gateway fell it would allow the Germans to pour down the Appian Way into the city, just as the Normans had done a thousand years earlier. Later, as he studied the area around the Porta San Giovanni, he informed May that in 1529 the Lutherans had chosen to storm Rome along a similar route. May had underscored the history lesson by saying, "Now it is the turn of Hitler's Huns."

They were not the only observers. Priests and nuns from religious houses were telephoning the Vatican to report what was happening. Every call brought news of how the Lateran Treaty, which under international law gave the pope temporal rights and jurisdiction over scores of properties within Rome, was being violated. The basilicas of St. John Lateran, St. Paul Outside-the-Walls, and St. Mary Major, had all been fired on. So had the palace of St. Calixtus and the Augustian College of Santa Monica and other buildings on the Janiculum, one of the seven hills of Rome. Elsewhere in the city various colleges, the Bambino Gesù hospital, the Gregorian university, and a number of research institutes were in the line of fire. So too were the hospices which provided accommodation for visitors in peacetime. All were under the protection of the pope, powerless now to stop the fighting.

Attempts by Maglione to contact Baron von Weizsäcker, the German ambassador to the Holy See, had failed. The telephone link to Villa Napoleon, the mission's headquarters, had been cut. Father Leiber had offered to take the pope's limousine and drive there. Pius forbade him; flying the Vatican flag would not guarantee safe passage. Father Leiber was asked to gather the pope's personal files and hide them in the basement of the Apostolic Palace. Maglione ordered his key staff to conceal all sensitive documents, including the codes used by the cryptographers. Late in the afternoon Pius had asked the cardinals living inside the Vatican to join him and his personal staff for prayers in the apartment's chapel.

———

In his office Count de Salis had been receiving telephone calls from Princess Enza Pignatelli Aragona Cortes. Her friends were telling her that slowly but surely the Germans were moving deeper into the city. German paratroopers who had earlier been driven back beyond Circus Maximus had regrouped to reach the Coliseum. In the Piazza Spagna, the Spanish Steps, a reporter in the office of the Fascist-run daily, *Il Messaggero* called a priest to tell him that units of the Italian garrison had set up a defense perimeter around the steps. The priest asked if there was any news of the Allies. The reporter's response became one of the quotable footnotes of the battle: "Do you know where God is when we need him?"

Sister Luke's reports to the hard-pressed nuns on the Vatican switchboard would also become memorable as she telephoned graphic accounts on what was happening outside the massive walls of her convent on Via Veneto. Her own mother superior had asked her to contact other religious houses. There could be injured needing attention, the elderly nun said, and Sister Luke and the convent's other nuns could offer help.

Sister Luke was told that on Via Veneto, as on many other roads and streets, that wherever Germans were seen they were set upon. Clashes were violent and armored cars were everywhere. "It is a mixture of riot, civil war, and anarchy," the calm-voiced nun reported.

Shops were being looted and soldiers were running back into the street carrying away wheels of cheese, parcels of pasta, and crates of wine. A priest on Via Massimo d'Azeglio had been shot when he ran to help a wounded woman. A Dominican father told Sister Luke that soldiers were commandeering handcarts to take away their spoils. A priest at San Camillo church reported there were several bodies in the road.

When Zolli had failed to gain access to St. Peter's, he made his way through the narrow lanes, hurrying as the gunfire echoed off the crooked roofs of the buildings to the home of Luigi and Carla Pierandello. More than once the whistle of shells had sent him ducking into a church, one of several he passed. Finally he reached the block of flats where the couple lived. He had met them almost a year ago as he emerged from the basilica after they sat beside him during Mass.

Several times since then Zolli had visited them, sometimes walking with them back to their home. On each visit he had learned more about them. Luigi was a post office worker, Carla was a shop assistant. They had shown him photos of their wedding day. Though they had not asked, he gradually told them about his life and what it meant to be a chief rabbi of Rome. Carla had stared at him wide-eyed and said it must be like being a pope. He had laughed and said the pope had the world to look after; he only had a few thousand Jews to care for. To his astonishment they never had asked him why he went to Mass.

A few weeks ago Carla suggested Zolli should bring his wife and children for a meal and he explained Emma was shy and never entertained. The subject had not been raised again until that Friday afternoon after Zolli had told them about St. Peter's being locked and the Guardia Palatina standing watch over the square and the entrances to the Vatican. It was then Carla said that after all he had told them about the Nazis he and his family would be safer in their apartment; a Catholic home was where the Nazis would never look for them.

Luigi added that several Jewish families were being sheltered after Mussolini had gone and Hitler had once more ranted on the wireless against the Jews. Zolli and his family should come now, urged Carla, before the Germans occupied Rome. Besides, Luigi said, the Allies would be here soon and everyone would be safe.

Zolli had thanked them but said that his own duties demanded he should remain with his people.

At seven o'clock that evening Radio Rome issued a proclamation on behalf of "*Feldmaresciallo* Kesselring."

"Rome is under my command and is declared to be war territory. It is subject to German martial law. Any crimes committed in this territory against my armed forces will be punished under German martial law. Those organizing strikes or sabotage, as well as snipers, will be shot immediately. Until further orders all private correspondence is suspended. All telephone conversations will be strictly supervised. The police and other civil authorities are responsible to the German authorities to help prevent all acts of passive resistance. A curfew will begin at nine-thirty every evening until seven o'clock in the morning. Only emergency services will be allowed to operate in that period."

The newscaster delivered his message in Italian with a German accent. Radio Rome, like the rest of the city, had been occupied.

That night the city had fallen silent apart from sudden screams, the grinding of breaks, and guttural commands. There was no traffic except for German trucks, armored cars, and ambulances taking the wounded to the hospital.

Father Patrick had lost count of the number of journeys he had made to collect the dead and the dying. All he knew in the darkness was there were more lying in the streets waiting to be collected.

He had learned during his long day that across the city there were men in hiding: Italian soldiers who had exchanged their uniforms for civilian clothes but kept their rifles; refugees and members of the Resistance.

"I was told there were at least fifty thousand people hiding. They were living under false names, as they huddled under the roofs or in cellars," Father Patrick would recall.

On that Friday evening he had a wounded teenager in the ambulance. She had been running barefoot down an alley to avoid being heard, when a soldier yelled at her to stop. She had turned into another alley and continued to run. He had given chase, his footsteps loud on the cobbles. Suddenly a hand grenade exploded behind her as she turned into another alley. She felt metal fragments strike her back and blood running down her legs. She ran on. Behind her the footsteps faded then stopped.

Father Patrick had been flagged down by an old woman carrying the girl. He brought her to the hospital then set off to search for more wounded.

D'Arcy Osborne had settled down after dinner on that Friday evening to turn the day's events into an encrypted report to London when John May announced that Anton Call had arrived. The minister had set aside his work and invited the policeman to sit while he fixed them drinks.

Call had transferred from the city police force to join the small Vatican force. When the Allied diplomats had moved into Santa Maria he had been assigned to patrol the entrance to the compound. May discovered Call had trained to be a veterinary surgeon and showed an affectionate interest in Jeremy, Osborne's terrier. When the dog developed a hernia problem, Call had brought his surgical bag to the apartment and helped May perform a life-saving operation while Osborne had watched anxiously. Since then the three men had become friends.

Neither Osborne nor Call knew their friendship had been betrayed to the Italian Secret Police, OVRA, by one of its informers in the Vatican. He was Monsignor Pucci, the seller of fake stories, who now worked as a translator for Cardinal Nicola Canali, the bewigged and cantankerous head of the Vatican administration. A dedicated Fascist and anti-British, he had opposed O'Flaherty's visits to prisoner-of-war camps claiming it would "only encourage them to escape and cause problems for the Vatican."

The armistice Italy had signed with the Allies allowed all prisoners of war to be freed before the Germans could transport them to camps in the Third Reich. But many were interned in central Italy and could be heading for Rome in the belief the city would hide them until the Allied armies arrived.

The minister had told Call he suspected "many of them could be leaderless and have no clear idea of where they could hide in Rome. Winter is coming and most of them were captured in North Africa in their desert clothes. But if they came into Rome in large numbers, the Vatican will simply be unable to feed, let alone hide them."

On Sunday morning, September 12, Dante Almansi, the former deputy police chief of Rome, hurried past the ruins of the arcade Emperor Augustus had built for his sister, Octavia in 23 B.C. Its magnificent marble columns were lost in the mist which during the night had spread like a fleecy blanket from the Tiber. Beneath it the city held its breath.

Almansi and his family lived on Piazza Quadrata, in an affluent district of houses and apartments; each had their domestic servants and the streets were daily swept by the *spazzini,* the city road cleaners.

At daylight when the curfew was lifted he had decided rather than drive to his meeting at the synagogue, he would walk, concerned his car would be confiscated by the Germans, and also to see for himself the extent of the damage.

The usual Roman traffic police had been replaced by German soldiers directing mostly trucks and armored cars. Vans with detection finder antennas on their roofs were moving slowly through the streets searching for illegal radios. Trams stood empty on their tracks where they were abandoned when last night's curfew had sounded and their drivers and passengers fled. Almansi's shoes crunched over glass and rubble smeared with blood. At regular intervals soldiers were pasting posters on walls. He stopped to read one. It was a printed version of the Radio Rome proclamation he had heard the previous evening issued in the name of Kesselring.

On Via del Portico d'Ottavia, the only shops open were two bakers, preparing the usual ration of 150 grams of bread for every customer. There were no street cleaners or peddlers setting off for the city. A few groups stood in knots talking among themselves. A man called out to Almansi asking what they should do. He told them to stay out of Rome to avoid the risk of arrest.

By the time he entered the synagogue the mist was lifting, burned off by the morning sun. Ugo Foa had called an emergency meeting in the synagogue's library with its magnificent collection not only for the study of Judaica but also of early Christianity. The shelves contained evidence of two thousand years of Jewish presence in Rome.

Rosina Sorani sat beside Foa as note taker. The *giunta* committee members sat on either side of the table. At the other end sat Zolli.

Foa's opening remarks were reassuring. He had finally been able to reach his contacts in the city administration and their consensus was that Kesselring had introduced nothing which specifically discriminated against Jews. While elsewhere in Europe there was harsh persecution of Jews, the best way to live alongside the occupiers was to regard their presence as little different to living under the racial laws. He reminded the *giunta* that he and Almansi had reduced the effect of many of those laws and he hoped it would not be long before they would succeed in doing so under the Germans.

Foa motioned for Zolli to speak. The chief rabbi rose to his feet and said it was reassuring to hear the president's words. But it would be wrong of him if he did not raise certain matters. He reminded them that soon the autumn high holidays would arrive, a time when the community would fill every space in the synagogue. The religious festivals would provide the Nazis with an opportunity to gather together the Jews and take them to concentration camps. He proposed that the celebrations should be postponed. Rosina would recall, "the silence was the silence only anger creates."

Zolli then proposed that the synagogue should withdraw all its deposits in various banks which paid for the community's school, the rabbinical college, the upkeep of the Jewish cemetery, and the salaries of synagogue staff. The money would be used to pay for Jews to be housed with Christian families. He was sure a number of them would welcome the additional income derived from renting. The Vatican should also be approached to provide shelter in convents and monasteries in the city and he would be willing to explore the idea with the Holy See.

Foa jumped to his feet, his face flushed with anger as he accused Zolli of being "thrown into a panic." Almansi said the chief rabbi "wanted to destroy the community." From around the table voices shouted their disapproval at Zolli.

Rosina noted: "Everyone was talking at once. Anselmo Colombo was shouting that Zolli should resign." She gave up trying to identify the protesters and what they said. It was left to Renzo Levi to call for a vote. Zolli's proposals were rejected.

That same Sunday afternoon, Pope Pius convened a meeting in the Apostolic Palace. Seated around a table in a salon were Maglione and his two assistants, Montini and Tardini. With them were Ottaviani, O'Flaherty, and Colonel de Pfyffer d'Altishofen, the commandant of the Guardia Palatina. Father Weber completed the group.

On the table before the pope were reports from priests and nuns in Rome. They included what had happened to two Vatican staff. One was a doctor who was wounded in the head by a bullet earlier that morning on his way to see a dying priest in a hospital and was now himself in critical condition. The other was an Apostolic Palace usher who was stopped at a German checkpoint and subjected to a body search despite producing his Vatican ID card and was robbed of his watch. Other reports described Romans being pulled off their bicycles or dragged from their cars, leaving their owners without transport. One report described the situation as "there is no redress, they are armed. It would be death for anyone to resist them."

Pius issued his first instructions. Maglione was to send a strong protest to the German ambassador, von Weizsäcker, that any further attacks on Vatican staff would be regarded as a serious violation of its neutrality. Commandant d'Altishofen was to contact Rome's police and press for the German authorities to investigate the shooting and robbery.

In the meantime St. Peter's would be reopened, but soldiers bearing arms were not to be admitted. The Gendarmerie around the perimeter of the square would be reduced so as not to alarm worshippers. The Vatican gates would also be unlocked and remain open during the curfew.

Pius turned to another matter. Earlier that morning he had received a telephone call from Count de Salis. The Red Cross director estimated that soon there could be up to four thousand Allied troops hiding in the city who, having walked out of their prison camps, would be waiting for British and American armies to reach Rome.

The pope turned to Father Weber. He said that during the summer hundreds of Jews had been provided with travel documents and smuggled across the Austrian and Slovenian boarders into Italy. But many had been caught by German forces and either had been shot or rounded up for transport to the concentration camps. Survivors were fleeing to Rome.

It was for that reason Pius said he had convened the meeting. In his view there was a very limited chance of moving those Jews farther south. They would be entering a war zone and would either be shot by the Germans or left to fend for themselves by the Allies. The only solution was for the Vatican to prepare to accept them. That itself would have its own problems. Reports from nuncios in the Third Reich indicated its ghettos had been systematically emptied of their Jews. There was no guarantee that would not happen in Rome, despite assurances from von Weizsäcker, the German ambassador, that its Jewish population would be allowed to continue their normal lives.

What was needed, continued Pius, was a properly organized system of safe places which were under the protection of the Lateran Treaty. In Germany and other parts of the Third Reich the Nazis had not respected church property. In Vienna troops had been billeted in a convent and the

St. Francis de Salles girls' school turned into a barracks. It was all part of the Nazi's systematic war against the church. The pope said that daily he received reports of priests and nuns in Poland and elsewhere being sent to concentration camps. They had all been accused of helping the Jews and speaking out against Nazism. More than ever the Vatican had a duty to protect the Jews on its doorstep. Just as the Nazis had taken over Catholic institutions in the Third Reich so the Vatican must turn every possible convent, monastery, and institution in Rome into a secret refuge for the Jews and escaped prisoners of war.

To provide such assistance would be difficult, even dangerous as the Germans would regard it as a breach of the Lateran Treaty. But it was a risk that must be taken.

The pope turned to Ottaviani and said that given O'Flaherty's experience in visiting prisoner-of-war camps he wanted him relieved of all but essential duties in the Holy Office and to concentrate on organizing a plan to provide sanctuary for both the Jews of Rome and the soldiers.

Bishop Alois Hudal had also been given a new assignment. Waldemar Meyer, his RSHA controller, had once more travelled from Berlin to ask him to find a suitable property in the city which could be converted into a religious college for Georgian students who had avoided Russian captivity and wished to complete their studies for the priesthood in Rome.

Hudal's increasingly pronounced pro-Nazi attitude made him no longer welcome among monsignori responsible for daily contact with the nuncios in the Third Reich; they had firmly refused to give him access to their reports and the pope's secretary, Father Leiber, insisted the bishop's sermons and lectures to his students must first be approved by the pope.

Only recently Hudal had been warned by Maglione to stop involving himself in Vatican-German affairs. This followed a memo Hudal had sent to the pope, volunteering to go to Berlin to discuss with Hitler how Pius could make a public statement about the danger of Bolshevism to Western civilization and, in doing so, would recognize the need for the Third Reich to deal with the threat from Moscow. The bishop had already sent the proposal to Meyer. He passed it to Ernst Kaltenbrunner, the head of the RSHA, who for over a year had been considering how best to get his spies inside the Vatican. He decided the first step was to send Meyer to Rome to see Hudal with a well-prepared cover story for the need of a college for Georgian students.

Hudal's sense of excitement could only have increased when Meyer shared with him some of the background to the search he would conduct.

Sofia Coghieli, a devout member of the Georgian congregation of Our Lady of Lourdes had been forced to flee her home in the Caucasus Mountains by Soviet persecution. She went to Brussels where she died in 1941. In her will she left a large sum of money to be used to open a college in Rome where young men from Georgia could train for the priesthood.

The bequest had come to Kaltenbrunner's notice. He arranged for the money to be removed from a Dutch bank where it was deposited and transferred to a Swiss bank account the RSHA had. From there it would be placed in yet another account the organization held in Rome to pay for the property once it was found. Meyer told Hudal that a number of Georgians were fighting for the Third Reich on the Russian front. To find them a suitable property where they could become priests was the least Germany could do.

Hudal was not told that the Georgian college would serve as an intelligence base to penetrate the Vatican. Outwardly it would operate under the same rules which applied to all the other dozen colleges. However the college students would be RSHA officers who would include linguists, cryptologists, and analysts. Their preparation would have included clerical studies to give them the essential cover of preparing to become priests. In reality they would spy on the Vatican.

The college would be under the control of Michael Kedia, a Georgian nationalist who had been recruited by AMT VI-G, the Russian desk in the foreign intelligence division of RSHA. Kedia's role was to ensure the clandestine side of the college would remain secret.

Hudal's search for a suitable property finally found one on Via Alessandro Brisse in the industrial district on the northern outskirts of Rome. The palazzo had once belonged to the Fascist publisher, Salvatore di Carlo, who had fled after the fall of Mussolini.

After Hudal and Meyer inspected the building a problem arose.

Kaltenbrunner wanted the property registered with the Vatican Administration for Ecclesiastical Properties to give the college legitimacy under
the Lateran Treaty; a protection that would stop inquiries by the Italian
authorities. But Hudal realized the registration would produce inquiries
in the Vatican. He knew Cardinal Eugene Tisserant, the head of the Congregation for the Eastern Churches would become involved and demand
Madam Coghieli's bequest be traced. The matter would inevitably come
to the attention of Maglione and lead to him taking action against Hudal
for why he had not kept the Vatican fully informed. The more he looked
at the request to have the property registered, the greater was Hudal's
alarm. He finally told Meyer he could no longer be involved. What had
been known as Operation Georgian Convent in the RSHA was dealt a
mortal blow. Meyer returned to Berlin, his own career in ruins. Kaltenbrunner ordered the operation to be stopped. Bishop Hudal spent the following weeks in a retreat house in Rome.

On Sunday afternoon, September 12, Princess Nina Pallavicini had gone to
the Excelsior Hotel for lunch. Her guest was Margarita de Wyss, a Swiss
journalist who was one of the few foreign reporters left in Rome. Both
women ignored the German officers occupying most of the other tables,
including those seated around a large table in the center of the room. The
princess recognized General Rainer Stahel from his photograph in *Popolo di
Roma*. The newspaper had named him as the city's military commander.
She saw his hair was more silvery and his lips fuller than in his photo.

Seated with him, among other uniformed officers, was SS *Obersturm-
bandführer* Herbert Kappler. His name and photo had also been in the newspaper, naming the thirty-seven-year-old as the head of the gestapo in Rome,
and the man who had planned the rescue of Mussolini from captivity.

That morning Rome Radio announced that in a daring action ninety
German glider-borne troops had plucked the duce from imprisonment at
the Hotel Campo Imperatore in Abruzzi. He would set up a neo-Fascist
regime in German-occupied Italy at Salo on Lake Garda. In the newspaper photo there was a menace about Kappler: the way he stared fixedly
into the camera, hair slicked back, his eyes half closed.

In the intervening years since he had come to Rome for the funeral of

Pope Pius XI, Kappler had been trained by the RSHA in the techniques of interrogation and how to create terror in all those he questioned. Jews in Austria, Poland, and other parts of the Third Reich had been broken by the time they were sent to the concentration camps.

In between he had acquired a wife, Leonore Janns, a twenty-seven-year-old typist in the party's office in Stuttgart. Unable to father a child, Kappler had applied to the *Lebensborn* program—Himmler's depraved plan to genetically engineer perfect Germans. The couple were given a baby boy they named Wolfgang. Fair haired with blue eyes and a muscular body the child could have been a model for the program.

The family had arrived in Rome with General Stahel's staff. Travelling with them was Kappler's mistress, Helen Brouwer, a buxom woman he had met at a gestapo training school and had arranged for her to come with him to Rome as his assistant.

After the pope's briefing, O'Flaherty and Ottaviani emerged from the Apostolic Palace onto St. Peter's Square. They paused to watch worshippers going into the basilica, walking quickly, talking among themselves and occasionally looking over their shoulders. At the edge of the square German soldiers stood before a newly painted white line separating Rome and the Vatican. Before anyone could cross the line they had their Italian identity card checked. Mounted on a truck a powerful telescope was scanning the Apostolic Palace. Standing inside the line were members of the Guardia Palatina, politely nodding to Romans as they made their way to the basilica.

The two priests looked at each other. Then, in step they walked across the white line, moved a few yards into Rome, turning and crossing back into the Vatican. The soldiers had looked bemused at this act of defiance.

"They must never forget we are a free country," Ottaviani said. O'Flaherty remarked it had taken the English centuries to remember that in Ireland.

Harold Tittmann had spent part of his Sunday afternoon strolling around the courtyard at Santa Marta with two priests who he had described in a message to the State Department as "my leg men." One was Father Joseph

McGeogh, a Boston Irishman with a fund of jokes which rivalled those of O'Flaherty's. The other was the French canon of St. Peter's, Monsignor Herisse. He lived on the far side of the Santa Marta compound, a spry white-haired man with a brisk stride and a fund of information he acquired from the basilica's congregation, which included news about the Jews of the ghetto and the activities of Delasem.

Both priests dispensed the monthly money transfers which came into the mission's account in the Vatican Bank. It had been transferred by Jewish relief organizations in New York. While the use of the State Department and the U.S. Treasury was a violation of the Vatican's neutrality, Tittmann regarded it as "charity aid to destitute prisoners."

On that Sunday afternoon Rabbi Zolli had decided he would go and visit Luigi and Carla Pierandello and see if they were still willing to shelter him and his family. He had not discussed the offer with Emma. Since the arrival of the Germans his wife had become close to a nervous collapse, weeping they should never have come to Rome. Zolli had assured Emma there was no cause for alarm and left the apartment. The day was hot and he was grateful for the shade of the back streets. A few food shops were open but there was little to buy.

The rattle of street trams was a reminder Rome was returning to normal, but Zolli decided not to risk travelling on them as soldiers were checking ID cards. His card identified him as the chief rabbi.

New posters warned that people caught looting or possessing stolen food would be punished by imprisonment. Near the Pantheon he had watched soldiers distributing loaves to a group of women while a German-uniformed newsreel cameraman urged them to smile into the lens. After he was satisfied the policemen took the loaves from the women and sent them on their way. The bread was loaded onto a truck with the cameraman and they drove off to find another setup for Goebbels's propaganda machine.

It was late afternoon when Zolli arrived at the apartment block where Luigi and Carla Pierandello lived. He climbed the stone steps to the floor and knocked on their door. There was no reply and he knocked again, louder than before. A door farther down the corridor opened and an old man stared at him. He said the couple had left.

Zolli asked where they had gone. "He said people were in a panic and leaving the city. Before I could ask any more he closed the door," recalled Zolli.

When he arrived home he found Emma crouched with their daughters in a corner of the storeroom where they kept the trunks in which they had brought their belongings from Trieste. He saw his wife had been in the process of filling one of the trunks with clothes when another panic attack had gripped her and she sobbed they were all going to die. Through her tears she told him a truck had driven down the street full of soldiers. As Zolli soothed his wife he would remember how Miriam looked at him. "There was trust in her eyes. She kissed her mother and said everything would be alright. I knew then I had to do something, find somewhere where they would be safe."

That night they all slept together in one bedroom.

In his room in the German college O'Flaherty studied the list of Vatican properties protected under the Lateran Treaty. It had been one of the first documents he had read when he came to the Vatican. But while it guaranteed the Holy See's extra-territorial properties would be protected he felt it unlikely the Germans would allow sovereignty to extend to providing shelter to Jews and Allied escapers.

In a notebook he had written the names of mother superiors and their convents and the heads of colleges and teaching institutes. Next he had gone down the list of parish priests in the city. Some he had met, others were new to their posts. Against names he placed a tick to remind himself to check their records more fully.

In her bedroom Princess Nina Pallavicini listened to the BBC late-night news broadcast start with the familiar words, "This is London calling." The bulletin began with the news that the remainder of the Italian fleet had escaped to Malta and surrendered to the Royal Navy, when her maid rushed in: A wireless detector van was at the end of the street. The princess switched off the set and returned it to its hiding place under the false floor in her wardrobe. She joined the maid at the bedroom window to watch the van moving slowly past the palazzo and turn around the corner.

Late on Sunday in the comfort of the library in Villa Napoleon Weizsäcker shared an Italian grappa with Kessel. Earlier that evening the ambassador had informed Maglione that he had been authorized by Ribbentrop to confirm that the neutrality of the Vatican would be fully respected. Kessel shrugged and asked for how long. Weizsäcker had smiled indulgently. In the weeks they had come to know each other he recognized they shared the same views and background. Neither were members of the Nazi Party and both were Catholics. The difference between them was that Kessel was headstrong and made no secret of his views.

Now, as they enjoyed their drinks, Weizsäcker told his young deputy that the arrival of Kappler in the city had made more certain the fate of Rome's Jews.

8

THE SANCTUARY SEEKERS

Shortly after dawn on Wednesday, September 16, 1943, escorted by side-car motorcyclists, a German staff car and five closed trucks drove through the streets of downtown Rome. During the night more posters put up by the occupiers had been torn down by the Resistance before its members disappeared back into the darkness of side streets.

The convoy came to a halt outside the Central Bank of Italy. Ugly pock-marks in its walls were a reminder of the fierce street fighting which had preceded the capture of the city, now gripped in a sullen silence, as stifling as the heat.

Waiting outside the double doors of the bank was its general manager; beside him stood an SS *Oberscharführer,* a staff sergeant (senior squad leader). He snapped to attention as a black-booted Kappler emerged in his immaculate uniform from the car. He stood for a moment looking at the building, the morning light catching the three-inch duelling scar on his cheek and, as he raised his hand to acknowledge the sergeant's salute, the steel ring on his index finger glinted. It was decorated with the death's-head and a swastika, the symbols of the gestapo.

When the paratroopers had jumped down from the trucks, Kappler led them to where the manager waited. He inclined his head as if greeting a valued client then opened the doors and led Kappler and the paratroopers

into the building. In the street the motorcyclists took up position, submachine guns at the ready.

Within an hour one hundred and ten metric tons of gold had been
brought up from the bank vaults and loaded onto the trucks by the paratroopers. In those sixty minutes the entire gold reserve of Italy had been
stolen. Later that day the paratroopers transferred the bullion onto two
freight railcars to begin the train journey north to Berlin. By then Kappler
had begun to plan how he could further steal more gold for the Third
Reich—this time from the Jews of Rome.

O'Flaherty had put together the Vatican network with the speed and skill
for which he was known. He had first spoken to Irish priests working in
the Vatican to check their Gaelic language skills. Priests who spoke their
native language had played an important role in those harsh years in Irish
history in the 1920s when they had used it to help Republicans fight the English Black and Tans who were seen by Catholics as "terrorists of the king."
O'Flaherty said the priests he chose would use Gaelic to outwit the
Germans.

Among the first recruits was Father Sean Quinlan, whose family were
neighbors of the O'Flahertys in County Kerry. Another was Monsignor
Thomas Ryan who said, "It's going to be more fun than saying morning
Mass." Father Owen Sneddon worked for Vatican Radio. O'Flaherty already knew he frequently slipped in messages during his broadcasts for
families of Allied prisoners.

Within days a dozen other priests had been recruited and Sneddon—a
lover of spy stories—suggested they should all have code names. O'Flaherty
became "Golf"; Sneddon chose to be known by his father's name, "Horace";
Quinlan "Kerry"; and Ryan "Rinso." Others were assigned names which
could have come from one of the prison camp stage reviews O'Flaherty
had watched. There was "Eyerish," "Fanny," "Emma," and "Whitebows,"
a priest in the De La Salle teaching order.

They would act as couriers between safe houses. For the most part he
had decided they would be convents. But on Princess Pallavicini's suggestion he had agreed she should negotiate for apartments to rent whose occupants had fled. They could be used to hide Allied soldiers who might

find it "a little uncomfortable being tucked away in a convent of nuns," she had told him.

One of his recruit's tasks would be to provide details of the network to rural priests who had parishes close to prisoner-of-war camps from where Allied prisoners had escaped and were heading for Rome.

O'Flaherty had made several visits over the years to the ghetto, attracted by its history and lifestyle. There was a poverty of centuries of difficult times but also a strong sense of spirituality that centered on the *tempio maggiore*, the synagogue. He had learned that their culture was as deeply rooted as that of Irelands's. His latest visit had been to meet Settimio Sorani, an introduction effected by Father Weber who had said after O'Flaherty had been appointed by the pope to head the Vatican network it would be good if it worked with Delasem.

Settimio had shown him evidence Delasem had received which confirmed the latest reports from nuncios of Nazi atrocities. They included grainy photographs of roundups in Lithuania, Latvia, and the Ukraine.

Through Rosina, O'Flaherty had met with Ugo Foa, Dante Almansi, Renzo Levi, and Israel Zolli.

It was the first time he had been inside a synagogue and Foa had shown him around, taking him to the library and explaining its importance in Jewish history before leading him to his office where the others were waiting. They greeted O'Flaherty warmly and listened intently when he told them of the pope's plans to help the Jews of Rome. O'Flaherty noticed everyone except Zolli expressed their satisfaction after O'Flaherty finished outlining Pius's intentions. The chief rabbi said if the Allies did not arrive soon there would be a bloodbath. According to Zolli, Almansi said to him, "How can a mind as clear as yours make such a prediction which can only disrupt the lives of our people? The Germans have not shown any sign yet of making a move against us!" The chief rabbi had shrugged and took no further part in the conversation.

That evening O'Flaherty had met with Princess Nina Pallavicini. She told him over a dozen apartments had been rented to house Allied soldiers and escapees and many more would be available shortly.

After she had given him the latest news from London on the BBC, the princess revealed she and her maid had spent the afternoon burying her valuables in the palazzo gardens in a tin box which was wrapped in oil-cloth. A number of her friends were doing the same now that looting had increased by street gangs. As he walked her back to the palazzo, the streets were already emptying before the curfew started.

One evening dressed as a Roman postman O'Flaherty had set out to visit Prince Filippo. The disguise had been his idea to avoid rising suspicion about why a monsignor was visiting Trastevere.

The prince was a member of the Black Nobility and a staunch anti-Fascist, a position which had cost him dearly. Mussolini had ordered him sent to a prison camp from which Filippo had been released following pressure from the pope. Filippo had gone into hiding to avoid being arrested by the Germans. O'Flaherty was among a small circle of friends who visited the prince in his small house in Trastevere. It was far removed from the family baroque palazzo on Rome's Via del Corso. With its thousand rooms it was rivalled in size only by the Apostolic Palace. On the bank of the Tiber, Filippo's neighbors were working-class families and a number belonged to the Resistance.

He had been his usual attentive host and when O'Flaherty had told him about the progress in setting up the network he handed him five hundred thousand lire to rent more apartments and stock them with food and clothes.

O'Flaherty's next move was to contact D'Arcy Osborne. His friendship with the British minister dated from the days they had played together at the exclusive Rome Golf Club. When Osborne moved into Santa Marta he had given O'Flaherty boxes of unused golf balls he had no use for in the Vatican and invited him to dinner. Osborne concluded there was no sign of any anti-British feelings in his guest; it was clear that O'Flaherty championed refugees and Jews and anti-Fascists.

On that September morning Osborne welcomed the monsignor to his office with his usual affected Irish greeting—"Top of the morning to you,

Hugh." O'Flaherty wasted no time in saying he had "come on the scrounge for money, the root of all evil." He told Osborne about the pope's decision to provide shelter for Jews and Allied escapers in Rome.

The minister sat making notes, interrupting to ask the occasional question. The more he was told, he realized he could not leave British escapers to roam the countryside trying to live off the land, let alone have to survive on the city streets. But if the Germans discovered he had helped them it would breach Britain's diplomatic status and lead to his expulsion from the Vatican. Yet he had to do something. He told O'Flaherty he would arrange to "open a facility account" with Vatican Bank which would be guaranteed by the Foreign Office in London and the money he borrowed to help support the network would be repaid within three month of the liberation of Rome.

A slightly bemused O'Flaherty asked what sum would be available to draw from the account. Osborne had replied, "How much do you want, two million, three million lire?"

O'Flaherty had not hesitated. "Let's go for the top number. There are a lot of people to take care of."

In London the request for money was accompanied by Osborne's promise it would be used to "save precious lives," and painted a graphic picture of "starving people being hunted by Nazis." The request landed on the desk of a senior Treasury official, Sir Horace Rumbold. The Foreign Office file—FO 371/37566—reveals a bureaucratic decision maker. What were the risks in opening a Vatican Bank account to save British prisoners? What danger could it create for His Majesty's government's relationship with the Holy See? How could Osborne guarantee the money would only be used to aid the "right people and not fall into the hands of crooks"? Would the money be used to aid other Allied escaped prisoners, such as the Russians or Greeks? If so would it be subsequently recovered from their governments at the end of the war? In the end Rumbold had advised, "It is worth taking a good many risks." A loan for three million lire was sanctioned on the terms and conditions Osborne had proposed.

Finally O'Flaherty discussed his own role with Maglione. He told the secretary of state he planned to stand on the top step of St. Peter's Basilica before morning and evening Mass. For members of the network it would be an opportunity for them to contact him to give him their latest news and receive his instructions. It would also be a spot where escapees and refugees could be brought and taken to their hiding places.

The cardinal sat back in his chair and said while the plan had been well prepared the risk was still there. The Germans had set up observation posts in buildings beyond the square. They would surely begin to wonder why he was standing there twice a day in his distinctive robes of black-and-red vestments which identified him as a member of the Holy Office.

O'Flaherty had said it was a risk he must take.

Pascalina had added to her weekly visits to the hospitals by making calls on convents which O'Flaherty had selected as safe houses. She told the mother superior of each convent that the pope had authorized she would have financial help to cover the costs of sheltering and feeding her guests. The money would be distributed through the Pallottine fathers.

At the convent of the order of Brigittines the abbess showed Pascalina the secret door which led to an underground refuge where in medieval years nuns had sheltered while Rome was under attack. It was being fitted out as dormitories where refugees could sleep. At the Augustine convent on the slope of the Caelian Hill the abbess took Pascalina to the small farm adjoining the building which would supply milk and meat for the asylum seekers. Pascalina told her that as the Nazis forbade ritual slaughter to the Jews, the pope would send a specially trained kosher butcher from the Vatican farm at Castel Gandolfo to prepare the meat as required by Jewish ritual slaughter.

In one convent Pascalina found plans were underway to store sufficient flour to bake for refugees. In another religious house the pantries were being stocked with tinned food. Sister Emilia Ameblow, the mother superior, had urged Pascalina: "Please bring as many Jews as you can. We will sleep on the floor to make room for them, and will also ensure they have a place to worship. After all, they are God's children."

That evening Pascalina wrote in her diary, "They all said it was good to be called upon by the Holy Father to open our doors, raise the grilles, and put aside the risk to save the lives of people in danger."

The pope sent his congratulations to O'Flaherty when he learned the Vatican network had begun to work closely with Delasem and the Pallottine fathers to help the refugees. Pius arranged for Settimio Sorani to use church buildings to set up secret offices in towns and cities across Italy which operated with the support of archbishops in Genoa, Turin, Florence, and Milan. He ordered diocese bank accounts to be used to distribute money Delasem received from Jewish relief organizations in the United States to provide documents and clothes for the fugitive Jews. Clearly identified Vatican trucks supplied food to convents and monasteries where the refugees sheltered.

Delasem had started to send small groups of Jews across the border into Switzerland. Some of the priests who had volunteered to act as guides were Pallottine fathers, and carried Vatican-stamped papers to show the Swiss border guards they were escorting home pilgrims from Rome. Jewish men were dressed with robes provided by religious orders. The women wore nun's habits and the children were listed as orphans from a Catholic home. If the guards suspected anything an envelope of money settled matters. Sorani had already arranged for members of the Swiss branch of Delasem to be waiting at the nearest border town to organize new lives in a neutral country for the refugees. Pius had sent several nuns and priests to Switzerland to assist with the resettlement.

Many of those waiting to make the journey there were moved from one religious house to another. Gisela Birach would remember that "nuns were kind, but they expected us to follow their work ethics. We had to wash and wax the corridor floors and our men would work in the fields. In some convents they had long periods of silence during which we had to remain in our rooms and not talk."

Ester Braunstein worked in a convent kitchen. "I was in charge of peeling potatoes and everyone was counted. Hunger defined our existence. While the sisters shared with us, there was never enough to meet our hunger. Unless you have chewed potato peel or radish leaves you don't know what hunger is."

By the end of the second week of occupation daily life seemed to have resumed in Rome. The shops had opened, trams ran, children returned to school, the black market continued. Only the newspapers and Radio Rome revealed the reality. They published the names of the "commissioners" appointed by General Stahel to run the city. They had been ordered to hand over all black marketers for "immediate execution." Other offenses included spreading Allied "propaganda," breaching the curfew, and removing public notices posted by the "German high command of southern Italy." Permits for nurses and doctors to be out during curfew hours had to be obtained from the Ministry of War office established at the city's police headquarters. Any misuse of the permits to communicate with the Resistance or support them in any way was punishable by death.

Every morning the station broadcast excerpts from Hitler's latest speeches and on Monday, September 20, announced it took "great pleasure" to confirm that Kesselring had been received by the pope. In the ten minutes' audience the pope obtained concessions from the field marshal: All vehicles bearing the Vatican City license plate, s.c.v, would pass unchallenged through the streets of Rome; all extraterritorial property would have a placard on their doors bearing the words PROPERTY OF THE HOLY SEE both in Italian and German and would not be entered by any German authority; the Vatican Railway train from Castel Gandolfo would not be stopped or searched; the German army would not cross the white line which marked its boundary with the Vatican.

Both *L'Osservatore Romano* and Vatican Radio reported the concessions without comment. But Dalla Torre, the newspaper's editor, told his staff that "whatever their motives the Germans are trying to make friends hoping it will help them when the Allies arrive."

As soon as he heard about the concessions Professor Borromeo had ordered a bold sign to be erected at the *Fatebenefratelli* entrance: ORDER OF ST. JOHN. PROPERTY OF THE HOLY SEE. In the past days he had learned that other hospitals in Rome not protected by the Lateran Treaty had been searched by German soldiers for injured Resistance fighters and wounded curfew breakers.

Several were already patients in the *Fatebenefratelli* recovering from wounds received in the battle for Rome or had been injured while breaking the curfew. After surgery they had been moved to an upper-floor ward identified as an isolation unit for tuberculosis patients.

They were young and spent their days lying immobile, staring up at the blank whiteness of the ceiling. Once they could move they were helped by a nurse to a day room where they could listen to the radio Dr. Vittorio Sacerdoti had brought them for news of the advancing Allies. Sometimes he sat with them during the evening and they told him how eager they were to go back to join the Resistance. He warned them they probably already had a price on their head and they replied that to save Rome it was one worth paying. He understood their feeling.

He never told them that twice already he had made his way through the dangerous night streets, carrying his surgeon's bag, to help a fighter whose family had been too frightened to bring him to the hospital. Instead he had used hot water to scrub clean a kitchen table, before giving the patient a local anesthetic and dealing with his wound.

His courage would make him one of the first heroes of the occupation.

Mose Spizzichino and his married daughters, Ada and Gentile, unloaded his handcart. Every day it was harder to find anything good to buy. People had left their homes and those who had something to sell haggled over an offer for an old dress, a coat, or a worn pair of shoes.

There had been no news from Umberto and Mario since they had left to join the Resistance. But Mose was reassuring. On his rounds he had heard that a number of fighters had headed south to join the partisans attacking the Germans preparing defenses against the advancing Allies. He had told his daughters their husbands would be too busy fighting to contact them.

Rome itself had undergone changes. Street names had been altered, including the ancient Via Marco Polo; it was now called Via Adolf Hitler.

The royal crest on letter boxes had been painted over with black and the swastika flag flew over all office buildings. Roadblocks were everywhere to check that all motor vehicles carried the new taxation discs which General Stahel had introduced. He had also ordered a proclamation to be broadcast on Radio Rome and published in all the newspapers that Italian soldiers who had fought alongside the Germans before the armistice could enlist in the German army, and have the same status including pay and food as Germans.

Stahel had also "invited" Italian workers to volunteer and join "labor brigades" to build defenses around the city "against an enemy who has taken possession of Italian soil and must be driven out." There was work for sixty thousand able-bodied men who would be well paid and treated "in the spirit of national and socialist justice which distinguished the new Germany being built," Stahel had promised.

When only three hundred Romans answered the call, Kesselring ordered a roundup. Streets were cordoned off and buildings searched, and trams and cars stopped, and physically fit men were bundled into waiting trucks.

Mose had twice managed to escape being conscripted by pushing his handcart down a side street.

Pascalina had visited the ghetto for the first time in weeks. She wanted to see how the Jews were coping. As she walked along the Via del Portico d'Ottavia people smiled and nodded in acknowledgment of her presence. "She was a reminder that the pope was close by and watching over us," Giogina Ajo, a cousin of Dr. Sacerdoti recalled.

Others told Pascalina that neighbors who had gone into hiding were returning to their homes to work and take their place in the food lines. A shopkeeper told her that milk had become short and mothers went from one dairy shop to another and often still returned home empty-handed, in tears.

Pascalina had returned to the Vatican and told the pope milk should be sent from the Vatican farm at Castel Gandolfo to the ghetto for its children. Pius had agreed.

From his vantage point on the top step of St. Peter's Basilica, O'Flaherty watched a German staff car park opposite St. Peter's Square. The driver opened the passenger door and Kappler emerged. He slowly walked along the white line dividing the Vatican from Rome, pausing to stare at the statues of saints on top of Bernini's colonnade. As he reached the far end of the boundary line Kappler stopped to look at the Apostolic Palace. Then he turned and walked briskly back to the limousine.

At this hour O'Flaherty knew the pope would be praying in his private chapel, where more than once O'Flaherty had himself knelt on a kneeler. He knew the pope would automatically have included the man who had taken a last sweeping look over the Vatican; in all his prayers Pius included every soul on earth. But it did nothing to reduce O'Flaherty's instinctive feeling as he watched the car drive away that it contained an implacable enemy.

That September evening Ambassador Ernst von Weizsäcker and his deputy, Albrecht von Kessel, sat in the comfort of the library in the Villa Napoleon discussing a potential imminent crisis in Vatican-German relations they were responsible for maintaining in Rome.

The previous day a Waffen SS unit had swooped on the small resort towns along the shores of Lake Maggiore in the north of Italy. Living there was a small Jewish community. Fifty-four of its men, women, and children had been taken to the lake and executed. Another twenty-two had been placed on a train and deported to Auschwitz.

A shocked Weizsäcker had received the details from Father Leiber, the pope's secretary. He asked the ambassador to provide Pius with a guarantee "such a war crime will not be repeated on Italian soil." The ambassador's attempts to reach either General Stahel or Field Marshal Kesselring had failed. Their aides told the ambassador that it was not a "diplomatic matter," but he could refer it to *Reichführer* Himmler in Berlin. He had been told that Himmler was "not available."

"The Jewish leaders of the Rome community must be warned of the need to go into hiding," insisted Kessel.

It would be impossible, they agreed, for either of them to do that. If it emerged they had made contact on that level with Jews it would almost certainly end their careers—and very likely their lives.

Kessel proposed a solution. Dr. Alfred Fahrener, who was a senior League of Nations official in Rome, was known to have contacts with Ugo Foa and Renzo Levi.

Weizsäcker telephoned him and said what had happened. Fahrener immediately agreed to call Foa and Levi. An hour later he called back. Both had rejected the suggestion that Jews "should go into hiding or flee." Fahrener had said he was himself inclined to agree there was no need for such dramatic action.

Weizsäcker had thanked him and put down the receiver.

PART III

WATCHING AND WAITING

9

HITLER'S PLOT

Wearing the white cotton gloves Ugo Foa had given Rosina to protect the priceless collection in the *Biblioteca Comunale,* the synagogue library, she carefully removed another book from its place on a shelf and wrote in a ledger its title and year of publication. Many of the books were centuries old in languages she could not read, nevertheless they had worked their spell on her in the months she had been cataloguing.

When Foa had asked her to update the library's inventory he explained it was a collection about the Jewish community in Rome, not only revered throughout the Diaspora but one only the Secret Archives of the Vatican, the world's largest collection of primary sources for two thousand years of religious and secular history, surpassed.

There were accounts by the early Jewish settlers along the Tiber who very likely had known Christ; documents of those who had converted to Christianity yet were content to remain living in the shadow of Judaism. There were descriptions of the arrival in Rome of the Apostles Paul in the spring of the year 61 and, a little later, the white-haired fisherman, Simon Peter. There were manuscripts in Greek dating back to the time of the Caesars and engravings of the emperor Nero who held orgies in the streets and squares of Rome. In every book or parchment she touched Rosina could feel the centuries of history.

She worked in the library in the afternoons when the synagogue was deserted except for a few employees. She had told Foa it would take her years to complete cataloguing and he smiled and said it was better to get it done properly than to hurry. He had given her permission to select a book to read at home in Hebrew and she had studied accounts of how Jews had been ordered to march under the Triumphal Arch of Titus depicting the destruction of Jerusalem and how in April 1753 papal authorities had entered the synagogue and filled thirty-eight carts with hundreds of books which had been taken into the Vatican.

Foa had assured Rosina that such an outrage would never happen again. The guarantee had been given by Pope Pius XI before his death in 1939.

With the Pierandello couple having left the city, Zolli had set out to find another haven for his family.

Emma's anxiety attacks made it increasingly difficult for him to work uninterrupted in his study, writing: She would constantly seek assurance that the Germans would not come and at nights she would awaken and start to cry and his daughter, Miriam, said he should take her to a doctor.

Professor Borromeo had prescribed a nerve-calming tonic and a sleeping draft. He also told Zolli he knew of a colleague in private practice, a Catholic, who was going to Mexico until the end of the war and was looking for someone to care take of his home in his absence.

Dr. Angelo Anaca, a bachelor, lived in an apartment on the fashionable Via del Mascherino. He was a gynecologist who, he reminded Zolli, Emma had once consulted. He was happy to have the family caretake his home. Zolli assured Emma and his daughters they would be safe until the Allies arrived.

Each day the pope asked Father Leiber to obtain the latest figure for the number of Jews who had been given shelter after arriving in Rome by train and bus. Each carried travel documents which identified them as Catholic pilgrims which Pius had arranged to be issued.

They arrived in small groups having been escorted en route by

Pallottine fathers and were met at the train station or bus terminus by priests from O'Flaherty's network who led them to the shelter of religious houses. Those with relatives in the ghetto or Trastevere were taken there by a member of Delasem.

Pius had also asked Pascalina to find further accommodation for Jews in the Vatican. On his daily afternoon walk he would pause and ask refugees if they needed anything. He was particularly concerned about the children, arranging for part of the gardens to be used as a playground; he also encouraged the older ones to visit Vatican Radio where they could stand in the control center and watch a program being transmitted. The Vatican Museum was also asked to arrange visits. He regularly met parents, asking where they came from, listening to the horrors they had experienced, and assuring them that now they were inside the Vatican and the Guardia Palatina were there to protect them. For Pascalina, Pope Pius was hands-on, "always ready to help our Jewish guests."

He had given her new duties in the network. Every day she telephoned the convents and other religious houses in Rome where an increasing number of Jews were hiding, to establish if they had any special needs. She had been given use of a Vatican Bank account to buy baby clothes and had arranged for doctors in Vatican-managed hospitals, who regularly made house calls to see nuns too old or sick to move into a hospital, to now include the Jews in their visits. When a child required hospital treatment the infant's mother would be brought there in a Vatican ambulance and the pope would ask Pascalina to keep him updated on the child's progress. Under his watchful eye the Vatican secret network operated at risk in the midst of the occupiers.

On Thursday morning, September 22, Kappler began the day in good humor. Radio Rome's promise of another blue sky was reinforced by congratulations from *Reichsführer* Himmler for the safe arrival in Berlin of Italy's gold bullion reserve. With the message had come a document stamped *Geheime Reichssache*—the highest form of secrecy emanating from Himmler's office. The single page was headed *Judenproblem in Rom*.

For Kappler a *Judenaktion* would be the first he had commanded. Until now he had only played a part in roundups in the northern cities of Europe.

His first step was to request *Stadtkommandant* Stahel to declare the ghetto out-of-bounds to troops; many had started to visit the bazaar-like shops to buy souvenirs to send home. Rome police were to patrol the approach road and allow only Jews to enter the ghetto. For his *Judenaktion* he wanted them all in one place.

By evening Jews were home before the curfew came into force, including many who had gone into hiding in Rome and now felt safe enough to return. Among them were Emma Zolli and her daughters. She had told her husband that after a week in the apartment she found it too small and the neighbors standoffish. The girls had returned to school and, with the aid of Professor Borromeo's medicine, Emma was calmer and Zolli had returned to his morning writing schedule.

Kappler continued with his preparation for *Judenaktion*. He had sent Helen Brouwer to the Questura, the Rome police headquarters on Via Della Grotta, to collect files he had requested.

They consisted of a list of the total number of Jews living in Rome on January 1, 1943, a street map of the ghetto and the surrounding area, and a street map of Rome, excluding the Vatican. Finally there was a file containing the names of criminal leaders of Rome's gangs.

He had spent hours studying names on the list while Helen Brouwer checked their addresses against streets on the two maps. A number of Jews lived in various areas of the city. However, those in the ghetto were crammed together and often bore the same name. The total number of Jews living in Rome at the start of the year numbered 9,290. Kappler knew that the figure was almost certainly out of date as it did not take into account Jews who would have left the city before it was occupied. There was also no way of knowing how many had been replaced by refugees.

Only two names in the file on criminal gang leaders had caught his attention. One was Giovanni Mezzaroma, the leader of the Black Panthers. The other was Pietro Koch, whose gang was named after him. Kappler asked his mistress to prepare reports on both men.

In the synagogue there was a mood of anticipation. On October 8, the ninth of Tishrei, 5704 on the Jewish calendar, it would be Yom Kippur, one of the holiest festivals of the year. For centuries the rituals and services in the synagogue had followed a traditional form. Ugo Foa contacted General Stahel's office and was told there was no reason for it not to go ahead, providing it did not break the curfew.

The Astrologo family, whose ancestors had smuggled out of Jerusalem the famous menorah lamp and some of the other treasures of the temple before Titus and his Romans had destroyed it, had long had a role in preparing the synagogue for Yom Kippur.

They were a prosperous family whose money came from buying and selling jewelry. No ghetto bride would get married without a Astrologo gold band on her ring finger. The family was known for its generosity to customers when it came to buying a broach or some other piece of jewelry; they had an instinct if somebody was selling to buy food or clothes for a growing son or daughter. From early on their own children were introduced to the world of hard work and tough bargaining and shown how to make decisions.

In preparing the synagogue for Yom Kippur the family polished every candle holder, plate, and wooden pew along with the *Risalt*, where the sacred Talmudic scrolls were kept and which would be borne aloft during the *Kol Nidrei* service on the eve of Yom Kippur. The day itself would be given over to prayers and fasting, followed by *minchah*, the service which included the reading of the entire Book of Jonah, the story of the prophet and the whale.

Fernando Astrologo, the family's seven-year-old son, its youngest child, had been told that the reading was a reminder that no one could escape God's will. On Yom Kippur the boy would sit beside his father for the service of *Ne'ila*, the final prayer of repentance. Then the *shofar* horn would sound and the family, like everyone else, would go home to break their fast.

On Sunday September 26, Professor Borromeo held his daily morning staff meeting at the *Fatebenefratelli*. The last of the curfew breakers who had been treated for gunshot wounds had been discharged. For the first time since the occupation there were empty beds.

Borromeo began by announcing an SS officer had delivered a poster that was to be displayed in every public building in Rome. It contained a list of penalties for breaching the latest laws of the German high command. The medical director read them out.

For harboring or helping escaped prisoners of war: death.

For owning a wireless transmitter: death.

For looting in evacuated areas: death.

For desertion of work, or sabotage: death.

For not fulfilling labor expectation: death.

For not acquainting the authorities of change of address: twenty years of prison.

For taking photographs out of doors: hard labor for life.

For printing or publishing or circulating news derogatory to the prestige of the Axis forces: penal servitude for life.

The document was signed: General Stahel.

Dr. Vittorio Sacerdoti broke the silence. While the Germans had so far made no serious move against the ghetto it could only be a matter of time before they did. Already young Romans were being snatched off the streets and sent to work in Germany. However it was significant that Jewish youths had been spared. Was another fate planned for them, for all the Jews of Rome? "But just as we have hidden and treated the curfew breakers we must do the same for our people," the young doctor said.

The other doctors and nurses considered what they had heard. Like Borromeo, a number of medical staff were Catholics and included several nuns. Sister Ester, the head nurse on the children's ward, recalled there was agreement that a priority be given to Jewish children and the elderly. "They could be admitted with a false diagnosis of tuberculosis," the nun suggested.

Sister Ester was known for her games to keep children amused during their stay in the hospital. She said she could teach her patients to make the "right coughing sound to fool the Germans." She had another idea. To complete the deception their illness should be given a new description to indicate how contagious it was. It should be known as *"morbo di K"*— the K-Syndrome."

Borromeo agreed. "After the scientist Koch, who discovered tuberculosis."

Sister Ester's reply brought smiles. "But we will know our 'K' refers to Kesselring, a reminder of all the bad things he has done."

Borromeo looked at Vittorio. Did he think it could work?

His deputy said that in the first days of the occupation the Germans had sent a medical inspection team to the hospital who had refused to go into the isolation wards where genuine tuberculosis patients were nursed. Once K-Syndrome patients were taught how to simulate the illness he suggested Borromeo should formally report to General Stahel's office that there was a outbreak of a deadly contagious disease. "It will be enough to keep his troops away," Vittorio predicted.

That afternoon he visited relatives in the Rome suburb of Viale Parioli and told them how he could select eight of them to become "K-Syndrome patients." They would be isolated from the other patients and though the nursing staff would know they were not ill they would be treated as having a contagious disease.

By the time he had returned to the hospital Vittorio had chosen sixty-five Jews, half of them children, to be brought to the *Fatebenefratelli*. He would recall: "Families were large, especially in the ghetto, and all were deserving of a chance to go into hiding. But there was only limited space in the hospital."

Within days the K-Syndrome cases were isolated on the hospital's second floor. On each of their doors hung a placard. MORBO DI K. From inside the rooms came the sound of coughs for a nonexistent illness.

After she joined the convent nuns in evening prayers, Sister Luke wrote in her diary. Rome's newspapers were publishing articles attacking people who "failed to collaborate with the German forces." The number of forced labor gangs had increased. Boys barely in their teens were being forced to dig trenches or stack sandbags. Others were being called up for military service.

The convent plumber had arrived one evening to say his only son, Antonio, had been caught in a roundup on his eighteenth birthday. He had been sent to a detention camp with several other youths. His wife had gone to try and find Antonio and had learned that he had been one of six youths who had tried to escape through a drain pipe. Their guards had sealed both ends of the pipe and left them to die.

Occasionally there was a touch of humor to record. "Soldiers around the German embassy have orders to fire without warning on anyone approaching the building at night. One of them, rather the worse for drink, saw figures on the adjacent roof, seemingly beckoning to each other. Outlined against the night sky they presented easy targets. He fired with no result. He fired again. Again no result. A platoon rushed to the spot and identified the 'beckoning men' as stone statues of saints above the entrance of the basilica of St. John Lateran."

Every Monday morning Helen Brouwer arranged the roses in Kappler's office which he cut from his garden. He prided himself on their cultivation and had told her their perfume would last a week. A more lasting reminder of his hobby were the photographs on the walls which he had taken. They included a picture of Wolfgang, the child he'd selected from the *Lebensborn* program.

Late one afternoon Kappler's mistress had shown into the office two visitors. One was Pietro Caruso, the Roman police chief Kappler had recommended Stahel should appoint. The forty-four-year-old was a veteran of Mussolini's march on Rome in 1922.

Beside him stood a tall figure with hollow cheeks, thin lips, a sallow complexion, and the watchful eyes of a wild animal. He was Pietro Koch, one of the two gang leaders Kappler had asked Brouwer to find out more about. After reading her report he had asked Caruso to bring Koch to his office.

The twenty-five-year-old gang leader was an ex-officer in the Fascist grenadiers of Sardinia, one of the toughest of the regiments in the Italian army. It was there Koch learned about Rome's underworld from those he commanded. With his education and society manners they respected him and after the armistice the grenadiers were dispanded and Koch took a number with him to Rome. Within weeks they had become a ruthless gang of thieves; their only rivals were the Black Panthers. Koch had met with its leader, Giovanni Mezzaroma, and they had agreed that there were sufficient spoils in Rome for them both.

It was that arrangement which had caused Kappler to have Caruso bring Koch to his office. He would decide how to use the Black Panther leader later.

Kappler led Koch to a window and pointed to a building across the road on the Via Tasso. He said it was his new gestapo headquarters and would have twenty cells in the basement along with two interrogation chambers. He explained he was appointing Koch as head of a new unit—*Reparto Speciale di Polizia*. It would have the same authority to investigate, enter premises, and arrest as Caruso's police force, but would only report to Kappler. It would hunt down the Resistance, hidden Allied soldiers, and Jews living in the city. Each captive would be brought to his new headquarters. For each prisoner he delivered there would be a bounty of five thousand lire. But they were not to be Jews from the ghetto until Kappler gave the order.

The elderly night-duty operator in the Vatican telephone exchange sat at the silent switchboard. She was a member of the pious Disciples of the Divine Master whose sisters, from dawn to midnight worked in shifts to handle the many thousands of calls which came and went through the switchboard. Now, in the early hours the switchboard was silent.

Before her was a list of numbers on a typed card. At the top was the bedside extension of the commandant of the Guardia Palatina. Next came the night number of the secretary of state, Maglione, followed by one for Sister Pascalina. The rest were the numbers of Father Leiber, Monsignor Montini, Monsignor Domenico Tardini, and Monsignor Alfredo Ottaviani.

She knew the list was part of the noticeable increase of security in and around the Vatican. The Guardia Palatina were now asking for identification from even long-serving Vatican employees at the gates and there were extra night patrols on the grounds and St. Peter's Square.

A light flashed on the switchboard and the voice of a Guardia Palatina reported all was well. The nun switched the call through to the guard-house behind the closed gate at the Arch of the Bells. In fifteen minutes' time she would repeat the process.

The operator, of course, had not been told that the calls were connected with a plot to kidnap Pope Pius.

Since the führer ranted in July 1943 that he intended to go into the Vatican and "clean out that gang of swine," he had remained obsessed with kidnapping the pope and bringing him to Germany. It was fuelled by his belief that Pius had been responsible for persuading King Victor Emmanuel III and Badoglio to abandon the Axis and join the Allies.

Hitler also believed the abduction would enable him to persuade Britain and the United States they were fighting the wrong war; that together they should join Germany and defeat the Soviet Union.

By September 13, Hitler's plot to kidnap the pope had reached the stage he decided it should be implemented. He had summoned to his headquarters—the *Wolfsschanze,* the Wolf's Lair near Rastenburg in East Prussia—General Karl Friedrich Otto Wolff. The steel-eyed and handsome forty-three-year-old had served as Himmler's chief of staff before becoming the SS liaison officer to Hitler. His anti-Semitic credentials were gilt-edged and he had played his part in ensuring that the SS dealt efficiently with the Jews. A month ago Hitler had bestowed on Wolff a unique title—general of the Waffen SS, and police leader of all Italy. Within the paranoid inner circle at the Wolf's Lair Hitler trusted Wolff completely.

But there was another side to the smiling, courteous, heel-clicking, and confident-sounding Wolff. He knew the war was lost. He had seen it on the faces of Hitler's top military advisers: Field Marshal Alfred Jodl and General Field Marshal Wilhelm Keitel. Even bombastic Luftwaffe minister, Hermann Goering, could not quite conceal that defeat was only a matter of time. His air force could do little to stop the Allies from bombing Germany day and night and the Red Army was racing westward and threatening to communize all of Europe.

But none of this was to be discussed on that Monday morning in Hitler's office. He had stood behind his desk, palms pressed down on its top, and told Wolff why he had sent for him. The general would later write in his diary the conversation which followed:

Wolff, I have a special mission for you. It will be your duty not to discuss it with anyone before I give you permission to do so.
I want you and your troops to occupy Vatican City as soon as possible, secure its files and art treasures, and bring the pope to Germany. I do not want him to fall into the hands of the Allies, or to be under their political pressure and influence. When is the earliest you think you will be able to fulfill this mission?

Wolff sat stunned into silence as his mind raced. He had renounced his Protestant faith upon joining the SS and his knowledge about Catholicism had been confined to listening to the ravings of Himmler. But what he did know was that the pope was the most powerful religious leader in the world. Wolff realized the kidnapping would guarantee he would be condemned for posterity. But to even give so much as a hint of refusal to Hitler would be fatal.

Wolff's response was calm. He could fulfill the mission—but he needed time to prepare it. Hitler asked how long Wolff needed. Wolff said four to six weeks.

The führer's eyes stared into Wolff's face. "Too long," he rasped.

Wolff's voice grew in confidence. He would need additional SS and police units transferred to Rome. Specialists in identifying precious art treasures. Translators in Latin and Greek to authenticate the documents in the Secret Archives of the Vatican.

Hitler had stopped Wolff with a wave of his hand. He could have whatever he wanted but the mission must be completed in a month.

Wolff stood up, clicked his heels, saluted, and left the office.

By the time he reached his headquarters on Lake Garda in the Alps Wolff saw what he must do.

Until now he would have carried out any order for Hitler; if he had been told to devise a plan to murder Stalin in Moscow or kill Churchill in London, he would have done so. That was his strength: The impossible was possible he had learned at military school. But kidnapping the pope and looting the Vatican was madness beyond anything he had envisaged.

From that conclusion he began to see how he could use the mission to win the gratitude of the pope and save his own life when the Allies won the war. It would mean delaying and sabotaging the kidnapping plan. To do so he would have to involve the German ambassador to the Holy See, Baron Ernst von Weizsäcker.

It was late evening when Giovanni Mezzaroma parked his car outside 155 Via Tasso, Kappler's new headquarters. The head of the Black Panthers and Celeste di Porto had arrived to keep their appointment with Kappler and were escorted to his office. He had greeted them politely, motioned for them to sit opposite him, and resumed his own seat behind the desk.

For the moment he concentrated on Mezzaroma, telling him what he had told Koch: that for every Jew or Allied soldier he caught there was a five-thousand-lire reward. He would have the same authority of arrest and search of premises as Koch. He was also similarly cautioned that the Black Panthers were to stay clear of the ghetto Jews.

Kappler turned to Celeste. She was to walk the streets of Rome and every time she recognized a Jew from previous contacts she was to greet them. Trailing her would be gestapo agents. The moment she ended her contact and walked on, they would arrest the people she had spoken to. She was also to trail Jews to their hiding places, as well as those where she suspected Allied soldiers were hiding. For each arrest she would also re-ceive not only a bounty of five thousand lire but would have permission to plunder the hiding places of whatever she wanted.

Celeste di Porto had accepted her role. No Jew in Rome would be safe from her smile and greeting.

In a prisoner-of-war camp to the east of Rome Major Sam Derry, a six-foot-three-inch-tall British gunnery officer in the Royal Artillery thought of little else but escaping and going to the city. He was among eight hundred prisoners held in Sulmona, one of many camps in Italy where the Ger-mans dumped their prisoners to be guarded by Italians. Shortly after the armistice the guards had deserted, leaving the gates at Sulmona open. But before the prisoners could walk out German soldiers had replaced them.

Derry sensed it would only be a matter of time before the Germans sent all prisoners to Germany. Lying on his bunk at night he planned his escape to Rome. He had never been there before; all he knew was it had the Vatican. And the Vatican had a priest who had become a legend among Allied prisoners of war. He had arranged that all their relatives knew they were safe. He had improved their morale. He had led them in songs and had taken their complaints to the camp commandants. He had brought them news of the war, how well it was going for the Allies. Then suddenly his visits had stopped. No one knew why. But nobody, least of all Derry, could forget his name. It was O'Flaherty.

Ugo Foa had been at home when there was a loud knock on his front door. Standing there was a uniformed gestapo officer who said he wanted Foa to accompany him to the synagogue. Parked in the street was a German truck. Behind Foa stood his two teenage sons and daughter. The officer smiled and said there was no cause for alarm as he had not come to arrest any of them. He told Foa he had been ordered to search the synagogue as there had been a report it was being used by the Resistance to store weapons. Foa protested that was not possible. The officer insisted he had orders. He glanced at the children and assured them their father would be home in no time, and motioned for Foa to follow him to the truck. Seated in the back were several soldiers.

The operation had been ordered by Kappler. It was another step in his preparation of *Judenaktion*. He wanted to create fear but not panic in the ghetto—"enough for them to hide in their homes," he had told Helen Brouwer.

Showing the community leader his power was part of a plan which Kappler had developed after emptying the Central Bank of Italy of its gold bullion. In Kappler's mind there could be enough gold in the ghetto to make a valuable contribution to Germany's war chest, an addition which would further impress his superiors. Kappler was subtle, shrewd, ruthless, and cunning—and he knew he would need all those qualities to lay his hands on the ghetto gold. He had considered, and discounted, various schemes before concluding that the best way was to convince the community leaders of an offer he would ask them to convey to their co-religionists.

In the meantime he would demonstrate his power by having one of his officers make Foa open up the synagogue and watch helplessly as the German went wherever he wanted to. It would prepare the ground for the offer Kappler intended to make: Jewish lives for Jewish gold.

Days after he had met Hitler, General Wolff flew to Rome in a Luftwaffe transport. During the flight he had devised a plan to show Hitler how he would kidnap the pope.

It called for two thousand Waffen SS soldiers to arrive in Rome and seal off the Vatican. A squad would then occupy Vatican Radio and take it off the air. Other squads would enter the Apostolic Palace and arrest the pope and his entourage. They would be taken to Rome's airport and flown to Munich. In the meantime another unit of experts would assess the Vatican's paintings and sculptures. Truckloads of books and documents would be removed from the Secret Archives. Together with the treasures they would be sent to Germany.

Wolff knew the plan would satisfy, even excite Hitler, but was determined it would never happen. The Waffen SS was already committed on all fronts and to find experts to evaluate the Vatican treasures would take considerable time to locate. By then the Allies could be close to Rome, forcing the Germans to withdraw and leaving the Vatican safe. To the Catholics he would be a hero and the Jews would see how sabotaging the plot helped to save the lives of those in Rome.

Wolff would give Hitler sufficient details to convince him preparations were underway and sent a coded message to that effect from the German embassy. Then he went to the Villa Napoleon to see Weizsäcker.

He had already studied the ambassador's file. He came from a prominent Württemberg family who included Ribbentrop in its circle. The foreign minister had found a place in his office for Weizsäcker and guided his career up through the ministry. Wolff also knew of the ambassador's growing relationship with Admiral Canaris. Since Hitler's rages that he was surrounded by traitors, Wolff had come to wonder if they included the head of the *Abwehr*. If so, could Weizsäcker have been sent to Rome to become involved in his machinations? Was that why Hitler wanted the pope kidnapped—to use him as a weapon against his enemies? Wolff later admitted those were the questions which still preoccupied him as he walked into Weizsäcker's office.

The ambassador and Kessel, his deputy, were waiting and Wolff sensed their tension. Weizsäcker wasted no time in explaining why. He had seen a copy of Kappler's *Judenaktion* order and asked if that was why Wolff was in Rome. If so, he should be aware that the pope was bound to protest and that could be the prelude to a popular uprising led by the Resistance, one possibly supported by the Allied escaped prisoners of war hiding in the city.

Wolff had not hesitated: He told the two diplomats of Hitler's order to kidnap the pope—and of his own intention to stop it.

Weizsäcker had thanked him. Wolff explained he must continue with its preparation so as not to arouse Hitler's suspicion.

Weizsäcker pressed, "But what if you fail?"

Wolff replied, "Then we are all finished."

10

GOLD RUSH

On Sunday evening, September 26, Foa and Almansi arrived at Kappler's headquarters on Via Tasso. He had sent his own staff car to collect them, saying it was the least he could do after disturbing their weekend at such short notice. Foa said it was no problem, and if there was any matter they could help with they would be glad to do so. Almansi remembered how Kappler had nodded affably and spoke about how he liked life in Rome, especially its culture. Suddenly he had leaned forward and when he spoke, in Foa's recall, his voice was cold.

"You and your co-religionists are Italian nationals, but that is of little importance to me. We Germans consider you only as Jews, and as such an enemy. Rather, to be more precise, we regard you as a distinctive group, but not wholly apart from the worst of the enemies against whom we are fighting. And we will treat you as such."

Almansi remembered how Kappler looked at each of them in turn, as if he was judging their reaction.

In Foa's later account, Kappler then said: "It is your lives or the lives of your children that we will take if you do not fulfill our demands. It is your gold we want in order to provide new arms for our country. Within thirty-six hours you will provide fifty kilograms of gold. If you do so no harm will come to you or your co-religionists."

Kappler invited them to discuss the matter between themselves in Hebrew. Foa and Almansi agreed it was pointless to ignore the demand. All they could do was to ask for the time limit to be extended. Kappler agreed to let it run from that evening to finish at 11 A.M. on Tuesday, September 28.

As he walked Foa and Almansi to the office door, Kappler paused. "Bear in mind that I have conducted a number of such operations and all but one ended well. That failure led to a few hundred of your coreligionists paying with their lives."

He wished them good evening and told his driver to take them back home.

Next morning, Monday, September 27, when Rosina and her brother, Settimio, arrived at the synagogue Foa, Almansi, and Rabbi Zolli were already there. Renzo Levi and members of the *giunta* soon arrived and joined the others around the conference table. Foa told them what had happened at the meeting with Kappler; there were shocked murmurs and Anselmo Colombo—one of the committee members, who had challenged Zolli over his expenses—shouted that he did not believe Kappler would keep his word. "They will take our gold and our people," he cried out. Another committee member wondered if it was possible to find that much gold in so short a time. A third voice said it was a trick to gather the Jews all in one place; they had done that in other countries during their roundups. Foa silenced the debate with a reminder that there was only a day to find the fifty kilograms.

The gold collection would be organized by Levi and would be set up on the second floor of the synagogue. In the meantime members of the *giunta* were to contact Jews living outside the ghetto and tell them to bring all the gold they possessed to the synagogue. People in the ghetto would be alerted to do the same. The ghetto goldsmith, Angelo Anticoli, would bring his scales to the synagogue to weigh the gold.

By eleven o'clock that morning all the preparations had been made for the collection.

Rosina was among the first to give a donation: It was a gold necklace her father had given her on her nineteenth birthday. It weighed two ounces.

Soon it was joined by other pieces of jewelry; each was weighed and put in a wooden chest.

By noon a line of donors had started to form outside the synagogue. The gifts were small: wedding rings, bracelets, or broaches. Rabbi Zolli contributed a gold chain, Anselmo Colombo matched him with another, Emma Zolli handed over a ring. Her daughter, Miriam, moved along the line with a tray collecting jewelry which she brought to Anticoli. Graziano Perugia, the ghetto's kosher butcher, donated a ring; Grazia Spizzichino and her husband, Mose, gave an antique broach he had given her on their wedding day. Tailor Serafino Pace gave a gold coin. For many their donations were the last precious items they had left. Eight years ago they loyally gave their gold when Mussolini had called for donations to finance Italy's war in Ethiopia.

Ounce by ounce the weight increased. Among some of the contributors were Christian neighbors who first asked if their contributions would be acceptable. They were quickly assured. A few required receipts which were politely provided by Rosina.

Jeweler Cesare del Monte gave his wife's wedding band he had made; Vittorio Astrologo selected several gold wedding rings from his stock. Angelo di Porto donated not only his own ring but his parents' wedding bands and his sister's earrings. Lello Perufia, a member of the Resistance, donated a family ring. Elena Sonnino Finzi, who taught in the ghetto school, had persuaded all her pupils to collect as many pieces of jewelry as they could. She had also spoken to President Foa asking whether, despite the gold being given to the Germans, should she still not leave home? He told her he saw "no necessity" to do so once the gold had been paid over. Nevertheless, after making her donation Elena decided to go into hiding in a convent which had offered her shelter.

Nurses and doctors from the *Fatebenefratelli* had come to the synagogue to hand over their donations. Dr. Vittorio Sacerdoti would remember that while waiting to have his contribution weighed some people had expressed doubts that their donation would make any difference. Others felt they *must* honor it: A deal had been made and the Germans *must* be paid. "Unless they were there was no knowing what they would do. Burn down the synagogue? No, it was better to contribute," a woman said.

As each item was placed on the scale and its weight recorded, it appeared that the fifty kilogram target would be reached. But at thirty-five kilograms there were no more contributions. It was now late in the afternoon.

Levi ordered the donations reweighed. There was no increase in the weight. The required total was fifteen kilograms short.

Foa was unable to hide his despair. It was then that Zolli spoke. He would go to the Vatican and ask the pope to make up the difference.

It was early on Monday evening when a car arrived at the Arch of the Bells gateway into the Vatican. One of the Guardia Palatina stepped forward. Count de Salis had shown him his Red Cross ID card and he was waved through. Beside him sat Rabbi Zolli. An hour ago he had telephoned the Red Cross director and explained the gold shortfall and why he hoped the pope would agree for the Vatican to bridge it. De Salis had collected Zolli from his home having arranged a meeting with Cardinal Maglione. The two men were ushered into the secretary of state's office and Zolli had explained the urgency of the situation. Visibly moved the cardinal rose and left the room. When he returned he said the pope would authorize the Holy See to provide the required kilos of gold. Within an hour the bars were handed over to Zolli. The chief rabbi asked for the gratitude of the Jewish community of Rome to be conveyed to His Holiness.

The transaction became the subject of controversy. There were claims that Pope Pius had argued over providing the money: that the Vatican Bank director had been asked for advice by the pope on the terms and conditions the money could be given. Should it be a term loan, repayable with interest? These were ugly questions that would emerge from critics over the pope's so-called "silence"—the claim he remained unwilling to offer any help for the Jews. The truth of how he responded to such claims would be confirmed by notes made by Maglione before his sudden death and subsequently found by his successor, Cardinal Montini. They make absolutely clear that Pius had immediately authorized "without any discussion" for the shortfall to be paid over.

Further confirmation came from Zolli on June 25, 1944, when he was

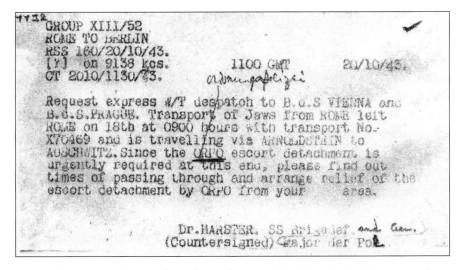

GROUP XIII/52
ROME TO BERLIN
RSS 180/20/10/43.
[Y] on 9138 kcs.   1100 GMT   20/10/43.
CT 2010/1130/43.   *adnungssolizei*

Request express W/T despatch to B.d.S VIENNA and
B.d.S.PRAGUE. Transport of Jews from ROME left
ROME on 18th at 0900 hours with transport No.-
X70469 and is travelling via ARNOLDSTEIN to
AUSCHWITZ. Since the ORPO escort detachment is
urgently required at this end, please find out
times of passing through and arrange relief of the
escort detachment by ORPO from your   area.

                    Dr.HARSTER, SS Brigadief and Gen.,
                    (Countersigned) Major der Pol.

Decoded intercept by British code-breakers at Bletchley Park of message from Theodor Dannecker, in charge of the *Judenaktion* of the Rome ghetto. Only fifteen of the 1,041 on the train to Auschwitz survived. *Author's Collection*

Dr. Vittorio Sacerdoti. The daring young doctor at the *Fatebenefratelli*, the Jewish hospital on Rome's Tiber Island. He risked his life to help wounded Resistance fighters but also created a fake illness he called "K-Syndrome" to deceive the Germans into believing that the Jews in the hospital had a deadly and contagious disease and could not be moved. *Luciana Tedesco*

Professor Giovanni Borromeo. Medical director of the *Fatebenefratelli*. During the bombing of Rome he became a hero to his patients and staff. *Luciana Tedesco*

Israel Zolli. The Chief Rabbi of Rome. On the eve of the roundup he fled with his family into the Vatican and hid there until the end of the war. After the war he converted to Catholicism and changed his first name to Eugenio, in honor of the Pope. Within the Jewish community, Zolli remains a controversial figure. *Courtesy Sister Margherita Marchione*

When the Jews of Rome fled from the roundup they found safety in the Vatican. Food halls were set up within the Apostolic Palace and other buildings on the grounds. *Courtesy Sister Margherita Marchione*

The Pope authorized his summer palace at Castel Gandolfo to be used to hide Roman Jews who had fled the roundup. Every available space was used, including the floor for sleeping. *Courtesy Sister Margherita Marchione*

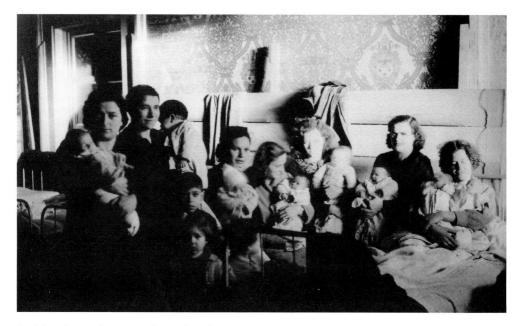

Jewish refugees from the ghetto found sanctuary in convents in Rome. *Courtesy Sister Margherita Marchione*

Vatican trucks delivered food to convents and religious houses and monasteries where Jews and Allied prisoners of war were being hidden. *Courtesy Sister Margherita Marchione*

After the bombing of Rome in 1943, Pope Pius left the Vatican for the first time during the war in order to visit bombed areas. *Courtesy Sister Margherita Marchione*

The Pope's study at Castel Gandolfo was hit by Allied bombers during a raid on German targets in the area. *Courtesy Sister Margherita Marchione*

The Pope's Christmas message in 1943 was an attack on the Nazis—but President Roosevelt felt it was not strong enough.
Courtesy Sister Margherita Marchione

The Pope addresses a postwar crowd in St. Peter's Square. On the upper left of the photo is the balcony from where Vatican staff and Allied diplomats had watched the air attacks on Rome.
Courtesy Sister Margherita Marchione

Vatican Secretary of State Cardinal Luigi Maglione, a powerful influence on Pope Pius. He followed the military movements of World War Two and discussed the strategy of generals with his two assistants, Monsignor Tardini and Monsignor Montini (later to become Paul VI). *Courtesy Sister Margherita Marchione*

Monsignor Alfredo Ottaviani, head of the Holy Office, O'Flaherty's link between the Pope and the secret organization to help the Jews and escaped prisoners of war. A stern disciplinarian, he also protected O'Flaherty from attacks inside the Vatican provoked by his activities. *Courtesy Sister Margherita Marchione*

The memorial to the victims of the Ardeatine Cave massacre. The mass murder was ordered by Hitler as revenge for the largest ever attack carried out by the Rome Resistance. For every German killed, he ordered that ten Roman hostages be executed. *Author's collection*

Baron Ernst von Weizsäcker. A member of a prominent old German family and an opponent of the Nazis. He was persuaded by Admiral Wilhelm Canaris, head of Germany's Abwehr, to go to Rome as Germany's ambassador to the Holy See and try to enlist the Pope in a plan to overthrow Hitler that Canaris was concocting. Both were uncomfortable with the ideologies of the Nazi regime. But the Pope did not become involved in the plot. Hitler ordered Canaris to be hanged for treason. Weizsäcker stood trial at the Nuremberg War Criminal Trials and was sentenced to seven years. He was released in 1950 and died a year later. *Courtesy Marianne Weizsäcker*

Herbert Kappler, Gestapo chief in Rome. Originally given the task of deporting Rome's Jews, he was replaced on Adolf Eichmann's order by Theodor Dannecker, the notorious *Judenaktion* expert on Eichmann's staff. Following the Resistance attack on Via Rasella, Kappler was ordered to carry out Hitler's order that led to the Ardeatine Cave massacre. Kappler was subsequently imprisoned in Rome, awaiting trial as a war criminal, when he was sentenced to fifteen years' imprisonment. He contracted cancer and his wife, a nurse, helped him escape to West Germany. Its government refused to return him to Italy and he died in 1978. *Author's collection*

received in an audience by Pius. "The pope confirmed to me there had been no discussion over the gold. He made it clear there was money in the Vatican treasury to help our people. No hero in all of history was more heroic than Pope Pius in his readiness to defend the children of God."

In her own account of that evening, Pascalina would recall, "Pius XII never wanted any of his good deeds revealed. When our guests were able to leave the Vatican to go to Canada or Brazil or elsewhere, he ordered me to withdraw from his personal funds sufficient money to give each family one thousand dollars in a sealed evelope."

That gesture would not be mentioned by his subsequent critics.

That evening Ugo Foa addressed the crowded congregation. He told them he had never known such generosity and how the pope, their neighbor, had helped. "This was a most providential and most generous intervention."

He paused and there was renewed certainty in his voice. During the day he had heard some people express doubts, wondering if the gold would guarantee their safety. There must be no doubt. In return for the fifty kilograms of gold he and Almansi had been given a guarantee they would remain safe. The donations they had made were a small price for them to live in peace and without fear.

Foa asked Rabbi Zolli to lead them all in a prayer of thanks that they could continue to live as their ancestors had done down the centuries in the ghetto.

An hour before the deadline expired on Tuesday morning, September 28, the gold arrived in a sealed box at Kappler's office. That evening it was put on a train to Berlin and addressed to *Obergruppenführer* Ernst Kaltenbrunner, the head of the RSHA. In his cover letter Kappler said he was providing the Reich with such "a good gift." It made no impression on Kaltenbrunner and the fifty kilograms of Jewish gold in its box was dumped in a corner of his office, gathering dust, unopened. In 1948, with the creation of the state of Israel, it was sent there.

———

Tony Simonds arrived in Rome the way he arrived everywhere: No one expected him and he would leave without telling anyone where he was going. He dressed to blend in with the role he had chosen. On his visit to Rome he decided to dress like a hill farmer. The farmer who had provided him with his garb was one of the names he kept on a list in his padlocked office overlooking the Nile in Cairo. The list identified names of trusted informers he had recruited and safe houses he had found in the past two years around the Mediterranean.

Lieutenant Colonel Simonds was in charge of a unit whose existence was a secret shared by few. He was head of N-Section, the most important department of MI9, a spin-off of MI6. Since the outbreak of war, its staff had devised every possible method of escape for captured Allied prisoners, smuggling into prison camps money, maps, clothes, compasses, and hacksaws.

Simonds's own background had made him an ideal choice to run N-Section. He had worked with Orde Wingate in Palestine to train the Jewish underground, the Haganah, who had terrified the Arabs during Britain's mandate in the 1930s.

In 1941 he was posted to Cairo to create escape lines across the Aegean, and on through Greece and Turkey. After the armistice what to do about Allied prisoners of war in Italy became a matter of concern. General Montgomery, the British commander appointed to lead the attack against Kesselring's forces, ordered that all the prisoners were to remain in their camps until his forces freed them.

Simonds was concerned prisoners who did not escape would be "packed into cattle trucks and sent off to concentration camps in Germany, Geneva Convention or no," he had warned MI9 in London.

He was summoned to Allied headquarters in Algiers as he later wrote, to "exert myself to the upmost to rescue Allied prisoners in Italy." He was told the order overruling Montgomery had come from Prime Minister Churchill. Shortly afterward came the news that a growing number of prisoners had escaped and were heading for Rome.

Simonds already knew about O'Flaherty's visits to the camps through reports D'Arcy Osborne had sent to the Foreign Office and he was certain that "our Good Samaritan priest is a beacon for escapers to head for the Vatican."

He had set out for Rome.

A week after leaving Cairo Simonds walked into the city smelling of the sheep he had slept among in the hills. Mass was about to start when he arrived on St. Peter's Square. Standing on the top step, where he had been told to expect to see him, was O'Flaherty cradling his breviary. Close by were two Guardia Palatina. They gave Simonds hardly a glance as he stepped closer to O'Flaherty who opened his prayer book and murmured, "Welcome". O'Flaherty had turned and walked back into the basilica, followed by Simonds. A side door brought them into the Vatican; a short walk led to the entrance of Santa Maria. Minutes later they were in D'Arcy Osborne's apartment.

Over dinner Simonds listened carefully as Osborne and O'Flaherty took turns briefing him on how the pope had ordered the Vatican to set up the network to hide Allied soldiers and Jewish refugees. Osborne told him about the money which Prince Filippo Pamphilj and other anti-Fascist aristocrats had provided and O'Flaherty explained how the princesses of the Black Nobility were ready to provide shelter. Simonds recognized that the network was amply worth supporting, but he also discussed the risk it faced. All over Europe men and women were being caught and executed by the Germans for operating similar organizations.

Osborne told Simonds that as a diplomat he would be safer than O'Flaherty if the Germans occupied the Vatican because, he would remind them, he was a descendent of the great Duke of Marlborough and the Earl of Danby who had taken a leading role in inviting William of Orange to invade England in 1688.

And, said O'Flaherty, his family came from an Irish Republican family who had also fought the English. The Germans would not want to harm him. But it could be a different matter for the pope: In recent weeks O'Flaherty had read reports from the nuncios in Lisbon and Madrid that Hitler wanted to invade the Vatican and imprison Pius. Were the reports credible, asked Simonds. True or not, replied O'Flaherty, could not the Allies make sure that would never happen?

Simonds said he would pass on the concerns. He had slept that night on Osborne's living room couch and slipped out of the Vatican with the first worshippers at the basilica's early morning Mass. Five days later he was back in Cairo.

In the early hours of Saturday, October 2, a train pulled into Rome station and a group of fourteen officers and NCOs together with forty troops emerged from their carriages. Each wore an insignia of the Waffen SS death's-head *Einsatzgruppen*, Himmler's mobile killing units. They had been responsible for the massacre of the Jews living around Lake Maggiore. Now they were the advance group for Kappler's *Judenaktion*. Though he did not yet know it, it was no longer under his command.

The decision to replace him had been taken by the SS *Obersturmbannführer* Adolf Eichmann. In his headquarters in Berlin's Tiergarten, Kurfuerstenstrasse, he headed a department with one function: the deportation of all Jews in the Third Reich to concentration camps. He would later describe his work to Rafi Eitan, the head of the Mossad team who captured him in Argentina and brought him to Jerusalem to face trial in 1961. "Whether they were bank directors or mental cases the people loaded onto the trains meant nothing to me."

Within the RSHA his IV-B-4 department was facing problems. Western European countries like Denmark were resisting the deportations. The Ministry of Transport was also refusing to give priority for trains needed to take Jews to the camps as they were needed to carry soldiers to the front lines.

A time table Eichmann provided at the Wannsee Conference to accomplish the Final Solution had fallen behind schedule. He promised Himmler in a top secret *Schlussverfügung,* a final decision, Rome's ghetto would "be cleaned out; at least eight thousand Jews will be deported."

However, since Kappler had received his order to carry out a *Judenaktion* he had informed Himmler's office of the difficulties he faced. There were not enough SS police in Rome to carry out the roundup. Those who were available were totally inexperienced in such operations. Further, the non-Jewish population of Rome could be expected to support the Resistance in stopping such an operation. Kappler had asked for sufficient troops from the Eastern front, veterans of *Judenaktionen,* to be sent to Rome. Himmler had passed the request to Eichmann. After looking up Kappler's previous record Eichmann decided that the gestapo chief did not have sufficient experience. He sent for SS *Hauptsturmführer* Theodor Dannecker, the most experienced of all *Judenaktion* experts in the department. He was to go to Rome with his own units and a letter signed by the head of gestapo, *Gruppenführer* Heinrich Mueller. It confirmed that Kappler was to be at Dannecker's disposal in the operation.

Sam Derry sat between a farmer and his daughter, a barefoot child, on a cart piled with cabbages heading for the market in Rome. Four days earlier the gunnery officer had jumped from the train carrying his fellow prisoners of war to Germany. He had hurled himself through a carriage door after shoving a guard aside. Dressed in his officer's shirt, trousers, and shoes he had no food, money, documents, maps, or any idea where he was. All he could think was that he was free. Soon, his wife, Nancy, should get his last letter he had written the day before jumping. What would the War Office tell her? That he was "missing." To reassure her was one more reason for Derry to get to Rome.

For three days he was hidden by a cabbage grower and his wife in their cottage on the outskirts of a village. They had fed him and tended to his bruises. At night he slept in a haystack. Their kindness was enough to convince Derry they would not betray him.

On the fourth day the village priest arrived. He greeted Derry warmly in English and listened intently as Derry explained who he was, how he had escaped, and why he wanted to go to Rome. The priest said he would make the arrangements. Next day he returned with the farmer and his daughter. Introductions were quick. The farmer was called Pietro, the girl was Marta. The priest called Derry, "Signor."

Together they loaded the grower's cabbages onto the cart and with the priest waving his hat and wishing them a safe journey, they set off for Rome.

At first the cart rattled over potholes, but as the hours passed the track became a road, and in the distance the dome of St. Peter's became clearer, dominating all the other domes and spires of the city.

Derry tapped Pietro's arm. Ahead a German truck was parked to one side of the road. Derry knew it was a checkpoint. Pietro spoke to his daughter who climbed onto the cabbages and began to move them aside. He made a sign for Derry to burrow into the hole and she arranged the vegetables over him. As the cart rattled forward then came to a stop Derry heard German voices. He breathed slowly, keeping perfectly still. There was a bang on the side of the cart. He held his breath: Had one of the soldiers spotted a movement in the cabbage? Any moment the sharp prod of a bayonet could come down through the vegetables. A commanding voice shouted. The cart began to move and the voices faded and the clip-clop of the pony's hooves grew faster. The cabbages above him began to move and the child's smiling face appeared and Derry eased his way out of the hole and took a deep gulp of Roman air and heard the sound of its bells.

In the warmth of early afternoon Rosina Sorani was replacing a book on its shelf in the synagogue library after noting its title and subject matter in her notebook when she realized she was not alone. Standing in the doorway were two men in gray suits. One was bald and wore spectacles. His companion was younger with a brush moustache who apologized if they had startled her. The older man said they were looking for President Foa. Rosina explained he was not there, but could she help? The men stepped into the library and said they would like to look around. Rosina asked if there was any particular book or subject they would like to see, remembering Foa had told her that in 1939, Fascists in Turin had forced their way into the Jewish community library, seized almost all of its collection, and used the books to fuel a bonfire in the city's Piazza Carlina.

Perhaps, sensing her concern, the older man said they were professors from the Einsatzstab Rosenberg Institute, ERR, claiming it was linked to the great universities of Europe, including the Sorbonne in Paris. The ERR was dedicated to the study of academic fields which until now had not been fully exploited. They were in Rome purely to assess the role the synagogue library could have as part of that program. The younger man added that under no circumstances was she to confuse them with the SS or any other military organization.

Somewhat reassured Rosina escorted them around the library, pointing out books produced by the earliest printers and documents handed down through the centuries. She decided their polite questions were those of cultured men who had spent their lives in scholarly pursuits, and far removed from the coarse-voiced soldiers who walked the streets of Rome. The older man revealed he was an Orientalist and had spent time in libraries in Palestine and other Middle East countries. His colleague said he was a specialist in Jewish literature and his language teacher had been a rabbi in Berlin before the war. He had spoken to Rosina in Hebrew and she was impressed. From time to time as she pointed out a book the two men spoke to each other in German.

After shaking her hand they left.

The ERR was a specialist unit formed in July 1940 by the official theoretician of the Nazi Party, Alfred Rosenberg, to assemble a library for the new educational and research institute for the party, the *Hohe Schule*, to be located at the Chiemsee in Bavaria. It would contain half a million volumes and would have an auditorium for three thousand people.

Rosenberg had laid down a rule for what ERR acquired for the institute: "If the desired object belongs to foreign 'Aryans' the owners are compelled to sell it; if it belongs to Jews it is confiscated. Material of no use is to be destroyed."

The Jewish library at Lublin in Poland was one of the first to be burned; Joseph Goebbels had sent a journalist from the Ministry of Propaganda to report the event.

"We brought the books to the marketplace where we set fire to them. The fire lasted twenty hours. The Jews assembled around wept bitterly, almost silencing us with their cries. We summoned the military band and with joyful shouts the soldiers drowned out the sounds of the Jewish cries."

A different fate had been earmarked for the Rome ghetto synagogue library.

In London, Simonds's report on Hitler's threat to kidnap the pope reached Stewart Menzies. The MI6 chief sent for Sefton Delmer. The former foreign correspondent for Lord Beaverbrook's *Daily Express* had interviewed Hitler before the war and had developed important connections across Europe. In his office on Fleet Street he had written newsbreaking stories few other reporters could equal. He spoke several languages and Beaverbrook called him "my source in the world".

He had arranged in 1942 for Delmer to join the Foreign Office political warfare department. It was there that Delmer picked up his first news of a plot to overthrow Hitler. It had been leaked to him by a long-standing source, who Delmer suspected was an opponent of the Nazi regime. In his diary Delmer would write: "Whether successful or not, even the suspicion of an anti-Hitler coup would help to hasten his defeat."

The story normally would have guaranteed Delmer the front page of the *Daily Express*. But he was told by Beaverbrook that he should hold it for a "more opportune time."

By October 1943 Delmer knew that moment had come, when he had been transferred from the Foreign Office to MI6. Menzies told him his new task "is to foment the maximum suspicion between Hitler and his generals."

Delmer was to head a unique intelligence operation. Using his journalistic skills he produced radio programs that supposedly originated from an undercover station in Germany. In reality they came from a country house outside London. Delmer had picked his team of German-speaking broadcasters with care. He described each one as a "loyal German dedicated to the fatherland but disturbed by the fanatical policies of Hitler." A number were Jews who had fled to England before the war. Others were students from German universities. All were told their broadcasts were not designed to attack Britain but to provide their listeners with news not broadcast to German audiences. To emphasize its role Delmer called the station Free Fascist Republican Radio (FFRR).

Menzies had shown Simonds's report to Delmer and told him to create a broadcast aimed at the Third Reich's Catholic populations.

On October 7, the station announced that "quarters have been prepared in Germany for Pope Pius where he will be taken and remain."

Pius was quoted as telling Secretary of State Maglione that "I was placed by the will of God here and therefore shall not leave. They would have to tie me up and carry me out because I intend to remain here!" The words were written by Sefton Delmer. The threat to the pope and his response was published in newspapers around the world, creating outrage in Catholic countries. Hitler's plot, which he had intended to remain secret until the last moment, was now in the public domain.

Realizing that the broadcast had provided an opportunity to abandon the plot, Wolff had flown to see Hitler and told him that the whole of Catholic Italy would defend the Vatican to protect the pope.

Warming to his argument, Wolff went on to tell Hitler that to deal with mass civil unrest would require German troops to be withdrawn from the southern front where they were engaged trying to hold back the advancing Allies.

The atmosphere in Hitler's office was captured in Wolff's account preserved in the Jesuit Curia library at the Borgo Santo Spirito in Rome: "Hitler, his hand trembling, stood at his office window staring out at the fir trees, the look on his face one when he received bad news." Wolff told him he had asked Bishop Alois Hudal to "persuade" Pius to leave the Vatican voluntarily. It emerged that Hudal actually went through the motions of exploring the idea with fellow Nazi sympathizers in the Vatican. But no doubt awed by the responsibility stemming from their mere knowledge of the proposal, they refused to take it any further. Only then had Hudal abandoned the idea.

Wolff recalled how Hitler had finally turned from his office window and cancelled the plot, "the madness in his eyes all too evident."

Derry had found it difficult to grasp what was happening to him since arriving in Rome. From time to time the cart had passed German foot patrols who gave them no more than a cursory look. In the marketplace a priest told him in a broad Irish accent he had come to collect him and led him through back streets. Standing in the doorway of a building adjoining a church another priest led Derry to a room where a tall man in a black clerical suit and collar said his name was Father Aldo and he had one question: How did he know O'Flaherty? Derry told him. Aldo said he would take him to the Vatican.

He led Derry back through more back streets before they caught a tramcar to the bottom of the Via della Conciliazione which led to St. Peter's Square. It was crowded with worshippers going to Mass. Ignoring the bored-looking German patrols, Father Aldo led the way toward the basilica steps. The tall distinctive figure in his red-and-black cassock of O'Flaherty, stood holding a prayer book in his hand. As they approached he turned away; Father Aldo had followed him nudging Derry to do the same.

Sensing his journey was coming to an end Derry walked under an archway into a courtyard surrounded by stone-walled buildings and followed the others across the yard to an open door. Derry stopped to glance up at the carved inscription above the lintel: COLLEGIO TEUTONICUM. He hesitated. He knew enough Latin to understand the words: German college.

From beyond the door came a powerful Irish lilt telling him to come in. They were the first words O'Flaherty spoke to Derry.

In the hallway there was no sign of Father Aldo when O'Flaherty introduced himself and led the way up a flight of stairs to a room. The furnishings were spartan and in a corner near a bed was a golf bag filled with clubs. Catching Derry's glance O'Flaherty asked if he played and was told that cricket was Derry's game. A booming laugh was followed by O'Flaherty saying they didn't play that at his seminary, Major Derry.

Derry gathered himself: It was the first time anyone had used his rank since he had jumped from the train. How did the priest know it? O'Flaherty said Derry was on the Vatican list of escaped prisoners of war which the Red Cross provided.

Derry had another question. In the camp he had been told that the British government, while no longer having an embassy in Rome, still had a diplomat attached to the Vatican. Could he see him? O'Flaherty asked if Derry knew his name. Derry nodded. Francis D'Arcy Godolphin Osborne, adding, "a name like that you don't forget."

O'Flaherty laughed again before going to a cupboard and producing a handful of clothes, including underpants and shoes before leading Derry down a corridor to a bathroom. The last time he'd had a bath was in Cairo over a year ago before he left to join the Eighth Army in the desert. Now he could relax in hot water, the guest of an Irish monsignor in a German college. Dressed in the priest's underpants, a smoking jacket which fit perfectly, trousers, and shirt, Derry returned to O'Flaherty's room.

Waiting, in a black coat and pin-striped trousers, was John May. He introduced himself and said he had come to bring Derry to the British envoy extraordinary and minister plenipotentiary to the Holy See—"my boss".

11

THE EXECUTIONER

Hauptsturmführer Theodor Dannecker arrived in Rome by train on the evening of October 8, 1943. He was thirty years old, a slim, lantern-jawed bachelor and his height, six feet three inches tall, did nothing to compensate for his poorly coordinated body movements, which included a tic that continually flicked his head to one side.

Early that year he had carried out deportations from Bulgaria, Greece, and Yugoslavia of over eleven thousand Jews to Auschwitz and Treblinka. Previously he had performed similar operations in France, Poland, Belgium, and Holland. In all, Dannecker had sent several hundred thousand Jews to their deaths. Ironically his first girlfriend, Lisbeth Stern, had been Jewish.

As usual Eichmann's office had arranged for him to travel alone in a reserved compartment to give him time to think how he would plan his latest mission. On the train he had read the dispatches Kappler had sent: his call for more troops to conduct the roundup and his concern about the Rome Resistance. Dannecker understood why Eichmann had decided Kappler was not capable of conducting a successful *Judenaktion*. Perhaps living in Rome had made him soft. Dannecker had seen that happen before when a local police chief in Belgrade had refused to carry out executions. Dannecker, then a member of the SS *Verfuegungstruppe*, a specialist combat support force, had shot him. After Eichmann selected him to head the *Judenreferat,* the Jewish department, Dannecker summed up his work in the words of his hobby. "Over the years I have learned which hook to use for which fish."

In his finely tailored SS uniform and polished boots he embodied someone to be feared and hated; a brutal, mean, crude man.

Following his usual custom of remaining unobtrusive on a mission Dannecker stayed in a small hotel on Via Po. The accommodation had been arranged for him by one of the *Judenaktion* officers who had arrived in Rome earlier; he had worked with Dannecker for a year and knew his habits.

Dannecker had changed out of his uniform into a suit and eaten alone at a nearby restaurant; the quality of the food was indifferent but it was still better than that offered in Berlin. Afterward he had walked around Rome, studying the solid marble statues and the sarcophagi. The city, he decided, was even more impressive than Paris. Rome had its priests in black, white, and purple robes and the Latin Mass which came from a church he passed. And, of course, there were the Romans: children sitting on the marble edges of fountains; the young women, their hair often the color of flame; old men and women sitting at their tables in pavement cafes. How many of those he had seen were Jews? How many would die under his orders?

Derry had decided that dinner with D'Arcy Osborne in the minister's apartment in Santa Marta came in three stages. First there were cocktails during which Osborne gave the impression he could handle any problem which could shake, even momentarily, his composure. He had welcomed Derry with English courtliness as if he was a long-expected guest returning from some distant land. O'Flaherty stood beside their host as Derry described life in a prisoner-of-war camp.

Hovering nearby, May was ready to refill glasses before announcing dinner. Osborne led his two guests to a table glistening with silver and crystal. While May started to serve the meal, Osborne revealed the number of escaped prisoners of war seeking refuge in Rome was increasing and were not only conspicuous because of their tattered clothes but were often in poor physical condition. Over coffee and brandy in the apartment's drawing room, the minister told Derry the Vatican was becoming understandably concerned about the danger of turning into a refuge for escaped soldiers.

The Holy See was a neutral state and under international law had to intern them. It neither would, nor could, do that; there was no space to imprison them, no guards to watch over them. But the pope could not allow a stream of escaped Allied prisoners to hide in the Vatican. The Germans would accuse the Holy See of sheltering their enemies and demand they were handed over.

Osborne waited for May to pour more drinks before he continued. From what he had heard—his source was Simonds, though he never mentioned his name—thousands of prisoners were still hiding in the Apennines. They were leaderless with no idea what to do except head for Rome and the Vatican. In part that was the fault of the BBC. In June it had advised escapers to do that.

The irritation in Osborne's voice was all too clear to Derry. "I was hauled over the coals by the secretary of state because of that broadcast and I told the Foreign Office it must not be repeated. But the cat was out of the bag and now we have escapers on the run hiding in Rome and hoping to get into the Vatican."

The minister told Derry how the pope had chosen O'Flaherty to set up the network of priests and Romans with its safe houses: sheltering the first hundreds of escaped prisoners. But there were still thousands more out in the hills making their way to Rome.

Derry asked his first question: What about money to buy food, provide escapers with suitable clothes?

Osborne explained sufficient sums had been provided by the Foreign Office via Vatican Bank and the Vatican itself. But while financial support was no longer a problem there was another one. The minister had once more looked at Derry, nodding as if coming to a decision. Years later Derry would recall his words.

"Major Derry, I have seen your military record. You are the ideal person to solve a problem of there being no senior British officer to command those escaped soldiers and the discipline which goes with that. You will work closely with the monsignor and John. You will, of course, stay with Monsignor O'Flaherty and have the appropriate papers."

Derry sat, too stunned to speak, overwhelmed with a sense of inadequacy, as the others continued to watch him. Finally Osborne sat back in his chair and asked Derry if he was prepared to take on the task.

Derry nodded.

Chief Rabbi Israel Zolli never missed a regular meeting of the Council of Administration at the *Fatebenefratelli* held in the hospital's boardroom under the chairmanship of Professor Giovanni Borromeo. The agenda for October had only one item for discussion: Should the list of Jewish patrons who contributed to the hospital's upkeep be destroyed in case it fell into the hands of the Germans? Renzo Levi had tabled the motion which had been carried over from the previous month's meeting. Borromeo reported he had discovered that since then two other lists of donors—one held at the Ministry of the Interior and the other at City Hall had been removed by Settimio Sorani for Delasem to use.

Zolli said the names of all those on the lists who were no longer making contributions to the hospital's upkeep should be used by Delasem to "fabricate documents to help those Jews who wish to leave Rome despite the assurance President Foa had given."

Around the conference table voices spoke against the rabbi. If the Germans discovered fake documents were being used they would take severe action.

Zolli made a further attempt to persuade the meeting. He argued that there were still people in the ghetto who did not believe the Germans would honor the promise made to Foa and Almansi after the gold collection. They all knew there had been rumors in Rome for some weeks that the Germans were considering evacuating Rome as the Allies began to slowly advance. People had asked him what would happen before the Germans left. Would they take the Jews with them? The Germans could use them as human shields while they retreated from the Allies. Or could they break their promise in some other way?

His questions were met with derision. Finally Borromeo called for a hand vote. Zolli was the only person who had voted in favor of not destroying the lists. He left the meeting knowing that the medical director had already secretly given all his Jewish staff ID cards provided by Delasem.

One by one the founding members of O'Flaherty's secret network made their way across the courtyard of the German college to his quarters. Derry was already there, drinking coffee which one of the college nuns served. If she wondered who he was and why he had been given a bedroom along the corridor she had long learned not to be curious about what the monsignor did.

Before the priests arrived O'Flaherty had given Derry two identity cards. One was in German and described him as a Vatican civil servant. It bore the stamp of the German embassy to the Holy See. The other card was written in Italian and identified him as a citizen of Dublin, Ireland, employed as a *scrittori*, a writer, in the Vatican library. Both documents were intended to satisfy any questions asked by Rome policemen and German patrols. Each gave his forename as "Patrick" and from now on Derry must use it. It couldn't be more Irish, O'Flaherty said, with another of his booming laughs.

He introduced the priests as they arrived, using each one's code name. Derry had nodded approvingly, saying codes were an important part of the role they would play. O'Flaherty said Derry would explain what was involved in helping escaped soldiers.

Derry began by describing the escape-and-evasion tactics which had enabled the soldiers to reach Rome; however, the one reason they were in hiding was because they saw it as a shortcut to finding their way back to their unit, regiment, or army. Those who helped them must never forget that to achieve that aim, escapers would do anything.

Their helpers must not put them in a position where they had to fight for their freedom by maiming or even killing an enemy soldier or anyone they felt stood in their way. Not only would that breach the Geneva Convention but it would have fatal reprisals for those helping them.

Derry had paused: If anybody wished to withdraw, now was the moment. Not one priest moved.

———

Emma Zolli steadily began to feel more relaxed since returning home with her daughters from the apartment which her husband had found for them in which to hide. He had coaxed her to walk with him through the ghetto where people greeted him as *professore,* in respect for his office, and he reminded them it was time for *attensimo,* waiting for the Allies to arrive. Foa had told him to repeat the word at the end of each *Tefilluth,* the daily service in the synagogue.

In his own discussions with the president, Zolli saw he was more re-laxed with every day which passed since the gold collection. Foa pointed out that there were still no German patrols in the ghetto and Zolli must do everything possible to reassure people there was no cause for alarm.

Zolli had kept to himself his discussion with Father Weber and Setti-mio Sorani. The Pallottine father said the calm atmosphere permeating the city was "unreal and something is going to happen." Sorani told Zolli he had completed going through the Delasem files and removed anything which could be compromising if it fell into German hands. He had also gone with Renzo Levi to Foa to discuss the situation. Once more the presi-dent had been reassuring. Levi and Sorani had concluded all they could do was visit their friends in the Jewish community and urge them to leave the city. Not one, it turned out, accepted their advice.

At their latest meeting Father Weber told Zolli he had received news from Stockholm of the roundup of sixteen hundred Danish Jews who had been transported by train and ship to Polish concentration camps.

Outwardly, Foa maintained his unshakable confident manner on his daily walk to the synagogue. People told each other their president had obtained the better part of the deal with Kappler. Many echoed the words of goldsmith Angelo Anticoli: *che de sense ne resta!* God willing, our gold could even bring misfortune to the Germans!

One morning Emma decided she would walk into the city, something she had not done for weeks. Reaching Via del Portico d'Ottavia she saw a famil-iar figure farther up the road talking to an elderly couple. It was Celeste di Porto and Emma recognized the couple as members of the congregation. Though they lived out in the suburbs they were regular worshippers at the synagogue and Emma guessed they were probably on their way home from morning service. But she wondered how they knew Celeste; Emma had not seen her in the synagogue for some time but she seemed to know the old couple very well, judging from the way they were listening intently as Celeste nodded and watched a car approaching. It pulled up beside Celeste and two uniformed gestapo officers stepped out and bundled the suddenly terrified couple into the vehicle. The Black Pantheress had earned another bounty for denouncing two more Jews.

Emma ran back to the ghetto shouting what she had seen.

Pope Pius continued to receive reports from the network.

In the monastery founded by Saint Francis of Assisi a synagogue had been opened in the basement where close to a hundred Jews in hiding could worship while the monks prayed above in the chapel. The Vatican information office, where Sister Luke worked, had opened a special unit to deal with overseas Jews seeking news of their relatives. By October 1943, the unit had answered twenty thousand inquiries in a month. The pope had appointed his own liason with Delasem, the Capucine Father Bourg D're. He had been given a "start-up" sum of five million lire to provide food, clothing, and medicine for Jewish refugees arriving in Rome.

The pope's response to every report contained the reminder that as well as saving Jews, every effort must be made to save the contents of synagogues and cultural centers, especially the libraries. "For Jewish people their history is as important to be protected as ours," Pius wrote.

On that October morning Rosina Sorani sat at her desk sorting through Foa's mail when she heard footsteps coming up the stairs from the ground floor. The tread was too heavy for Foa and he usually called up to have his coffee ready. A stocky, barrel-chested, middle-aged man stood in the doorway. He gave her a snaggletoothed smile and introduced himself as a paleographer from the ERR who had come to inspect numerous texts in the library. He handed her a typed sheet.

Rosina looked at the paper and saw it listed the rarest works in the library: books from the famous Soncino publishing house dating from the fifteenth century; original texts from sixteenth-century Constantinople and Salonika; manuscripts which were histories of the literary and intellectual life of Rome; a record of how the kabala came to replace already existing philosophy; a thirteenth-century mathematics text and an extremely rare Hebrew-Italian-Arabic vocabulary published in Naples in 1488. Finally there were twenty-one Talmudic tracts.

He asked Rosina to take him to the library and locate the books for him.

Rosina hesitated. The precious texts were kept in a locked area at the back of the library and though she had a key to open it she wondered whether she needed Foa's permission to admit a stranger. The officer said she should accompany him to the library and reassure herself that he'd handle the manuscripts and books with proper care. Foa had not arrived and she decided he would probably have no objection; besides, in the past she had allowed Rabbi Zolli and one or two of the senior students at the rabbinical college to look at some of the books to research papers they were writing. She led the way to the library, gave the officer a pair of white cotton gloves, and unlocked the door to the room where the books were kept.

She saw he was an expert, in the way he opened a book, softly touching the paper and leafing through the pages, the way she had seen Rabbi Zolli do. The man had the same attention to touch, running a gloved hand down a page, stopping at a special point of interest to him before moving on to another page. At times he would smile at Rosina as she handed him a document, identifying it as a codex or a palimpsest. He would stand there, sometimes moving a hand above the page as if he was giving it some sort of benediction.

Much of what he asked to see was written in obscure alphabets. She had asked him about one and he told her it was Armenian, a branch of the old Christian church. But mostly he remained silent, his eyes fixed on a page, his eyes widening and brightening. Occasionally he would breathe in, the way Rabbi Zolli did when he seemed to know where to look for a particular text.

Finally he finished. Rosina locked the door behind them and walked him back to her desk; he turned to her and delivered a terrifying sentence. "You will please inform your president that the library is under sequester and if any books are missing you will have to pay with your life."

He turned and walked down the stairs.

When Foa arrived later that morning she told him about the latest visit of the ERR official.

He dictated four letters for her to type. The first was to General Stahel; the others were to the neo-Fascist city administration: the minister of interior, the minister of education, and the director general of public safety. Each had the same text: an account of the ERR visits; the sequestering of the library; its unique value. It concluded by asking that immediate and appropriate action be taken to protect the library. After signing the letters Foa told Rosina to hand deliver them to the various addresses. He would never receive a reply.

For Dannecker security had been a problem in Paris when he discovered that the French police who had been recruited to help with the roundup had warned wealthy Jews, in return for money, of their impending arrest enabling them to escape the trains to Auschwitz. From what he had read in Kappler's intelligence reports Rome could provide a similar problem.

For that reason he had billeted his *Judenaktion* team in the *Collegio Militare*. The fortress-like complex stood on Janiculum Hill and overlooked the Tiber. The SS group occupied one of the buildings around the college's huge parade grounds where army recruits had been drilled under a towering statue of the emperor Julius Caesar. The college was empty and in a decrepit condition. But Dannecker had decided it would be ideal as a holding pen for the start of his *Judenaktion*.

It was both close to the ghetto and secure to hold his captives before they were put on a train to Auschwitz. But until he could provide the Ministry of Transport in Berlin with the timing for his roundup and its approximate numbers it would not provide a train.

Dannecker's hope that his mission would remain secret failed through a regulation General Stahel had introduced. Like every hotel guest in Rome, Dannecker had to register. As a serving officer he was only required to provide his name, rank, and unit on the form which was routinely collected and brought to the *Stadtkommandant*'s headquarters at the Hotel Flora. There it was checked against a list of names of expected military officers arriving in the city; they were usually on leave or on their way to another posting.

But Dannecker's name was not listed. Its absence might had been ignored in some other headquarters, but Stahel from the outset of his appointment as *Stadtkommandant* had ordered that any oversight was to be tracked down and rectified. One of his staff officers was ordered to call Berlin and was told Dannecker was in Rome on the order of *Obersturmbannführer* Eichmann and his presence was to remain secret, a classification approved by *Reichführer* Himmler.

Stahel was furious. For him no one could come to Rome on even a secret mission without him being told its purpose. It had been infuriating to learn over the radio and newspapers of a plot to kidnap the pope of which he had known nothing beforehand and which had caused such an outcry. But now to find that Eichmann—a man Stahel strongly disliked—had somehow enlisted Himmler's backing for some secret mission was too much; Stahel's instinct told him it could only bring trouble for him. He had called Kesselring at his headquarters in Frascati. The commander-in-chief had been firm: Dannecker's mission must remain *Geheime Reichssache*—a secret affair of the Reich.

Stahel sent detailed daily reports to Berlin and to other Nazi and Fascist authorities in Rome. They included Weizsäcker and the new ambassador to the German embassy to Italy, Eitel Frederich Moellhausen. He noticed the latest report had mentioned the arrival of Dannecker.

The slim, elegantly dressed, thirty-year-old bachelor had quickly caught the eye of more than one Roman woman and was currently conducting an affair with a wealthy young widow. She had told him about the family of Jewish refugees she was hiding in her palazzo basement and how increasingly it was getting harder to feed them as they had no ration books. He had immediately arranged for them to be provided through the embassy.

Sensing Weizsäcker shared the same opposition to Nazism, Moellhausen regarded him as his mentor and mentioned Dannecker's name on Stahel's list. His fellow ambassador asked Moellhausen to come and discuss the matter with him and Kessel.

Weizsäcker said he was certain Dannecker was in Rome for only one reason and produced the copy of the *Judenaktion* he had shown General Wolff. Dannecker was either there to ensure Kappler carried out the *Judenaktion* or to take charge of the operation himself.

Moellhausen's career had been devoted to avoiding what he called "difficult situations." He knew colleagues in the embassy looked on him as a diplomat who had quickly climbed the promotion ladder while so many others still languished on the bottom rungs. Though Moellhausen avoided any discussion with embassy staff about what they called the "Jewish Question," the document shocked him. All that mattered was what steps could they take to stop it?

Kessel suggested a warning had to be conveyed to the Jews from the one voice they would listen to: the pope. He could contact Dr. Hermione Spier. She was a German Jew and employed by the Vatican as an archeological consultant. Kessel said he could try to persuade her to go to the ghetto and warn its people "as a representative of the pope" about the threat.

Weizsäcker told Kessel to call her. There was no reply. Kessel then dialed the number of the director of the German Archeological Institute in Rome.

"I let it be known that the present situation for Jews in Rome was difficult and I wanted Dr. Spier to know. I intended this to be a signal to be passed on by her to the Jewish community leaders. But I was given to understand that she had never had any contact with the community," Kessel would recall.

Kappler was in his office when Dannecker walked in, saluted, and introduced himself before handing over SS *Gruppenführer* Mueller's letter empowering him to take command of the *Judenaktion*. Kappler read the letter and handed it back. Inwardly, he said later, he was seething: He had not been told of a change of command and saw it as an insult to the way he had carried out his duties in Rome so far—especially after the successful gold collection. He had intended that operation to be the perfect precursor to the roundup.

Reports he received from the gang bosses, Giovanni Mezzaroma and Pietro Koch, confirmed that the ghetto remained calm. Both men had

also collected their financial rewards after updating Kappler on the number of Jews snatched off the streets and who were now held in Regina Coeli
prison waiting to be included in the roundup. For moments longer Kappler sat looking at Dannecker, the scar on his face more livid than usual.

Dannecker was used to such a reaction from local gestapo chiefs. While
Kappler outranked him, Dannecker knew he would also be aware that in
his final report on the mission to Eichmann he could seriously damage
Kappler's future career. More than one officer had been posted to the Russian front after Dannecker complained about his lack of cooperation.

However, after studying Kappler's and Stahel's files in Berlin, Dannecker decided both were two of a kind when it came to protecting their
own positions. He knew if his *Judenaktion* went wrong they would ensure they avoided criticism. He would need to bring Kappler onto his
side. Dannecker told Kappler he would welcome his unrivalled local
knowledge. Kappler said he would offer all the assistance he could.

Dannecker told him about billeting his men in the *Collegio Militare*,
and the role it would play as a holding pen. In Paris he made "the mistake"
of scheduling his *Judenaktion* on Bastile Day, when the city was celebrating its most patriotic national holiday. It was only when an informer drew
his attention to the possibility of Parisians disrupting his operation that
he postponed it for two whole days. He would not want that to happen
in Rome.

Kappler assured him it would not. The Jews had just celebrated their
Yom Kippur.

Dannecker's smile of relief came and went. But, he admitted, there were
other matters on which he would welcome Kappler's guidance.

Kappler produced the lists he had obtained from the Questura. Dannecker's facial tic increased as he studied them: There were more Jews than
he had anticipated. He may have to ask the Transport Ministry to schedule
more than one train and he would need more men than the number he
had brought.

Kappler claimed later: "I told him that I had no men who could be
placed at his disposal. When he asked for topographical information in
order to organize his operation I said none of my officers knew the city
well enough. Instead I gave him a street map of the ghetto."

Once more Dannecker expressed his gratitude. Kappler felt there "was something of the dark" about the man seated opposite him. Certainly they must have looked a forbidding pair: Kappler with his tightly combed blond hair and receding forehead, piercing gray-blue eyes, and a duelling scar; Dannecker, his tic constantly turning his head from one side to another as he studied the documents.

After marking various points on the map he asked Kappler what his relationship was with the police. Kappler normally did not like being questioned but he recognized Dannecker was making an effort to be amiable. He told him that Pietro Caruso, the force's chief, was a loyal Fascist and could be counted on to help in any way possible. Dannecker asked if it would be possible to use police in the roundup to close off roads leading to the ghetto, and provide guards at the *Collegio Militare*.

Kappler hesitated. He had appointed Caruso and did not wish to lose control over him by allowing Dannecker to deal directly with the police chief. He picked up his desk phone and dialled the Questura to speak to Caruso. He ordered him to place forty of his men on "special duty." Until they were required they were to be kept in a German compound so as not to draw any attention. He put down the phone and turned to Dannecker. The SS officer had more questions. In Berlin he had been told that the Vatican was run by "Jew lovers, including the pope." How would that affect the roundup? Kappler said there was a need to be careful.

The gestapo chief delivered a short lecture on the Vatican's neutrality; the *Stadtkommandant*'s refusal to deal firmly with the Resistance who were mostly Communists; how the Reich's diplomats in the city were "young and soft." Finally there was tension in Kappler's voice as he said, "In Rome this has all led to the belief that the relationship between the Jews and the Vatican is close. The Jews believe it, the Resistance believe it, and most Romans believe it. That is why you have to be careful in how your operation is carried out."

PART IV

MAGNIFICENT HEROES

12

FINAL PREPARATIONS

At first Luciana Tedesco found it strange to be in the *Fatebenefratelli*, feeling there was nothing wrong with her yet having to cough regularly in the hospital ward like the rest of her family. All the other Jews in the isolation area on the second floor did the same.

She had asked her cousin, Dr. Vittorio Sacerdoti, why they all had to cough and he said it was to keep her safe—keep everyone safe. She asked if he could give her some medicine and he listened to her chest with his stethoscope and said in his gentle voice he always used with patients that as long as she coughed and breathed deeply she would be fine.

She heard him tell her parents the Germans had come to the hospital and he had met them at the entrance and shown them a file containing the case notes of all the K-Syndrome patients who had been admitted. Each was listed as "contagious" and he laughed as he said the soldiers had quickly left.

There were books for Luciana to read and in the afternoons Sister Ester, one of the nuns, took all the children to a side room and played games with them. In the ward the adults either napped on their beds or played cards and talked among themselves. To Luciana they were one big family.

There were her parents, Gabrielle and Alvise, and her younger brother Claudio; her aunty Georgina and her son Pierluigi, a chubby-cheeked five-year-old. They ate together at the table in the center of the ward with another family. The food was brought up from the kitchen by the nuns.

Every morning when Vittorio came Luciana would proudly demonstrate her cough and he would laugh and listen to the other children show off their coughing. He always told them they were the best.

Afterward he would check the adults, calling out their names in turn. On admission they had each been given a false non-Jewish name. At first there had been confusion when he had tested them to see if they remembered their new identities. But after a few days they were name-perfect and each patient had shot up a hand at once. He had gone from ward to ward repeating the process, the children trailing behind him as if he was the Pied Piper of the *Fatebenefratelli*.

By October O'Flaherty had recruited three women to join his network of priests and nuns. They were princess Nina Pallavicini; Yvette Bruccoler, who worked in the office of the Red Cross director, Count de Salis; and a woman who asked to be known as "Frau K" to the others. The only clue to her background was that she still spoke Italian with a German accent after living in Rome for twenty years. Like the others she was a widow and all were regular worshippers at St. Peter's.

O'Flaherty knew them all well before finally enlisting them: the princess from her regular visits to bring him news from the illegal radio broadcasts from London; Yvette Brucoller from his visits to see Count de Salis where she worked as his secretary; Sister Pascalina, the pope's housekeeper, had introduced him to Frau K.

She had been the first to offer her help, explaining she was a trained calligrapher and would like to use her skill to forge food coupons. She had shown him a sample of her work and O'Flaherty immediately saw the coupon was identical to the real ones, and could be used to buy food for the hidden soldiers and Jews. Yvette had offered to distribute the forged coupons through the Red Cross.

It had been left to Princess Nina to astonish him. One evening after she had delivered her latest news from the BBC she told him that she had mastered the art of faking documents for staff of the Black Nobility who had fled underground fearing arrest by the Fascists; to survive in hiding they needed ID cards and other papers to avoid arrest. She could provide the same documents for the Jewish refugees.

He had welcomed her with open arms and Nina had returned to her palace to begin work at once.

Two old friends had also offered their services. They were Delia Murphy, the wife of the Irish minister who maintained his country's strict neutrality, and their daughter, Blon, a striking nineteen-year-old. They had turned up at the German college with two stuffed sacks which they emptied on O'Flaherty's floor. They were newly repaired shoes and boots. He had stood there, too startled to speak, before asking where in the name of God they had come from. Delia explained they had discovered a building backing onto the embassy residence that was used as a German boot repair shop and was left unguarded at night. The two women had scrambled over the embassy wall, entered the unlocked shop, gathered up a selection of shoes and boots, and thrown them back into the embassy grounds. O'Flaherty had shaken his head in wonder. He had fetched Derry and John May who began to sort out the footwear for distribution. Blon impishly said she believed they could supply a sack a week.

That night, as usual, the priests of Rome's parishes were out bringing food and clothes to the convents and safe houses where Jewish refugees were hiding. Some of the priests had become experts in working the black market, bartering for a dress for a little girl, a pair of trousers for a growing boy. The priests hid their purchases under their robes or carried them in bags holding the goblets and wafers they used for Holy Communion. Father Patrick Carroll-Abbing would remember "the darkness was a nightmare sound of German boots patrolling."

It was the sound of boots running toward the palazzo front door which had first warned Princess Pallavicini. She was alone: having sent her cook and maid south to her country home, together with her chauffeur and gardener. She knew that if she was discovered forging documents they would be imprisoned—or even executed as collaborators.

Already her friend, Princess Virginia Agnelli, the widow of Edoardo Agnelli, the Turin Fiat heir, was imprisoned in the San Gregorio Convent; in spite of the Lateran Treaty, the building had been turned by the Fascists into a prison for the ladies of the Black Nobility. Virginia had smuggled out a message to Nina that she was "reasonably comfortable and I can use the chapel."

The kicking of boots against the front door and shouts in German sent Nina racing to the back of the palace to jump out of a ground floor window. Knowing the penalty of death faced her when her illegal wireless was discovered she ran through the streets to the only person and place she knew would provide sanctuary—Monsignor O'Flaherty in the German college.

That night O'Flaherty found her a bedroom in the nun's quarters. Hours later Radio Rome broadcast that she was to be arrested on sight for using an illegal radio and working for the enemy. A substantial reward was announced for her capture. O'Flaherty told Nina he had obtained permission for her to stay in the college for the foreseeable future where she would continue to produce her documents until the Allies arrived. Nina worked from a basement room and the special paper and equipment she had left behind in the palazzo was replaced by an old friend of O'Flaherty's, Count Giuseppe Dalla Torre, the editor of *L'Osservatore Romano*.

The three German diplomats—Weizsäcker, Kessel, and Moellhausen— had met in locked-door secrecy for a further meeting in Villa Napoleon to discuss a new approach after their attempts had failed to alert the ghetto Jews. The two Holy See diplomats said it was essential that Berlin understood *Judenaktion* would have serious consequences for the Vatican's relationship with Berlin. At a time when the war was going badly for Germany the loss of any possibility of support from the pope would be a serious blow to German policy. It was agreed that the foreign minister, von Ribbentrop should be alerted.

Moellhausen suggested General Stahel was the right person to communicate with Ribbentrop; in his capacity as *Stadtkommandant* he had a responsibility to keep Rome peaceful and avoid an uprising. The others agreed and Moellhausen said he would go and see him. He would bring with him Weizsäcker's copy of the *Judenaktion*. At the same time Moellhausen would tell the general what was known about Dannecker.

Stahel had erupted as soon as he read the order. Moellhausen would remember him shouting, "Why was I not told? The order was directly sent to Kappler. I will pretend to know nothing about it!"

The ambassador told Stahel about Dannecker. His anger deepened: "I want nothing to do with this kind of filth."

Moellhausen reported back to the others and they agreed their next move should be to send a telegram to the foreign ministry. Moellhausen proposed that in his capacity as representing the interests of the Reich in Italy, it should be addressed to von Ribbentrop personally. He would transmit the message in his own name and use the secret code which German ambassadors possessed to deal with matters that require the foreign minister's immediate attention.

If Weizsäker or Kessel wondered about his decision they may well have assumed that Moellhausen saw it as a step up the promotion ladder. They made no attempt to enjoin him as co-signatures because Moellhausen had insisted on passages in the telegram they were nervous about. But he had insisted they must be included if they were to succeed in averting the *Judenaktion*.

The telegram was encoded and marked *"supercitissime!"*—"very, very urgent." That in itself was a remarkable classification as it did not exist in the German code book; the highest was *"citissime"*—"very urgent." Moellhausen had added the prefix "super" to give it extra emphasis. Additionally it was marked for the attention of the *Reichminister "personally."*

This additional direction had caused raised eyebrows in the Wilhelmstrasse communications department. The telegram was decoded, typed, and three carbon copies made. One was sent to Ribbentrop's office. As it referred to a matter outside the normal province of diplomacy, copies were transmitted to Himmler's and Eichmann's offices. The text read:

> *Obersturmbannführer* Kappler has been commissioned from Berlin, to seize the eight thousand Jews resident in Rome and take them to northern Italy where they are to be liquidated. General Stahel, city commander of Rome, said that this action is to be permitted only with the approval of the German foreign minister. I am personally of the opinion that it would be better business to transport the Jews for work on fortifications. I will propose this to Field Marshal Kesselring. Please advise. Moellhausen.

The telegram caused consternation in Berlin—though not quite as Moellhausen expected. No ambassador had sent the foreign minister a *personal* letter that included the word "liquidated" in an official document; any reference to the Jewish Question was forbidden. The telegram had also involved the foreign minister in an operation that would be strictly under the command of the SS.

The fallout was swift. Stahel denied he had made any statement to Moellhausen. A furious and embarrassed Ribbentrop apologized to Himmler for this "unfortunate telegram" assuring the *Reichführer* that he would never again allow such overstepping of authority by any of his staff. He sent a message to Moellhausen:

> The *Reichminister* for foreign affairs insists that you keep out of all questions concerning the Jews. Such questions, in accordance with an agreement between the Foreign Office and the RSHA, are within the exclusive competence of the SS and any further interference in these questions could cause serious difficulties for the minister of foreign affairs."

Moellhausen realized his diplomatic career was seriously damaged along with his attempt to save the Jews. He had already decided not to contact Kesselring to avoid fomenting more trouble.

In 2000 the Nazi War Crime Disclosure Act allowed the National Archives in Washington, D.C. to release some 400,000 pages of documents from the Office of Strategic Studies, the wartime OSS. Among the material were British interceptions of messages of radio traffic between Rome and Berlin in October 1943. Among them was Moellhausen's telegram to von Ribbentrop and the response it had generated. The intercepts had been picked up by the code breakers at Bletchley Park.

Their release would raise a disturbing question. Could the Allies have used the information at the time to try and save the Jews of Rome? The question would become part of the endless debate on what could have been done with intelligence during war. Those millions of words began the focus, not for the first time, on the role of the war leaders, Churchill and Roosevelt. Could they have done more to warn the Jews? Inevitably, the codes were interpreted by some writers to level an accusation that both *must* have known in advance the impending fate of Rome's Jews and did nothing to save them.

The truth is otherwise. In those 400,000 pages that require months of careful reading, there is nothing to show that Franklin Roosevelt received sufficient *advance* information about Nazi intentions in Rome to enable him to have acted. It was not until December, 1943, that Allen Dulles, head of the OSS, obtained a copy of Moellhausen's telegram to Ribbentrop and had it sent from his headquarters in Bern, Switzerland to Roosevelt.

Churchill's intelligence files at the Public Records Office in Kew, London, show that while he did receive daily digests of information from Bletchley intercepts, there is nothing in the files to indicate he knew in *advance* of the fate of the ghetto Jews until the end of October. However earlier that month the prime minister had discussed at a war cabinet meeting on October 6, whether he should once more denounce all Nazi atrocities. Foreign Minister Anthony Eden had opposed the idea. "I am most anxious not to get into the position of breathing fire and slaughter against war criminals and promising condign punishment and a year or two hence having to find pretexts for doing nothing."

Eichmann's office had informed Dannecker of the fruitless attempt by Moellhausen to intervene in the *Judenaktion* assuring the SS officer there would be no further attempt made to interfere in his work.

Dannecker asked Kappler to provide him with an office in the gestapo headquarters on Via Tasso. On trestle tables Dannecker laid out the ghetto and city street maps which Kappler provided. On the ghetto map he created thirty *Judenaktionbezirke*—"precincts." He then repeated the process on the city map, producing forty-five further squares.

Dannecker had made a geographical map of the locations of the Jews of Rome. The most densely filled squares were on the ghetto map, often spilling over into an adjoining square. In Trastevere some of the squares were empty, indicating where non-Jews lived. The city street map squares were mostly vacant; those with only a few names were close to the northern wall of the Vatican. When the time came he would be able to assign the correct number of men to visit each square. It would also enable the lorries to be correctly sent to pick up the Jews and to complete the roundup as quickly as possible. Preparation like this had made Dannecker Eichmann's vaunted "Jew catcher."

Dannecker was also realistic. He did not expect to catch every Jew in Rome. Past experience had shown him there would always be some who would escape. There were also the latest fuel limitations on deportation trains imposed by the Ministry of Transport. It meant there was a limit on the distance a train could travel, which in turn reduced the number of carriages it could pull. The usual limit in 1943 was twenty cars, sufficient to carry one thousand people. If no more could be crammed on board they could be held in Regina Ceoli prison for the next train. Before Dannecker had come to Rome he was told that Eichmann's office had arranged for the prison to be emptied of all short-term Italian prisoners to make room in anticipation of an overflow from the deportation train.

In Dannecker's calculations time was of utmost importance: The timing of when the train would arrive should be as close as possible to the completion of the roundup to avoid the Resistance attacking it; the start of the operation should be in the early hours and before dawn, when people were asleep and in the least likely position to try and escape.

He had found there was another element to a successful roundup. It was to convince people they were only being "transferred" to work in the German war effort. It had worked before; he expected it to work now. He had asked Kappler to have translated into Italian a text which would be mimeographed on paper the size and shape of postcards. These would be presented to each Jew who was head of a household.

1. You and your family and all other Jews belonging to your household are to be transferred.
2. You are to bring with you:
   a) Food for at least eight days
   b) Ration books
   c) Identity cards
3. You may bring:
   a) A small suitcase with personal effects, clothing, blankets, etc.
   b) Money and jewelry

4. Close and lock the apartment/house. Take the key with you.
5. Invalids, even the severest cases, may not for any reason remain behind. There are infirmaries in the camp.
6. Twenty minutes after presentation of this card the family must be ready to depart.

When Dannecker had completed his pre-planning he had shown Kappler the result. The gestapo chief had expressed himself suitably impressed but he had warned it would be important to ensure that every deportee was in fact a Jew as defined under German law, and had reminded Dannecker that the city was full of Allied escapers his own men were trying to capture and if they were caught in the roundup, with the enemy so close, it could have harmful consequences for captured German soldiers.

Dannecker promised he would bear that in mind.

Settimio Sorani met with Father Anton Weber at the general house of the Pallottine fathers on Pettinari Street. Rome had suddenly become more dangerous: The Germans had looted the Villa Savoy, the deserted palace of King Victor Emmanuel. German crews were working to restore cut telephone lines linking command posts around the city. The palace looting fuelled rumors the Germans were preparing to leave Rome stealing what they could, and that the Resistance had disrupted communications to hasten their departure.

As he walked down the long entry hall to the priest's office, flanked on either side by the busts of dead Pallottine priests, the director of Delasem wondered what he would hear.

The answer stunned him. Father Weber said that in Germany the Nazis had arrested several fathers in Hamburg and incarcerated them in Dachau for helping Jews. He had been told to close down the network bringing out refugees from northern Europe. He urged Sorani to do the same with Delasem.

Sorani had met Renzo Levi. They both agreed it was time to close down the agency and go into hiding. They took with them any incriminating documents for burning. That night Settimio had collected Rosina from the synagogue and together they took a tramcar to their new hiding place he had found in the suburbs. She had tried to call Foa but there was no reply. It was only later she would learn he had found a hiding place for his children and himself.

Pope Pius had also asked Father Leiber to contact the community leader. He intended to offer Foa accommodation in the Vatican for both his family and what space was still available for those Foa would select.

The decision had been made after Pius had discussed the matter with two of the Jewish scholars he had moved into the ghetto. Both Professor Tullio Levi-Civita and Professor Giorgio del Vecchio had told Pius that the demand for the fifty kilograms of gold would be the start of other demands on the ghetto population. Given what was happening to Jews in other ghettos both said it would have been better if they had already left. But in del Vecchio's experience, "our ghetto people are stubborn to listen to any advice—let alone moving."

Nevertheless Pius had insisted that space would be available should it be required. But Leiber had failed to find Foa.

On the evening of Thursday, October 14, the synagogue caretaker telephoned Zolli. Getting no reply he hurried to the chief rabbi's home and found neighbors gathering outside. Zolli's front door was ajar and a neighbor told the caretaker that Zolli and the family had left earlier that morning and in the afternoon German soldiers had arrived with a locksmith who had opened the front door. Between them they had carried out books and files and driven off in their truck. The caretaker had gone inside and found the apartment had been thoroughly searched and family belongings scattered everywhere. He had used Zolli's phone to call Foa, Almansi, and Rosina. Each time there was no reply. Not knowing what else to do the caretaker had closed the door behind him and hurried back to the synagogue. He would spend the night sitting by a telephone that never rang.

After Emma Zolli had rushed home in understandable terror having witnessed the elderly couple bundled into the car by the gestapo men and

Celeste di Porto walking away, Emma had told her husband they must return to the apartment loaned to them by her gynecologist. He immediately agreed. While his wife and children repacked their suitcases he gathered together his favorite books, writing paper, and his typewriter on which he wrote his articles. The family crowded into one of the few taxis still plying for hire in the ghetto and the chief rabbi of Rome disappeared. It was a time above all when his congregation needed him.

It was evening when Dannecker went to the *Collegio Militare* to brief his troops. He had taken them over the maps and assigned the appropriate numbers of soldiers for each one. Trucks had arrived and were parked on the parade grounds inside the college. Finally he had given them the start date and time for the mission: Saturday, October 16, 5:30 A.M.

In her diary Sister Luke noted that the Vatican had ordered an increase in the number of guards on all the extraterritorial properties throughout Rome. With an eye for fashion she noted, "They each have a dashing magenta beret, very wide and floppy, caught up with the pontifical cockade of yellow and white and a swirling military cloak of dark blue. One does see some of them with civilian trousers beneath this glory but you cannot have everything with the present shortage of materials. They also carry rifles and ammunition."

In his private dining room Bishop Alois Hudal was entertaining to dinner SS *Sturmbannführer* Eugen Dollmann. It had become a regular occasion since Dollmann had come to Rome in 1937, assigned to be *Reichführer* Himmler's personal representative to Mussolini's Fascist government and now to the Vatican. The post was not officially recognized by the Holy See, but Dollmann regarded himself as he later told OSS Chief Allen Dulles, "as a kind of top link between the Germans and the church." Multilingual, tall, and elegant in his customized suits, he wore his long black hair combed back and had an effeminate manner.

In the debacle following the Moellhausen telegram he had been told by Himmler's office he was to become the link between the new *Stadt-kommandant*, Kurt Mälzer, and the Vatican. Dollmann regarded Mälzer as coarse and a drunk, though they both quickly learned they shared a common dislike for Kappler and Ambassador Weizsäcker.

However Dollmann had developed a close relationship with the Bavarian-born Father Pankratius Pfeiffer, the abbot-general of the Order of Salvatorians, who Pope Pius had made his own personal liaison with the German occupiers; the two had first met when Pius had been nuncio in Munich where Pfeiffer had been a parish priest. Allen Dulles would later say, "Dollmann knew how to be everybody's man, but only in high places."

Soon the silver-tongued Dollmann would be called upon to once more show his self-serving skills.

13

ROUNDUP

Early on Wednesday, October 13, Mose Spizzichino had stopped pushing his handcart along Lungotevere dei Cenci, the broad road which would bring him into the city. Coming slowly toward him were two large freight cars trundling along the trolley tracks which were part of the city's public transport network. Towing them was a smaller motorized vehicle and walking alongside were a group of men in overalls; they were employees of Rome's leading removal firm. With them was a squad of armed soldiers. Behind the freight cars was an open military car with a uniformed driver and three men in gray suits.

Mose pushed his cart into an alley and watched the procession pass. The freight cars were identical to those he saw on his visits to the streets around the marshalling yards: Each had a swastika and a German railroad emblem stamped on their sides. He turned and hurried back along the alley into the ghetto to report what he had seen.

From her office window in the synagogue Rosina watched the approaching freight cars. She knew why they were there and did not know what to do. Apart from the caretaker she was the only person in the building.

Rosina had hardly slept in the small apartment Settimio had found them. They discussed late into the night what Father Weber had told her brother after she helped to burn the documents Settimio had brought from his office.

The priest had assured him he would take care of the remaining refugees in Delasem's care, mostly women and children. Settimio had given him a list of their names and addresses. He had begun to worry about the Germans finding it. She had tried to reassure him, though she herself had become increasingly uneasy: First Almansi and now Foa and Rabbi Zolli had disappeared. There had still been no reply as she had continued to call the numbers of the president and the chief rabbi into the early hours. She knew there was no point in calling Almansi. He had said he would never answer the phone in his hiding place, instead he would call the synagogue and leave a message where he could be found at a different place every evening in the city "in order to deal with matters relevant to carrying out my duties."

The freight cars were now parked outside the synagogue and she recognized the three officers from the ERR who had descended from the car and were leading the overalled men into the synagogue.

The younger of the officers, who had spoken to her in Hebrew the first time he came to the synagogue, politely asked her to lead them to the library. Rosina had said it was locked. The officer who had threatened her ordered her to open it. Rosina said she did not have the key. He motioned to one of the soldiers to follow him and moments later there was the sound of the library door being forced open. The looting of the library was about to start.

A crowd had begun to form in the street below. Among them was Umberto di Veroli, who had come out from his shop opposite the synagogue to see what was happening. The soldiers had formed a line to hold back people.

As the removal men emerged with books the ERR men supervised their storage in the freight cars. Sheets of corrugated paper were placed between the books to protect them. Slowly and carefully the piles of irreplaceable literature filled each car to its roof. A total of 26,568 volumes were ready for their long train journey to Germany. It was early evening when the work was finished.

The Hebrew-speaking officer thanked Rosina for her "patience and understanding." She told him it was not appropriate to thank her for what had been done. He gave her a Heil Hitler salute and joined the others in the car. As the freight cars trundled back up the road Umberto di Veroli handed her a sheet of paper on which he had written the stencilled numbers on the freight cars; saying he hoped that one day they could help to trace the stolen library. Close to tears he called it a crime against history.

Four years would pass until in October 1947 an officer in the monuments, fine arts, and archives section of the Allied military government in West Germany was assigned to discover the fate of the books. Major Seymour J. Pomerenze, a former archivist at the National Archives in Washington, found they had been shipped to the ERR *Institute der NSDP fuer Erforschung der Judenfrage* in the small village of Hungen. From there Pomerenze traced them to the Rothschild Library in Frankfurt and they were shipped back to Rome. Like so many books they had survived being sacrificed as a burnt offering to racial hatred in Nazi Germany.

On that Wednesday evening when the freight cars had departed, Foa arrived at the synagogue with its caretaker. Rosina was waiting for them and together they went to the Treasury, the repository of the gold articles used in religious sermons. They carried them down to the synagogue's *mikvah*, the ritual bath. While Rosina stood guard at the entrance the men began to place the precious pieces in the tank of holy water which supplied the bath. That night back in his hiding place, Foa wrote, "With the help of God they are saved and kept intact." But the fate of many of those who used them was drawing closer.

Sister Pascalina had taken upon herself the task of keeping track of the number of Jews who had been rescued by the Vatican since October 1942, when Italy's leading Fascist newspaper, *Regime Fascista,* had reminded its readers that "we should not forget that in the long run the pope is a greater enemy of National Socialism than Churchill or Roosevelt. It is incomprehensible that the Catholic clergy should today support so many protests against the elimination of the Jews."

Pascalina's own record keeping would include details of a secret letter the pope wrote to the Catholic bishops of Europe in 1942 after the Wannsee Conference. Headed *Opere et caritate* (by work and charity), it asked them to "save the Jews and other victims of persecution." Pius requested his letter remain secret "for the same reason the International Red Cross and the World Council of Churches had avoided making any public statement which would increase the suffering of Jews."

Pascalina's records also showed that in the late summer of 1943 over two thousand Jews in Hungary were given documents by the Vatican which identified them as baptized Catholics. The cardinal of Genoa had been told to have his priests issue baptism certificates to eight hundred Jews hidden in the city. In every city, town, and village where Jews were hidden, Pius had sanctioned priests to provide the certificates and, in some cases, make Jews citizens of the Vatican. All told, there were over four thousand Jews hidden in convents and monasteries across Italy.

In Rome the number of Jewish families being sheltered had increased since Father Weber had brought those on the Delasem list to convents. Many arrived in the ambulance driven by Monsignor Patrick Carroll-Abbing. The vehicle now bore Vatican license plates to protect it from being stopped by German police.

Nevertheless, a different problem had arisen one October morning when Father Patrick arrived at the convent of Our Lady of Sion and found a group of Jewish families he had earlier brought to the convent in an uproar. The mother superior had told them their menfolk could not stay in the convent because the order's rule forbade it. Father Patrick asked the nun to keep the men until he returned. He had driven to the Vatican and explained the situation to Father Leiber. He had immediately telephoned the mother superior to say she was absolved from the order's rule as the Holy Father had decreed that "given the grave situation, nuns are allowed to give hospitality in their convent to Jewish men as well as their families." By the end of the day over a hundred and fifty mother superiors had been contacted and given the same ruling.

By the second week of October O'Flaherty's organization had found secure hiding places for close to five hundred Allied soldiers. The number would have been greater but for the number of escapees caught on the streets by the Koch or Black Panther gangs who were incarcerated in an old palace near the Pantheon.

Derry told O'Flaherty it was time the escapees in hiding were reminded they "are under British military discipline and not to damn well go wandering through the streets like tourists. They need to understand that feeding, clothing, and finding them hiding places is a dangerous game."

O'Flaherty suggested that Derry should visit the safe houses.

His ID card in his suit pocket and escorted by Father Owen Sneddon—the New Zealand priest who had chosen "Horace" as his code name—Derry's tour of the safe houses gave him an insight into the courage of Romans risking their lives to help escapees. Before he left each safe house Derry firmly impressed on the soldiers they were in a position of great responsibility to ensure their helpers were not caught.

After once more installing his family in the apartment his wife's gynecologist had loaned them, Zolli had gone to see Father Borsarelli, the abbot of the Sacred Heart monastery in Rome. The priest had become a confidante of the chief rabbi after Zolli visited the monastery to see its small but important collection of religious paintings. After several visits Zolli had eventually told Borsarelli of his spiritual journey through prayer and meditation which had brought him from devout Judaism to wishing to convert to Catholicism.

Now, the abbot had asked him to wait while he went to make a telephone call. When he returned he told Zolli they would go and collect his wife and children and take them to the Vatican where they could stay with the full blessing of the pope. The abbot told Zolli that among the pope's favorite saints was Saint Neri, "who had always prayed for the Hebrews and so intense was his desire to see the Jews united to Christ that at the sight of one of them still outside the fold, he would weep."

It was dusk when the monastery's old car drove into the Vatican. Inside its walls the chief rabbi and his family would become the latest of three hundred Jews who had so far been given sanctuary.

Ugo Foa had ordered the synagogue caretaker to remain in the building after he locked up in case Zolli telephoned; if he did he was to be given the president's new number at his hiding place and told to call at once. During the night no call came to disturb the rain spattering on the cobbles of the Temple Square.

By dawn on Friday, October 15, the rain stopped and daylight spilled into the caretaker's room. He had left the door open so that he could hear if the telephone rang in Foa's office on the floor above.

A clock chimed ending the caretaker's remnants of uneasy sleep. In between listening to the small sounds of the building, he tried to make sense of all that had happened: the theft of the books, the burial of the precious gold vessels in the water tank, the anger of the president over where the chief rabbi had gone.

Across the street Umberto di Veroli paused in opening up his shop to exchange greetings with the caretaker. As he opened the synagogue doors both agreed if Zolli did not appear to take the Sabbath service it would be a serious matter.

With less than a day left before launching *Judenaktion,* Kappler told Dannecker he needed more soldiers to guarantee the operation's success. Overnight there had been an increase in Resistance attacks which could be a prelude to interrupting the deportation.

Dannecker telephoned Eichmann's office. Inside an hour two SS police companies attached to Stahel's headquarters were transferred to Dannecker. By early Friday afternoon, Eichmann's "Jewish specialist" had a total of 365 Waffen SS troops to carry out his operation together with those forty Rome police officers.

By late afternoon Mose Spizzichino was making his way home. It had started to rain again and his near-empty cart showed it had been a poor day for peddling; only a handful of old clothes and a few boots were under the blanket he used to protect them against the weather. Shopkeepers were closing early, knowing the weather would not bring out late customers. The Sabbath was coming and families were at home preparing for it.

The sounds of hurrying footsteps faded and in the windows seven-branch candlesticks flickered on tables being set for the Sabbath meal. By the time Mose reached the Via del Tempio it was dark, the only sound the rain striking the cobbles. He saw the synagogue doors were closed and the building in darkness. Pinned to a side door was a note that the evening service was cancelled.

Mose wondered if it was further proof of what he had heard: that the chief rabbi and his family had disappeared.

A woman was standing on a street corner. In the dark she looked more forbidding than usual in her ragged black dress, soaked to her skin and her matted hair in tangles over her face. Pitifully thin with wild eyes and stumps for teeth she looked what everyone called her: Celeste the crazy one. He knew she lived somewhere in Trastevere and said she had relatives in the ghetto, but no one claimed kinship. She was known to laugh at funerals and cry outside the synagogue at weddings and she would gossip with anyone who would listen.

Celeste ran toward Mose, gesticulating and shouting with spittle dribbling from her mouth. She had news, she cried, grabbing his arm.

Mose was a kind man and one of the few who didn't laugh at her and asked what was the news.

Celeste said the woman she cleaned for had told her that the Germans were coming to take everyone away. Her employer herself had heard it from a friend of her own husband, a guard at Regina Coeli prison. They were coming that night, Celeste gabbled. She swore it was the truth. She had come all the way from Trastevere to bring the news. Instead people had closed their doors in her face.

Mose thanked her for her warning and pushed his cart homeward. He was too tired to know whether he believed her as she shouted after him to believe her.

It was nightfall and the curfew had started when trucks arrived at the *Collegio Militare* with the two SS companies and the forty Rome *carabinieri*.

———

In her diary Sister Luke had devoted the space for October 15 to note in the past days hundreds of slogans had appeared all over the city, daubed on walls and shop fronts, on what seemed every available space. They were all in the same dark red and had been painted, she guessed, under cover of darkness "by courageous men who must have known they faced death if caught. They had worked at speed as the letters dripped paint before they dried. They were a protest against the tyranny that surrounded everyone in Rome."

The words made her feel, for the first time, uneasy about what the partisans intended to do after the war. Each inscription praised Communism. *VIVA LA RUSSIA! VIVA STALIN!* She wondered, as she completed her diary entry, what the pope felt about those slogans.

Dr. Sacerdoti's shift on that Friday night in the *Fatebenefratelli* had passed with few calls on his skills. But shortly before midnight a man rushed into the hospital. His hands were smeared with red paint and he told the doctor he was one of a group of partisans who had been painting slogans on the bridges and walls along the Tiber when a German patrol spotted them. He had dropped his paint and brush and ran into the darkness. Now he needed to wash the evidence from his hands and clothes. Dr. Sacerdoti had taken him to a bathroom and found him a room in the basement while his clothes were washed and dried by one of the nurses.

As the doctor returned to his on-call room the wall clock struck midnight, the start of October 16.

Kosher butcher Graziano Perugia had sat up late discussing with his wife, Sara, what to make of the warning which Celeste had cried out as she ran on through the ghetto that the Germans were coming to deport them. They had watched her from their bedroom window as she had paused to stand outside in the rain shouting in her hoarse voice that they would all be sorry if they did not listen to her, that if she was a *signora,* she would be believed, but because she had no money to buy fine clothes she had to wear rags—and she had ran on repeating herself.

If not mad, she is close to it, Graziano had told his wife. Sara was less sure, reminding her husband that at times Celeste had shown a strange foresight: There had been her warning one year that a flood tide in the Tiber would be higher than usual and several streets had been flooded; another time she predicted there would be an outbreak of illness sixth months before several babies in the ghetto died from diphtheria.

The butcher and his wife finally went to bed and fell asleep still unable to agree over Celeste's warning.

In a low-rent ghetto apartment lived Lazzaro Anticoli, a garage mechanic and cousin of the ghetto goldsmith, with his petite wife, the mother of their twins. Lazzaro decided after Emma gave birth to Mario and Rosa, shortly after the Germans occupied Rome, that the ghetto was no longer safe to bring up a family. A friend at work, a Catholic, said they could move in with his family.

Their new home was cramped and their hosts were also poor. The Anticoli family slept on the floor in one room. Suddenly Rosa was taken ill. Lazzaro's friend sent for the doctor. By the time he arrived Rosa had a high temperature and could hardly breathe. He told her parents that she had pneumonia and would not live long. Lazzaro decided that Rosa's only hope was to go back to the ghetto and sleep in her own bed. Helped by their Catholic friends the family had returned to their own apartment the previous day. As Saturday morning arrived, they sat around Rosa's cot praying she would live.

Count de Salis had completed his weekly report to the International Red Cross headquarters in Geneva. Suspecting his communications were intercepted by both the Allies and the Germans, de Salis concluded: "The pope continues to espouse the Jewish cause and remains regarded as its most influential defender. He continues to direct innumerable rescue missions by his priests and provides funds for Father Leiber to obtain visas and other requirements. There are now close to three thousand Jewish refugees in Rome's convents, parish churches, religious institutions, as well as those in the ghetto and inside the Vatican. The latest figure for Allied escapers is now close to four thousand."

———————

In the early hours of Saturday, the ghetto once more slept. An hour before, the sound of shots had awoken people, followed by boots pounding over the cobblestones and loud German voices shouting. Those courageous enough to do so had gone to their windows and glimpsed the *rashanim*, ghetto slang for soldiers, followed by the sound of a vehicle driving away before silence returned to the ghetto.

In her bed Settimia Spizzichino wondered if whoever the shots had been fired at managed to escape. Within the house there was only the sound of her father, Mose, turning on the bedsprings in the room above. In the bed beside her, her sister Guiditta slept deeply.

Settimia started to count the seconds, but sleep would not come even though her eyelids were heavy. All she could hear was a fly buzzing, wanting to escape. In the dark she couldn't see it, only hear the buzzing as it flew around the room. She wondered again about what her father had told the family over dinner about Celeste's warning. It was strange, to come all that way from Trastevere to say such things. Maybe she had meant those soldiers who had now gone away. The thought helped Settimia to finally drift back to sleep.

It was around 5 A.M. when on Saturday Prince Filippo Doria Pamphilj awoke. For days now he had knelt on his prie-dieu and prayed about whether it was time to tell the Resistance to place the detonators in the tunnel beneath his family palazzo on the Via del Corso to ensure the enormous baroque edifice, with its thousand rooms, which had become the Waffen SS headquarters and barracks in Rome, would be totally destroyed.

Over the past weeks, the forty-three-year-old prince, dressed in a coalman's clothes, had led the demolition team through the tunnels as they worked by the light of a lantern placing the explosives beneath a palace where for centuries the family had lived and welcomed monarchs, popes, and rulers of Europe with two exceptions: Prince Filippo had refused to entertain Mussolini or Hitler when they came to Rome.

His decision had cost the prince his liberty—imprisoned in one of Mussolini's concentration camps. After pressure from the Vatican to free him, Pope Pius had advised Filippo to go into hiding from the furious Fascists.

The palace gardener, by then a member of the Resistance, had found the prince a home in Trastevere among its working-class population, and introduced him to the partisan leaders, who promised he would be safe among them. They showed him some of their hideouts. He had told them about the tunnels. When the Germans arrived he proposed the palace should be blown up.

Even hard-bitten men of the Resistance had hesitated. The damage could be widespread, the revenge of the Germans guaranteed, and he would become a prime target, together with his family.

Prince Filippo discussed the matter with his wife, Gesine, and their daughter, Princess Orietta. Gesine had reminded her husband that the palace would eventually pass to Orietta as their only child and she would be entitled to an inheritance which would include four princedoms, two dukedoms, and immense estates including a castle, a thirteenth-century abbey, and the church of St. Agnes in Rome's Piazza Navona.

Orietta told her father he must do what he felt was right.

Since then Prince Filippo knelt every morning as dawn broke on his prie-dieu and prayed to make the right decision.

On that morning his devotions were interrupted by the roar of trucks emerging from the *Collegio Militare* and moving down the road on the opposite bank of the Tiber.

Dr. Sacerdoti stood in a window above the staff entrance to the *Fatebenefratelli* watching the canvas-topped trucks coming down Lungotevere dei Vallati as the rain swept off the Tiber against the hospital walls. A truck would stop and soldiers jump down and run into a side street. Further down the road another truck would repeat the process. Dr. Sacerdoti had seen enough to recognize what was about to happen: another roundup.

He told one of the night nurses to alert all the staff to remain in the hospital. He dispatched porters to stand watch in the entrance and to call him if any Germans approached. His next task was to phone professor Borromeo to alert him to what was happening. That done, Dr. Sacerdoti went to the second floor where the K-Syndrome "patients" were housed. They were all asleep. Elsewhere nurses were checking on other patients.

Before the medical director returned to the hospital to take charge, he had his own telephone calls to make. The first was to Ugo Foa. There was no reply. Neither was there a response from Dante Almansi's number. Rabbi Zolli's number rang out. He remembered that after the last meeting of the hospital management committee one of its members, Alina Cavaliera, had taken him aside and said she had urged the chief rabbi to go into hiding. Borromeo's next call was to Count de Salis. He was still asleep but when he heard what was happening he made what he later said was "the one call that mattered—to Secretary of State Maglione to alert him."

The cardinal informed Sister Pascalina that as soon as the pope awakened he must see him. Until then no one else in the Vatican would know that just over a mile away Rome's first *Judenaktion* was under way.

The rain had stopped when Graziano Perugia awoke sometime before 6 A.M. It was the hour he usually rose, dressed, and went downstairs to prepare the meat for the shop counter. But this was not a normal day. From out in the street came the cadence of boots. He knew Sara was awake and watching him. He went to the bedroom window and lifted a corner of the shutter. Soldiers in helmets and carrying rifles were marching down the street. He lowered the shutter and told Sara they must leave at once.

Sara didn't have to say that Celeste's warning had been right; it was there on her husband's face.

They slipped out of the back door into an alley and made their way down past the ruins of the Theater of Marcellus to the bank of the Tiber and on past the Pyramid of Cestius and out into the countryside.

It was a route others would follow. Still more would flee into the city to find sanctuary in convents and other religious houses before the trap closed on the ghetto.

Roadblocks had been set up at the entrance to the Portico d'Ottavia, where some of the Rome police stood guard. Their orders were to put anyone who approached into one of the waiting trucks. Other *carabiniere* stood guard outside the synagogue and at the bridges across the Tiber, Ponte Cestio, and Ponte Garibaldi. More trucks waited there for the same purpose.

The Waffen SS soldiers, working in pairs, began to go in search of their targets. By 6 A.M. the operation was fully under way.

Arminio Wachsberger was a slim and polite twenty-nine-year-old specialist in repairing cameras and watches. Born in the Austrian province of Fiume before it became part of Italy, he had come to Rome before the war, enlisted in the Italian air force, and met and married a Trastevere girl, Regina. His father, a rabbi, had performed the ceremony. In 1938 their daughter, Clara, was born. When she was three she had developed poliomyelitis. Arminio's business had expanded and, with the help of two Catholic friends, he had established a small workshop for his photo-optical and watch repair work.

Clients came from all over Rome to have their cameras or watches repaired including Germans from a nearby barracks. He spoke to them in their mother tongue and, with his name and still a trace of an Austrian accent, he allowed them to assume he was a German.

Though he lived outside the ghetto in a spacious apartment on Via Lungotevere, he was regarded within the ghetto as a devout member of the synagogue and the family attended every Sabbath service. Regina's parents lived with them and her father worked in her husband's workshop.

There had been family discussions about whether they should all move closer to the workshop. Arminio had said there were a number of apartments available in the district, but Regina and her parents were reluctant to live there. The district was a long-established area for Fascists and to move that far into the city would increase the distance for Clara to go to school. Besides all their friends lived in Trastevere. Arminio had proposed a compromise: They should remain where they were but his wife should "prepare to move when the Allies arrived."

There the matter lay on that Saturday morning when there was an insistent knocking on their apartment's front door.

Standing there were two soldiers with the double-lightning symbol of the Waffen SS picked out on their collars. One of them handed Wachsberger the postcard-size paper with the instructions Dannecker had prepared.

Arminio read the words and shook his head, saying in German there must be a mistake. One of the soldiers glanced at the piece of paper in his hand, looked at the apartment number on the door, and said: *"Kein Fehler"*—no mistake.

Behind Arminio in the corridor stood Regina, Clara, and her parents. Wachsberger would later testify one of the soldiers had glanced at the family and said: *"Alle müssen kommen"*—everyone has to come.

The other soldier was reassuring. He said Regina's parents would be expected to do only light work at the labor camp where they were being transferred. Clara would be looked after at the nursery. They should bring with them anything of value and all their money to buy things at the camp store.

The soldiers stood in the doorway watching the family packing. Arminio asked them to dress in their best clothes so as to make a good impression when they arrived at the camp. He chose his new suit and a pair of shoes he had recently bought. Within the twenty-minute time limit the family were ready to leave. The adults carried suitcases. Clara clutched a doll. Arminio locked the apartment behind him as other doors opened in the corridor and their non-Jewish neighbors stood there in their nightclothes too stunned to speak.

Down in the street the family was pushed into a truck. Arminio was pulled aside by one of the soldiers and ordered to tell everyone who was already in the truck they would be shot if they tried to jump. He prodded Arminio with his rifle into the truck.

All across the ghetto the arresting teams went about their business. A description of their work has survived.

"From a doorway of Via del Tempio several women with children are pushed brusquely toward the street. The children are crying. Everywhere you hear the heartbreaking cries and pleading of the victims while the thugs—some violent, some indifferent—perform their duty without any sign of human pity. One group of people, mostly women and children, are piled into a truck. It all seems like a scene out of Purgatory."

Seated beside the driver of one of the trucks was Celeste di Porto. Kappler had recommended her to Dannecker as a guide around the ghetto.

On her way to morning Mass Marchesa Ripa di Meana had seen a truck coming out of the ghetto filled with women and children. She was to remember, "I saw their terror-stricken eyes, their faces grown pale as if with pain, their quivering hands that clung to the side of the truck, the maddening fear that had overtaken them by what they had seen and heard and the atrocious anguish in their hearts in anticipation of what awaited them.". She was among the first to telephone the Vatican and alert Father Leiber.

Shortly after eight o'clock that Saturday morning the secretary of state, Maglione, telephoned Ambassador Ernst Weizsaecker to request information about reports that a roundup was underway of Rome's Jews. The ambassador said he had no knowledge of "any such operation" but would make immediate inquiries.

In the meantime Princess Enza Pignatelli Aragona Cortes had also seen trucks carrying men, women, and children into the *Collegio Militare,* close to where she lived. More trucks passed her as she drove to the Vatican.

A close friend of Pius, she was admitted at once to the papal apartment, where the pope and Maglione listened in silence as she described what she had seen for herself.

The pope's first orders were given calmly. Maglione was to continue to stay in contact with Weizsäcker. Father Pankratius was to obtain information from the German high command in Rome. The secretary of state's two assistants—Montini and Tardini—were to work together to contact the religious houses where Jews were being sheltered and told what was happening. Father Leiber was to inform Osborne and Tittmann and ask them if their governments would protest to Berlin; the pope's secretary would make a similar request to neutral missions to the Holy See. Pascalina was to inform Chief Rabbi Zolli and ask him to convey the news to all the other Jews hiding in the Vatican. D'Altishofen, the Guardia Palatina commander, was to contact the Rome police for information. Ottaviani was to inform O'Flaherty, who should send his priests out into the streets to establish what was happening. The Vatican switchboard was alerted and it began to handle priority calls from the network Pius had mobilized to help the Jews.

Through the long day Pius remained in his office receiving reports and issuing new orders. To Father Leiber he was "leading the smallest state on earth to challenge the military masters of Rome. It was clear that upon his courage and decision-making would depend the lives of those being taken into the military college."

14

BLACK SATURDAY

Ambassador von Weizsäcker had turned his office into a command post. He had called Kesselring's headquarters at Frascati and was told that the field marshal was in a planning meeting and could not be disturbed. A call to the German embassy in Rome produced the news that Moellhausen had been summond to Berlin and the embassy was now in the charge of its first secretary, Gerhard Gumpert. He was a thirty-three-year-old lawyer whose post as economic attaché was to organize food supplies to be sent from Italy to Germany.

Weizsäcker decided to send Kessel to the embassy to see what Gumpert was doing. He found Gumpert fielding a call from one of the city's Fascist newspapers inquiring about the roundup. Kessel told him to stop taking any further calls—"even if it is the pope himself"—before they decided what to do and say.

When Gumpert had hesitated and suggested he should contact the foreign ministry in Berlin Kessel would recall: "I told him there was no time for that. Unless we could find a way to halt this operation it would have a serious effect on Germany's relations with the Vatican."

If Gumpert wished to contact anyone it should be *Stadtkommandant* Stahel and Kessel said he would help him to compose a letter to the general.

———

Sometime on Saturday Dannecker received news in his temporary office in the *Collegio Militare* that the deportation train would arrive on Monday morning. The timing carried the usual caveat—"subject to surviving air attacks." There would be sufficient freight cars to carry a thousand people.

Dannecker realized to fulfill his original quota he would have to leave behind several thousand Jews. In the past they would have been held in a local prison until they could be transported; he had ordered his men to do that in several cities in eastern Europe. But in Rome such action would provoke a citywide uprising; neither did he have the men to guard them in the nearby Regina Coeli prison until another train could arrive. The two SS companies were due to be returned to General Stahel's command to assist Kappler in dealing with the Resistance.

Dannecker summoned his officer in charge of the Jews already in the *Collegio Militare*. He reported that close to five hundred had been rounded up in the past four hours. Dannecker came to a decision. The roundup would continue until 2 P.M. when by then another five hundred could have been arrested. The barracks could then be prepared to defend itself until Monday against any attacks by the Resistance. While a thousand Jews was far less than he had originally planned to arrest, Dannecker knew it would still be a significant number for Eichmann.

Angelo Anticoli, the ghetto goldsmith who had weighed the gold collection, was arrested with his wife and their two young sons. They found themselves on the same truck as their cousin, Lazzaro Anticoli. His wife, Emma, held Rosa close to her to keep her warm; her husband sat beside her with Mario on his knee, stroking the child's hair and reassuring everyone around them that everything would be alright.

Throughout the ghetto and selected addresses in Trastevere the SS troopers hammered on doors, presented a postcard with its instructions, waited while the occupants packed in the prescribed time, and escorted them to a truck.

Mose Spizzichino and his family were in their kitchen when the knocking came on the front door and two soldiers came in. Settimia pointed to her married sister, Gentile, and to her small son and said they were not even Jews but Catholics who worked for the family. Mose and the others chorused confirmation. One of the Germans asked Gentile if she was a Catholic. She made a passable sign of the cross. The soldiers looked at each other. One used his rifle to motion toward the front door and said: *"Raus"*—out. Mose yelled at his daughter in Hebrew to leave. She scooped up her son and ran from the house.

In the German embassy in Villa Wolkonsky, Kessel and Gumpert studied their copies of the typed letter addressed to *Stadtkommandant* Stahel. It read:

"I must speak to you on a matter of great urgency. An authoritative dignitary who is close to the Holy Father has just told me that this morning a series of arrests of Jews of Italian nationality has been initiated. In the interests of good relations that have existed until now between the Vatican and the high command of the German armed forces—and above all thanks to the political wisdom and magnanimity of Your Excellency, which will one day go down in the history of Rome—I earnestly request that you order the immediate suspension of these arrests both in Rome and its environs. Otherwise I fear that the pope will take a position in public as being against this action, one which would undoubtedly be used by the anti-German propagandists as a weapon against us Germans."

Kessel said it should be signed by Gumpert as pro tem ambassador and a copy was to be hand carried to Weizsäcker in the Villa Napoleon.

Bishop Alois Hudal was awakened with news of the roundup by Father Pankratius Pfeiffer who said the pope was "very concerned" about what was happening.

Hudal asked what steps had been taken so far. Pfeiffer said Pius was in constant conference with his senior advisors.

The bishop, so long banished from papal circles, saw an opportunity to regain favor when Pfeiffer explained about the letter written under Gumpert's signature to Stahel. Hudal told Pfeiffer the letter must not be sent until he read it. Pfeiffer said he would bring a copy to Hudal within an hour.

It was midmorning when Weizsäcker was shown into Maglione's office. The secretary of state said the ambassador must intervene with the foreign minister in Berlin to have the roundup cancelled "for the sake of humanity and Christian charity."

Weizsäcker's response came after a pause. "It would be more powerful if the pope was to publicly protest against the deportation."

The words would form part of the claims and counterclaims of what followed in the short meeting between the two diplomats. Weizsäcker claimed he praised the Holy See for its balanced attitude throughout the war and asked if it "was worthwhile putting everything in danger just as the ship is reaching port?"

Maglione would insist, "I reminded him that the Holy See had no wish to be put in a position where it is necessary to protest but if the Holy See is obliged to do so I trust the consequences to divine providence."

In the ghetto a long line of people waited for the trucks to return empty from the *Collegio Militare*. They included a disabled man in a chair which his two sons were carrying and women who were weeping. One was cradling her bag of belongings and talking to it as if it was a child. A mother carrying a baby knelt before a trooper, imploring him to let her find water for her infant to drink. But the soldier shoved her back into the line and threatened to drown the baby in the Tiber.

All along the line came the sound of praying and the half-mad cries of the demented. When people begged to know where they were going, the soldiers pointed to the trucks and shouted for them to climb on board. The man in the chair was lifted, chair and all, onto the truck by his sons. He thanked them profusely for not leaving him behind.

In another truck Settimia Spizzichino sat with her sisters and her mother, who was crying. On the way to the truck Mose had quickly kissed his wife and suddenly rushed into an alley. Before a soldier could shoot the peddler had disappeared into another alley. The troopers had shrugged, shouting he would not get far.

On the second floor of the *Fatebenefratelli*, the K-Syndrome "patients" watched from the ward windows as the trucks roared up and down alongside the Tiber and wondered what was happening. Professor Boromeo had instructed no patient was to be told in case it caused panic.

Alina Cavaliera was arrested as she came out of her apartment by members of the Koch gang, who had been given a police van for the purpose. She had spent the previous evening studying plans for a hospital extension she was going to finance and wanted to show them to Professor Borromeo.

Elsewhere Giovanni Mezzaroma, head of the Black Panthers, had also been provided with a van. By noon he calculated he had earned over fifty thousand lire from hunting down wealthy Jews he had brought to the Regina Coeli prison.

They included Lionello Alatri and his wife, owners of Rome's largest department store and the father-in-law of Enrico Fermi, the Nobel physicist. On that day he was in the United States, part of the team developing the atomic bomb at Los Alamos. He would later admit his one ambition was to get the bomb ready in time to drop on Hitler's bunker in Berlin.

Hudal had been given a seat around the table for the noon meeting on Saturday which the pope regularly held in a salon in the Apostolic Palace with his senior advisors. They included Maglione, Montini and Tardini, Monsignor Leiber, Monsignor Ottaviani, and Father Pfeiffer.

After Maglione had reviewed his meeting with Weizsäcker, Ottaviani reported that the convents and religious houses were sheltering ghetto Jews who had managed to escape and Father Weber had brought a number into the Vatican.

Each person had before him a copy of the letter Gumpert and Kessel had composed and which Pankratius had brought to Hudal. It now became the subject of discussion.

Hudal said he found the content acceptable but that the signatory was too low-ranking to represent the views expressed. As it involved the Holy See it should be signed by someone with a suitable rank in the Vatican as he was certain then that General Stahel would transmit the letter to Berlin. Further it should be brought to the *Stadtkommandant* by Father Pfeiffer to reinforce the letter represented the Holy See's position.

While agreeing to this approach, Maglione had a question: Who should sign the letter? Hudal said he would be honored to put his name to the letter. It was left to the pope to say the document should not be written on Vatican stationery but on Bishop Hudal's German college notepaper as its rector. This would be interpreted by his critics as "evidence" that the pope did not wish to be further involved in the fate of the Jews.

Count de Salis had driven his car as far as Via del Portico d'Ottavia, the entrance to the ghetto, where he was stopped by Rome police. Farther down the road he saw people being pushed onto a truck. He had followed the vehicle to the *Collegio Militare* to find his way blocked by more police. He returned to his office and telephoned the Red Cross headquarters in Geneva. He was told to continue his efforts to contact the Jews and discover the extent of the roundup.

By 2 p.m. Dannecker was informed there were 1,259 people in the barracks compound, 859 of which were women and children. From past experience he concluded that many Jewish men, believing the Germans were only interested in able-bodied males, would have gone into hiding at the start of the operation.

On those occasions he had his troops lay in wait for days, knowing the men would return to search for their families. But he didn't have time to do that now. In thirty-six hours the train would have come and gone on its way to Auschwitz.

What he needed now was an interpreter. One of his officers had told him there was a German-speaking Jew in the roundup. He even had a German name—Wachsberger. Dannecker asked for him to be brought to his office.

———

D'Arcy Osborne tried to keep track of the roundup and had sent a telegram to the Foreign Office containing the scant details he had obtained from May's contact with O'Flaherty.

He had met with Tittmann and agreed the barracks was only a temporary holding point to the deportation and discussed if it would be possible for the Allies to bomb the railroad and halt it long enough for the SOE and OSS to free the Jews. Osborne had been told by Derry they were operating in Italy.

Unknown to the minister the code breakers at Bletchley Park had been tracking messages between Dannecker, Eichmann's office, and on that Saturday morning, a signal from SS Commander Wilhelm Harster, chief of the security police in Italy, confirming the deportation train would be numbered X70469 and Dannecker was to give two copies of his list of passengers to the head of the SS guard unit on board. His name was SS *Oberscharführer* Arndze. Dannecker was instructed to inform him to "hand over the copies upon arrival at Auschwitz."

While the intercept was being decoded at Bletchley Park, D'Arcy Osborne continued to seek an audience with the pope. On Saturday afternoon he was told it would be on Monday.

In the barracks square, watched by Dannecker, Wachsberger carried out his first order as a translator. Standing on a table he told the crowd, first in Italian and then in Hebrew, that they were to be divided into groups, each no more than seventy-five persons, with women and children separated from the men. They would be taken to classrooms where they would receive food to supplement what they had brought with them.

From among the crowd people started to wave their identity papers and shout they were not Jews and should be released. Wachsberger translated the request to Dannecker. His tic flicking his head from side to side, he said their papers would be examined later and if genuine they would be set free. The shouting stopped when the translation was completed.

Dannecker continued to bark out his orders which Wachsberger translated. They would be remaining in the college until Monday when they would be taken to the station where a train would bring them to the labor camp. In the meantime if anyone attempted to escape they would be shot. A similar fate awaited those who tried to attack the guards.

At 5 P.M. Father Pfeiffer arrived at General Stahel's office in the Hotel Flora and handed over the letter bearing Hudal's signature. After reading it Stahel sighed, shook his head, and summoned his aide to take it to the communications room to have it encoded and transmitted to the Foreign Office in Berlin. The matter was now in other hands, the general said.

Back in his office in the Apostolic Palace Father Pfeiffer informed Maglione and Hudal of Stahel's decision. The secretary of state told Father Pfeiffer to inform Weizsäcker.

Pfeiffer's confirmation it was on its way to Berlin was the signal for Weizsäcker to prepare his own response to the roundup. He began to write in a fine copperplate.

"With regards to Bishop Hudal's letter I can confirm that this represents the Vatican's reaction to the deportation of the Jews of Rome. The Curia is especially upset considering that the action took place, in a manner of speaking, under the pope's own window. The reaction could be dampened somewhat if the Jews were to be employed in labor service here in Italy. Hostile circles in Rome are using this event as a means of pressuring the Vatican to drop its reserve. It is being said that when analogous incidents took place in French cities, the bishops there took a clear stand. Thus the pope, as the supreme leader of the church and as bishop of Rome, cannot but do the same. The pope is also being compared with his predecessor, Pius XI, a man of more spontaneous temperament. Enemy propaganda abroad will certainly view this event in the same way, in order to disturb the Curia and ourselves."

He signed and sealed the letter and put it aside to go in the diplomatic pouch to Wilhelmstrasse in Berlin. That decision would later arouse more speculation than anything else Weizsäcker had done during his tenure in Rome. Was the letter a clear indication he was prepared to risk his career, and very likely his life, to try and save the Jews? If so, knowing the urgency of the situation, why had he not immediately encoded it and sent it to Berlin? The diplomatic pouch would not leave until Monday. By then, he could reasonably deduce, the fate of the Jews would be settled. From what he had heard *Judenaktionen* were swift operations.

Elsewhere on that Saturday evening others were expressing their views. The military council of the Resistance met in secret to review the reports of partisans who had watched the Jews being brought to the *Collegio Militare*. Several knew the barracks from their days as students there and ruled out an attack. Even dynamite would not breach the massive stone block walls of the old military school, and an assault would also undoubtedly lead to the Jews being slaughtered by their guards. It was decided that attacks on German targets in the city should be increased to make the occupiers hesitate about holding the Jews. The council was however short of a crucial piece of intelligence. When did the Germans intend to move the Jews out of Rome and to where? To know that would provide an opportunity to destroy the rail tracks.

In another quarter of the city the latest edition of the underground newspaper *L'Italia Libera* was being prepared for press. A powerful front-page editorial was intended to arouse the fury of readers against the Germans.

"They have gone around Rome seizing Italians for their furnaces in the north. The Germans would like us to believe that these people are in some way alien to us, that they are from another race. But we feel them as part of our flesh and blood. They have always lived, fought, and suffered with us. Not only able-bodied men, but old people, children, women, and babies were crowded into covered trucks and taken away to meet their fate. There is not a single heart that does not shudder at the thought of what that fate might be.

"But the soldiers who carried out such an inhuman task, so coldly, so fearlessly, and without a shred of pity in their eyes also have loved ones, far away: mothers, wives, children, sisters. And even they sometimes warm with nostalgia when they hear a song of their youth. Any party or national discipline that dehydrates and petrifies a man's heart to such an extent, that muffles every human feeling, that degrades man into automation, is a poison that must be cauterized with fire and iron.

"We do not hate anymore; we are horrified. Not until Europe is freed of this nightmare, can there be any hope for peace. No one thinks of taking revenge against women and children, but these Nazi soldiers, their lackeys, spies, and cutthroat Fascists, must be silenced for all time, buried forever in this very land they dared to profane with so much shame."

The words would reach Radio Bari, the voice of King Victor Emmanuel broadcasting from behind Allied lines. In turn the station's broadcast was picked up by the BBC in London and passed to the United Press International wire service. Its story reached the United States in time for the Sunday edition of its newspapers. Americans were told what was happening to the Jews of Rome.

In the *Collegio Militare* Dannecker had ordered three tables to be set up in the square. On the center one stood Wachsberger with a bullhorn in his hand so that his voice carried into the classrooms around the square. At the middle table sat a young woman before a typewriter; she had answered a call for someone to do secretarial work. On the third table were two large boxes before which Dannecker stood, his head flicking from side to side as he watched the Jews gathering. The captain told his translator to order them to form a line which began to snake around the square and whose head ended before the table.

Dannecker broke the silence. Each person was to place in his or her right hand all the valuables—jewelry and cash—they had brought with them. They were then to come forward and give their name to the typist and state if they were a Jew or non-Jew. After giving their name and religion they were to deposit their jewelry in one box and money in the other.

What followed would be captured in Wachsberger's later words.

"Through me he told us that we were to be transported to Germany to a camp where according to our skill, we would have a job to do. Since the old, the invalid, and women with children would naturally be unable to work and since the German government had no intention of maintaining them free of charge, all money, jewelry, and other objects of value that we had brought with us had to be surrendered to create a communal fund. He concluded by saying that the rich Jews among us must pay for the poor Jews."

One by one people shuffled forward, the fit and ill, the old and young, the weeping and the strong-faced, the silent and the shocked, the rich and the poor. They gave their names and admitted their faith; many with pride and courage.

From this vantage position Wachsberger watched them coming forward. His words conveyed the horror of what was happening.

"Whenever someone deposited a piece of jewelry of particular value, Dannecker put it in his pocket and we soon caught on that it had all been a trick to strip us of our goods."

In the Vatican, Secretary of State Maglione waited in his office for news of a response to Hudal's letter. He had told the switchboard to immediately put through any call from Weizsäcker. Montini and Tardini remained at their desks ready to deal with any calls from Osborne, Tittmann, or any of the other foreign diplomats in Santa Marta. So far there had been none.

Hudal asked Dollmann to join him in his college office and encouraged him to use the bishop's telephone to call his contacts in Rome to gauge their responses to the roundup. Several had told him that it would make the Germans increase their hold over the city if the Resistance launched a full-scale attack.

Father Pfeiffer was still in his office in the Apostolic Palace and had arranged with Sister Pascalina to call him once there were any developments. She had told him the pope was at prayer in his chapel. In the meantime the priest was carefully reading the editorials in Rome's two leading newspapers. Neither mentioned the roundup.

That night the peace of Rome was broken by the Resistance mounting its largest attack against the Germans and their collaborators, the Fascist street gangs. Pitched battles took place around the Pantheon, the Piazza Navona, and along the Corso. Members of the Koch gang and the Black Panthers, who had taken to wearing black berets with a silver skull, were shot and their bodies left in the road. By the time German armored cars arrived the Resistance had vanished to reappear elsewhere to launch another attack.

Inside the *Collegio Militare* people sleeping on the classroom floors awoke to the sound of gunfire. They huddled together, listening and fearful.

Settimia Spizzichino and her sisters grouped themselves around their mother, stroked her face, and wiped her tears and offered reassurance that their father was alive and in hiding. Grazia had nodded, too exhausted to speak. In other groups people were similarly trying to comfort each other—if their relatives were not there, they must have escaped.

There were forty-one members of Umberto di Veroli's relatives in the barracks, the largest number of a family caught in the roundup. But he and his wife and their eleven children had managed to flee at the outset of the roundup.

In the darkness men and women recalled other escapes they had seen: the family who had jumped, one after the other out of a window; men running along rooftops; a mother throwing her baby down to a neighbor; the youth who had carried his mother on his back. All had vanished before the Germans could catch them.

Rosina Sorani and her brother, Settimio, had spent the day in their apartment wondering what they should do. She had been on her way to work when she saw the trucks parking on the Via del Portico d'Ottavia. She had calmly turned round and retraced her steps. From then on they had taken turns to use the telephone; Rosina to try and contact Foa, her brother to reach Father Weber and Renzo Levi. Settimio finally contacted the Pallottine priest late in the afternoon who said he would come at once. When he arrived he explained he had been in the Vatican all day helping to deal with the situation.

Weber said he would take them to where Foa, Almansi, and Levi met after going into hiding. It was a dairy shop run by a Catholic widow and her daughter. While she provided them with coffee, the three most powerful men in the Jewish community listened to Weber's news.

They had discussed how they could save the Jews. Foa suggested he should write an appeal to the pope to intervene. Weber said Pius was doing all he could. Levi proposed a direct approach should be made to either the German embassy or its mission to the Holy See to ask for the freedom for the old and sick and the women and children. He would personally guarantee to pay any sum of money in exchange for their release. The money would be raised from America. Weber had asked how long it would take to find such a sum. Levi thought it would take "a few days." The Pallottine father had looked at the others and said he feared there were only hours left in which to negotiate any deal.

Nevertheless Ugo Foa decided he would still write to the pope and Weber said he would bring the letter to the Vatican. When he gave it to Pfeiffer it contained a sentence which caught his attention. Foa had written there were a number of people in the ghetto who were classified under the racial laws as *Mischlinge*—the offspring of parents who were of mixed religion. Some, Foa wrote, had even been baptized and while they still lived in the ghetto were regarded as Catholics. They should be allowed to go free.

Pfeiffer hurried to see Maglione. After reading the letter the secretary of state produced a copy of the racial laws and found the relevant passage. He had taken the book and Foa's letter with him to the pope. Pius told Maglione to inform Weizsäcker and asked to intervene to have the *Mischlinge* freed and arrange for a senior member of the Vatican to go to the *Collegio Militare*, taking with him a copy of the racial laws to show to the officer in charge. Maglione proposed sending Bishop Hudal, given he was the signatory of the letter to Stahel.

Hudal's role in the roundup has remained secret until now. In his own notes of the matter Maglione only referred to him as a "Vatican official."

On Sunday morning, dressed in his bishop's robes, Hudal introduced himself to Dannecker at the entrance to the *Collegio Militare* as "the most senior Reverend Alois Hudal, the senior German-speaking bishop abroad."

Twenty-one months later he would use similar words to receive Heinrich Mueller in his palatial office in the Pan-Germanic college to discuss with the former German gestapo chief the help Nazi war criminals needed from Hudal to obtain travel documents to hide in South America.

There is no evidence the pope and the Vatican were implicated in the matter—let alone an organization which became known as ODESSA, which appears to have been the brainchild of Hudal. In 2011 Mossad files show that figures like Franz Stangl, the *commandant* of Treblinka; Klaus Barbie; Martin Bormann; and Adolf Eichmann were all assisted with false papers and hiding places provided by Hudal while they were en route to hide in Latin America at the end of the war.

The details emerged in 1945 when Dannecker was captured and interrogated by American forces. He had been hiding in Bad Tölz in Bavaria organizing Nazi resistance to the Allied occupation. He had already instructed his wife to poison their two children; one died, the other was saved. Dannecker was found hanging in his cell awaiting trial.

That Sunday morning at the *Collegio Militare* what passed between them ended with Dannecker agreeing with Hudal that 274 "non-Jews"—spouses and offspring—caught in the roundup were to be set free.

They left the barracks soon after the bishop drove back to the Vatican. In the meantime Weizsäcker had told Maglione he was unable to help free the non-Jews.

After the excitement following the departure of the *Mischlinge*, Sunday passed slowly in the barracks. Beyond the walls the city was quiet and some people wrote letters with no idea if they would be allowed to post them. Others lay on the ground, curled up, trying to sleep or waiting for the next food to be handed out. Small groups sat together and discussed what kind of work they would have to do when they reached the labor camp.

Sunday had been a busy one for Count de Salis. He had gone to the ghetto and found it deserted. However by noon some of the *Mischlinge* had returned home to collect precious items they had been forced to leave behind before they left again to go into hiding. Several had told the Red Cross director they were terrified the Germans would arrive to bring them back to the barracks and he drove several families to convents where they were warmly welcomed.

By early afternoon he had been joined by Father Patrick Carroll-Abbing and his ambulance, Father Borsarelli driving the Sacret Heart monastery car to carry people into hiding.

De Salis had also contacted the German embassy. The acting ambassador, Gerhard Gumpert, told him he had no news regarding when the Jews would leave the barracks—or their destination. Another call to General Stahel's office produced the same response. That evening de Salis visited Princess Enza Pignatelli and the Marchesa Ripa di Meana. They had been promised by Sister Pascalina they would be kept informed of any developments.

Sister Luke wrote in her diary for Sunday: "We know nothing about their destination. It is an absolute horror. People you know and esteem, brave, kind, upright people, just because they have Jewish blood, are treated like this."

In the barracks Settimia Spizzichino awoke into a Monday dawn in which everything remained as beyond her control as it had been when she had fallen asleep. All around her people were sitting up in response to the shouts of the soldiers walking among them. Those who did not move fast enough were kicked or prodded with rifles.

From the courtyard came a roar of truck engines starting. Settimia helped her mother to her feet, her body stiff from lying on the cold floor. Children had started to cry as they were ordered to move out into the courtyard.

Settimia led the way. In the light her mother looked like a ghost, moving slowly as a soldier pushed them to a truck. It quickly filled with fearful people; even the children were now too frightened to cry. A shout came from outside and the truck lurched forward past the life-sized statue of Julius Caesar and under the archway with its motto, ROMANA VIRTUS ROMANA DISCITUR—Roman virtues are learned in Rome.

The truck crossed the Tiber and into the city that was still waiting for the curfew to be lifted. As they were filled other trucks followed, and the convoy passed landmarks familiar to every Jew on board: the piazzas, the monuments, and the palaces. Finally they reached Rome's marshalling rail yards, still bearing the scars of the first American bombing. The trucks halted before a solitary freight train, its sliding doors open. Lined up before each car were SS troopers. Standing to one side was SS *Ober-scharführer* Arndze, the train commander, and Dannecker. He handed over the two lists he had prepared of the Jews to be deported. It totalled 1,007 men, women, and children.

The two officers exchanged Heil Hitler salutes and Dannecker walked past the trucks to the waiting car. His role in the deportation was finished. After a few days' leave in Rome he would travel to Florence to prepare another *Judenaktion*.

As each freight car filled the door was rolled shut.

President Foa had left Rome. He had concluded there was no more he could do after the "non-Jews had been freed." His destination was Leghorn, the Tuscany town of his birth. He would later insist he felt no guilt for not having urged the Jews of Rome to leave. The last of the 1,007 of Foa's community who had answered his appeal for gold under the guarantee of their safety were forced into the freight cars.

In 1998 a document released under the Nazi War Crimes Disclosure Act concluded Foa had "hoped for the best from Kappler but only received misleading information during the gestapo chief's demand for the fifty kilograms of gold."

D'Arcy Osborne's scheduled audience with the pope for that Monday had been brought forward to midday. He began by thanking the pope for the sanctuary he was providing Jews and Allied prisoners which had saved so many lives.

The minister explained there was nothing practical Britain could do except to use the BBC to castigate the roundup. The Allies' land forces were still some distance from reaching Rome, and while they regularly flew north on bombing missions it would be difficult to persuade the strategic planners to divert aircraft to disrupt a deportation train. Similar requests to bomb Nazi death camps in Germany had been made and rejected.

Rome's rumor mill was beginning to spin that Hitler would soon abandon the city to fight in the hills in the north. Osborne doubted it was likely to happen in the near future. But if the Resistance used the roundup as an opportunity to repeat what they had been doing for the past few days, it was possible the Nazis would launch a bloodbath in retaliation.

Osborne decided he would ask the pope a question.

However he phrased it—and Osborne was a master at subtlety—he knew he was asking the pope if he would consider leaving the Vatican as a mark of protest over the roundup.

Pius was emphatic: He would never leave, not after the plot to kidnap him, not for any reason.

Osborne's encoded telegram that evening to London about the deportation concluded, "The pope underestimates his own moral authority. Everything he says and does is done with the knowledge he would have to answer to God. No person can have done more to help the Jews."

By then the last freight car had been loaded and sealed and the deportation train had moved out of the marshalling yard on its journey to Auschwitz.

15

BEFORE THE DAWN

Neither Radio Rome nor the city newspapers reported the deportation. Nevertheless the news spread across the city and there was growing fury.

The military council of the Resistance met in an emergency session to discuss what action to take. It was agreed the train was by now out of range to launch any form of rescue from Rome. Even if the partisans in Florence, the train's first refuelling stop, were alerted there was no guarantee the Resistance in the city would have the resources to act in time before the train continued its journey out of Italy. But the decision was taken to continue attacking the German forces in Rome.

Those who had escaped the ghetto roundup disappeared into the countryside and equipped themselves with false names and documents. Others joined the Resistance. Many still hesitated to seek shelter in various religious houses. Giuseppe Gay, a ghetto taxi driver, had decided he and his wife would hide in the city's lunatic asylum because he feared being in a convent would require them to convert to Catholicism.

———

On Wednesday, October 20, Maglione had informed the pope that any response to Hudal's letter to Stahel would not be forthcoming. The bishop had been told by Eugen Dollmann that in his own conversation with Weizsäcker the ambassador had said it was no longer a matter for discussion.

Five days after the train had left Rome it had passed through the Reich protectorate of Bohemia and Moravia, crossed the border into Czechoslovakia, and entered Poland on the Jewish Sabbath. A week after the roundup the train reached Auschwitz.

Within hours of their arrival all but 196 Jews of the ghetto were gassed.

In his office in *L'Osservatore Romano* editor Count Giuseppe Dalla Torre proofread an editorial for the next edition:

"The pontiff has not desisted for one moment in employing all the means in his power to alleviate the suffering, which whatever form it may take, is the consequence of this cruel conflagration. With so much evil, the universal and paternal charity of the pontiff has become, it could be said, even more active; it knows neither boundaries, religion, or race. This manifold and ceaseless activity on the part of Pius XII has intensified even more in recent times in regard for the increased suffering of so many unfortunate people."

As usual the publication was the first newspaper Weizsäcker read on its arrival in Villa Napoleon on Sunday morning.

That afternoon he sat in his office and drafted what would be seen as a self-serving telegram to von Ribbentrop. It read:

"The pope, although under pressure from all sides, has not permitted himself to be pushed into demonstrative censure of the deportation of the Jews of Rome. Although he must know that such an attitude will be used against him by our adversaries and will be exploited by Protestant circles in the Anglo-Saxon countries for the purpose of anti-Catholic propaganda. He has nonetheless done everything possible even in this delicate matter in order not to strain relations with the German government and the German authorities in Rome. As there apparently will be no further

German action taken on the Jewish Question here, it may be said that this matter, so unpleasant as it regards German-Vatican relations, has been liquidated."

The document would form part of Weizsäcker's war crimes trial in 1948 in Nuremberg. Among those who wrote testimonials presented to the court were Pope Pius XII thanking the ambassador for "trying to help the Jews." Another affidavit was written by Bishop Hudal in which he spoke of the ambassador's "courage." Von Kessel testified how Weizsäcker had tried to help the Jews. But the prosecutors showed Weizsäcker had signed the minutes of the Wannsee Conference which launched the Final Solution. Weizsäcker was convicted and sentenced to seven years in prison. In 1950 he was released and wrote his memoirs. It contained no reference to the Jews of Rome. He died in 1951.

In his daily meetings with Maglione the issue of public order had become a constant concern to the pope. In the weeks following the deportation Resistance attacks had increased, with partisans throwing homemade bombs from the backs of trucks. A trattoria near a German barracks was hit, killing eight soldiers; six more died as they came out of a cinema reserved exclusively for occupying troops. In another attack a hand grenade was hurled by a cyclist into a van filled with troops. Six died as the youth zigzagged into the safety of a dark alley.

The city's new *Stadtkommandant,* General Kurt Mälzer, had the walls of Rome plastered with a new poster warning that anyone attacking soldiers would be shot on the spot if caught no matter their age or sex.

He had also ordered troops to check the city's hospitals for wounded partisans who were to be taken to Regina Coeli jail to await execution. However when a patrol arrived at the *Fatebenefratelli* Professor Borromeo told them that while he would permit them to enter they must sign a paper absolving the hospital if they contracted the deadly K-Syndrome illness. The soldiers hurriedly left.

The pope asked the priests of Rome to appeal from their pulpits for a halt to the fighting. The attacks continued and slogans were daubed on walls that the Resistance would never forget the Jews of the ghetto.

Thousands were now in hiding either in the Vatican or in religious

houses across Rome. With them were anti-Nazis, Rome politicians, diplomats, and lawyers; all were Catholics with a price on their heads.

One of the Jews who had escaped the roundup was Michael Tagliacozzo. Twenty-two years old in October 1943, he would survive to become
a notable Jewish historian describing his time in hiding in the basilica of
St. John Lateran. He recalled:

"I remember fondly a priest turned to me, knowing that among the
refugees I was the closest to the Jewish traditions. He begged me to in-
struct him in the Jewish dietary laws, so that the sentiments of the refugees would not be offended. He gave me a Bible in Hebrew that inspired
me with faith and hope."

The Gregorian University could only take male refugees. Father Leiber,
the pope's secretary, arranged for them to have Vatican identification cards
with their photographs and the signature and seal of the assistant vicar of
Rome. They were all described as students of philosophy.

Jewish families—some from the ghetto, others refugees that Father
Weber's organization had smuggled into Rome—were also hidden in sem-
inaries. For both the priests and their students the presence of men, women,
and children required adjustment on both sides.

In the *Seminario Lombardo* space was limited and newcomers were often young and boisterous. To accommodate the seminary's strict rules the
rector insisted the Jews must maintain their own rooms, keep to the time-
table for eating, and practice going quickly to their hiding place behind a
secret door in the basement. The seminary organized lectures by its tu-
tors and concerts by the seminarians and a room was set aside to celebrate
the Sabbath. A similar lifestyle was happening in all the religious houses
where Jews were hiding.

On November 1, 1943, Romans had been told that one of the defining
features of the occupation, the curfew, had once again been changed; it
was now fixed from midnight to 5 A.M., a period when everyone must be
inside unless they had a new pass which must be obtained from police
headquarters.

Romans saw the change as linked to General Mälzer's promise to
hunt down the Resistance. In his first broadcast on Radio Rome the

Stadtkommandant said he would catch "the rats in our midst" and that all those who helped him would be rewarded.

In the five hours of the new nightly curfew the Banda Koch and the Black Panthers, led by Kappler's gestapo, had roamed the streets. In a few days they had struck with deadly effect.

They uncovered a Resistance bomb-making factory on the Via Giulia. The discovery was important enough to awaken Kappler and bring him rushing from the bed of his mistress, Helen Brouwer. His report to Mälzer claimed, "We found enough explosives to blow up half of Rome." The two bomb makers were taken to Kappler's interrogation center and tortured before being brought to Rome's Fort Bravetta and shot in the prison yard.

Two nights later the Koch gang were led to the printing press of *L'Italia Libera* by Francesco Argentino, a former officer of Mussolini's secret detail. Editor Leone Ginzberg, who had written his powerful article on the fate of the ghetto Jews, was tortured in his office and shot before the printing press was destroyed. Names found in the newspaper office were passed to Kappler and his gestapo rounded up a number of the Resistance. All would be executed.

But a bigger coup was under way. The target was the monastery adjoining the basilica St. Paul Outside the Walls. Argentino had revealed the monastery was a hiding place for Jews and other escapers.

Kappler had told Koch and Mezzaroma that for every Jew they caught their fee was now increased by one thousand lire, to six thousand lire. However, when the two gang leaders said they needed more men to carry out the raid, Kappler hesitated: To involve his officers in an attack on Vatican property could have serious problems for him. He ordered Police Chief Pietro Caruso to provide a senior officer to lead the operation together with policemen to support the criminal gangs. It made a total of sixty armed men.

A fascist monk, Don Ildefonso, known as the Koch gang's priest, hammered on the monastery door and shouted he wanted sanctuary because he was being chased by the Germans. A priest peered through the door's Judas window, saw the figure in monk's robes, and opened the door.

The attackers rushed in and began to search the monastery. Inside an hour they had caught an Italian air force general dressed as a monk, nine army officers, and eleven Jews.

On Friday, November 5, the pope and Father Leiber had their weekly supper served by Sister Pascalina. As usual there would be much to discuss. A few days ago troops had tried to search the Oriental Institute, the Vatican's center for the study of eastern churches, run by Jesuits. The rector of the institute had "forcefully" told the soldiers they were breaking international law and he had demanded their names. Stunned by his attitude, the troops withdrew. In the institute's dormitory in the basement thirty Jewish families slept unaware of how close they had come to discovery.

After the raid the pope had ordered that nuns and priests living in buildings under the Lateran Treaty were to maintain their guard during the night and immediately telephone the Vatican if any attempt to enter was made. A squad of auxiliary Gendarmerie was on standby to go to any protected building.

Sister Pascalina had served the meal when there was the sound of a plane. The pope and his secretary had gone to a window as it passed above St. Peter's Square and on over the Vatican gardens. In the darkness there was no sight of the aircraft. Suddenly there was an explosion. Then another, followed by a third and fourth. As quickly as it had appeared the aircraft disappeared.

Vatican firemen and Gendarmeries were running toward where fires had broken out. A bomb had fallen on a storage building near the railway station. Another fell close to a workshop. The third and fourth dropped between the Ethiopian college, where Jewish refugees were hiding, and Vatican Radio. The force of one explosion had broken windows in the Vatican museum and the sacristy of the Sistine Chapel.

Harold Tittmann and his wife, Eleanor, were playing their customary Friday evening game of bridge when the first explosion rocked their apartment in Santa Marta. They dived under the dining table to shelter from any falling debris. After the drone of the plane faded, the veteran Great War fighter pilot helped Eleanor to her feet and led the way down to the Santa Marta courtyard.

D'Arcy Osborne and John May were organizing people to follow them out into the Vatican gardens. Most of the windows in the convent on the far side of the courtyard had been blown out, but the building itself had

shielded the apartment block where the diplomats lived from blast damage and the nuns were already sweeping up broken glass and debris. A
doctor from the medical center was going from group to group to establish if anyone was injured. It turned out there was only one casualty, a
Guardia Palatina who had been on patrol on the grounds. Osborne remarked to May that "it's nothing compared to the Blitz." Picking his way
around bomb craters, the minister invited anyone who needed a drink to
join him in his apartment.

Several German officers arrived at the Bronze Door entrance to the
Vatican to express their readiness to provide men to help with rescue
work and make safe any damage. They were politely thanked by Father
Leiber and told the Vatican had everything under control.

Within hours Radio Rome announced that the attack had been carried
out by a British bomber. By then Sam Derry had gone with O'Flaherty to
cast his professional eye over the bomb-casing fragments: He concluded
the explosives were from fragmentation bombs.

Next morning Tittmann and Osborne made a more detailed examination of the damage. The Vatican *Governatorato,* its administration building,
had suffered considerable damage, as had the mosaic factory. The Bernini
stained-glass windows in St. Peter's were broken in several places. Monsignor Herisse, the canon of the basilica, who had been Tittmann's "leg-
man" with Delasem, estimated it would take a week to repair the damage.

Cardinal Maglione had asked Tittmann, Osborne, and Weizsäcker to
request their governments to conduct an immediate investigation into the
responsibility for the attack.

All three governments requested pieces of bomb fragments. On November 9, the State Department in Washington declared that no Allied
aircraft had flown over Rome on the evening of November 5. However a
number of British planes had carried out raids in the vicinity of Rome at
that time. Weizsäcker said Berlin was satisfied there was no German in-
volvement.

In his diary, Tittmann wrote on November 16: "The bomb fragments
did not lead to any conclusion to their origin. The identity of the airplane
that bombed the Vatican has remained a mystery, although the most
likely theory is that the bombs were jettisoned by a British aircraft
in distress."

Tittman would further claim on December 8, that anxiety in the Vatican increased as a "lone, single-engine plane reappeared on clear nights, flying low over Rome and over the Vatican. It became known as *la vedova nera,* the black widow."

Whatever its mission it dropped no bombs.

Sister Luke, whose contact with Pascalina gave her an insight into thinking in the Apostolic Palace, wrote that the bombing was the work of Roberto Farinacci who had flown a biplane in Mussolini's air force and was considered by Eugen Dollmann in his own debriefing by his OSS interrogators in 1945, as "the boldest and most determined Fascist of all."

He seemed a more likely candidate for the bombing of the Vatican than Tittmann's "British bomber in distress."

The Pope had asked Sister Pascalina to arrange for convents and monasteries hiding Jews to provide them with calendars to mark the weeks as they passed through *Cheshvan* (October), *Kislev* (November), and *Chanukah* (December), when, on the tenth of that month, to mark a feast day, the nuns and priests would provide candles in the rooms where their guests worshipped.

During Christmas week *Stadtkommandant* Mälzer announced he would allow extra provisions to be bought on ration cards, but to sell the goods on the black market would be punishable.

Throughout December the Resistance continued their attacks in retaliation for the roundup. Criminal gangs caught looting the ghetto had been shot by the partisans. A time bomb had been smuggled into the Excelsior Hotel where Field Marshal Kesselring stayed on his visits to Rome. The bomb had been placed in the elevator shaft and exploded shortly after Kesselring left to return to his headquarters. A German officer and a woman had been killed and the planned Christmas celebrations at the hotel were cancelled. Kappler had increased the manhunt for Resistance fighters. In the street battles a number of partisans were killed.

All bicycles—a favored means of escape by bomb throwers—were banned; anyone using one would be arrested. The traditional midnight Masses during Christmas week in all Rome parishes had already been changed to take place at 5 P.M., then were cancelled altogether. The only nativity service would be in St. Peter's.

Vatican Radio engineers had completed repairs from the November bomb damage and made a final test linking the station between the transmitter and the microphone in the pope's study from where Pius would make his third Christmas broadcast to the world.

A year ago, Christmas 1942, part of his message had finally seemed to be a response to a previous request by President Roosevelt for the pope to condemn the mass killing of Jews in the Nazi death camps. Toward the end of the broadcast he had spoken of "the hundreds and thousands who, through no fault of their own, and solely because of their nation or race, have been condemned to death or are progressively wasting away."

His words were seen as still lacking clarity in the State Department and Tittmann had been asked to discover exactly what the pope had meant. The envoy was firmly told in a short audience that Pius had spoken without a further need to explain he was referring to the Jews.

It was not until 1961, when he retired, that Tittmann revealed the pope's attitude. In his speech at St. Louis University the diplomat quoted Pius as saying to him:

"If I should denounce the Nazis by name as you desire and Germany should lose the war, Germans everywhere would feel that I had contributed to the defeat, not only of the Nazis, but of Germany herself; for the German people not to be able to make the distinction between the fatherland would only be human in the confusion and distress of defeat. I cannot afford to alienate so many of the faithful. Second, if I did denounce the Nazis by name, I must in all justice to do the same as regards the Bolsheviks whose principles are strikingly similar. You would not wish me to say such things about an ally of yours at whose side you are engaged today in a death struggle."

It was an attitude that would haunt the pope for the rest of his life and help to label him as "Hitler's pope." The perceptive Tittmann believed Pius could have avoided the smear if, at the start of the war he had said he intended to denounce "all atrocities without exception, in doing so he would not have been taking sides, nor would they affect in any way his traditional position of neutrality."

At noon on December 24 all the Allied diplomats and their families had gathered in the Santa Marta refractory to listen to the pope's radio broadcast. His address was short and dignified and dealt with the evils of war. He mentioned no names or nations. Sister Pascalina sat listening in the corner of his study.

In the Villa Napoleon First Secretary von Kessel decided the pope was trying to "influence the Western powers by aiming his message as a direct appeal to their people to end the war and see the dawning of a new spirit of world brotherhood." For Kappler, at home with his family, the words were "unlikely to provide any change of direction." In her convent Sister Luke had gathered with other nuns to listen to the broadcast as was happening in religious houses all over Rome. While she thought "the pope spoke clearly and distinctly and delivered sound Christian principles. I wonder will they be acted upon?"

On December 26, General Kurt Mälzer had promulgated his last order of 1943. There would be a census of the Romans. With the bucolic grin that became his trademark he had told his staff it would remind Romans of Herod's census of the Jews and the slaughter of their infants. Hours later the Koch gang broke into the college of the Russian church, the Russicum. The search of the building unearthed three elderly Jews hiding in the basement. Their fate would remain unknown.

Luciana Tedesco and the other children on the K-Syndrome wards had become used to the sound of gunfire and the regular crumps of bombs falling in the industrial suburbs and out in the hills. The nights would be suddenly brightly lit all over the city by parachute flares. Often the wind carried them onto Tiber Island and the nurses would rush out and cut off the parachutes from the spent flares. More than one nurse turned the silk into a blouse.

Dr. Sacerdoti brought regular news to the second-floor K-Syndrome "patients." The Vatican had sent a fleet of trucks to bring food from the countryside and a priority was given to hospitals. On another morning he said the Vatican had sent a squad of its Palatine Guards to help the Guardia Palatina protect all its extraterritorial properties including the hospital. They would live on the premises and guard the hospital entrances in their military cloaks with rifles with fixed bayonets.

St. Stephen's Day—Ireland's traditional second day of Christmas, O'Flaherty kept "open house" in his German college suite. His guests included parish priests in the city, Sam Derry, John May, and Count de Salis. Sir D'Arcy Osborne and Harold Tittmann dropped in for a drink, along with the Irish ambassador, Thomas Kiernan and his family. Monsignor Ottaviani and several members of the secretariat of state came. Sister Pascalina brought a cake.

Father Patrick Carroll-Abbing arrived with a banjo. O'Flaherty led the carol singing and ensured no one was without a drink. Some of the college nuns served jugs of coffee from their kitchen.

Apart from praise for the pope's broadcast there was no mention of the war, though its sound was never far away; outside heavy military vehicles were a constant background roar.

After the other guests left, Monsignor O'Flaherty's booming voice said it was business as usual.

Sam Derry said the census would have a serious effect on their work. Nuns and priests would have to post the name of everyone under their roof on the building's front door. Failure to do so would lead to a search of the premises. At most risk would be the safe houses run by Romans. Discovery of Allied soldiers or Jews inside would mean death for their hosts.

O'Flaherty was reassuring: The citizens of Rome would not let the Jews or the Allied escapees fall into the hands of those hunting them. But everyone knew the manhunts were increasing.

A number of young Jews had come out of hiding to join the Resistance. Among them were Rosina and Settimio Sorani; they became couriers between the various groups in a city which had become even more dangerous.

More than once they were caught in air raids. Rosina would recall that by February 1944 Rome had been bombed more than forty times since she had seen those American bombers passing overhead last July to bomb the marshalling yards.

Settimio had been on his way back to a new hideout he shared with his sister and several other young partisans in an already bomb-damaged building overlooking the Coliseum when the siren wailed. At the far end of the street a troop carrier received a direct hit and body parts were scattered over the road.

Skirmishes between the Germans and the Resistance were day and night, and the German high command had moved from the Flora and the Excelsior hotels to a heavily protected building on the Corso d'Italia. Roadblocks had been set up at each end of the street and armored cars blocked off side streets.

From his rooftop vantage point in Santa Marta, D'Arcy Osborne watched the almost daily raids on the city and surrounding countryside. The bombing had increasingly affected his relationship with the Holy See and he was regularly summoned to Secretary of State Maglione's office to receive a written protest to convey to London. One document detailed how several hundred Jews the pope had ordered should be hidden at his summer residence in Castel Gandolfo were killed by bombs dropped on a building in the papal complex along with seventeen nuns. During a bombing raid on Rome, a clinic was struck resulting in a number of deaths. Maglione had pointed out that all the buildings were protected under the Lateran Treaty.

Though Osborne had apologized each time, it had led to stress on his relationship with Maglione, a diplomat he admired. He had warned the Foreign Office that the continuous bombing was turning Italian public opinion away from "our side, as all reports indicate that the destruction of civilian life and property is altogether disproportionate to the military results attained."

Tittmann also felt the "cold anger" of Maglione after American bombers had finally destroyed the monastery on top of Monte Casino.

"I told the cardinal I did not believe for a minute the Allies would have

destroyed the monastery had there not been overwhelming military reasons. To this he replied, 'Pardon me if I say so, but I know what I am talking
about and have access to sources of information that you are probably not
open to.' I was forced to admit that my own source so far was the radio."

Osborne, more than Tittmann, was personally upset at the ruthless-
ness of the Allies. He finally told the pope that he "could not but sympa-
thize with some of the Holy See's grievances."

But the air raids went on. Meanwhile the cells of Regina Coeli prison
were filling with Jews who had been rounded up. On March 14 Celeste di
Porto had reached her eighteenth birthday and later would be accused of
having been responsible for the arrest of over fifty Jews since the roundup.

PART V

LIBERATION

16

LIVING WITH GOD
AND THE DEVIL

On that mild March morning in 1944, Dr. Sacerdoti sensed the growing fear, despair, and hunger as he walked to work. Every day the
bombings had destroyed more tram lines and left new craters for the labor
gangs to refill with rubble from toppled buildings.

In the hospital drinking water was rationed and visitors smelled of the
carbolic disinfectant they were dabbed with to try and kill lice and other
germs before they entered the wards. It was a battle waged all over Rome:
in the food lines, public bathhouses, restaurants where people wiped their
cutlery, in cinemas and theaters where contact could lead to the spread of
bacteria. There had also been a loss of illusion, symbolized by a slogan
scrawled on walls: ALLIES HOLD ON! WE'LL BE HERE SOON TO LIBERATE YOU!

Increasingly Romans felt left to fend for themselves. The excitement
following the departure of Mussolini had faded as fast as the memories
of those golden days after Italy had conquered Ethiopia in 1936. Most
people—clerks, shopkeepers, market workers—had little revolutionary
bent though they were supportive of the Resistance, even if many partisans were Communists. Romans who were churchgoing members of the
Christian Democratic Party knew that the pope was increasingly concerned that the Communist leaders in the Resistance were growing more
determined to control Rome's destiny, not to be shaped by it. The most

militant of all were the *Bandiera Rossa,* the Red Flag Party. Its sabotage and military actions had given it a power in the Resistance.

Professor Borromeo may well have spoken for many Romans when he had told his staff at morning conference he could not understand why the Allies were taking so long to break out of their Anzio beachhead when they were confronted by no mountains, no wide rivers to cross, and the flat ground was ideal for tanks. Daily "Axis Sally"—the American-born Mildred Gillars who had become the radio voice of the Germans in Italy— taunted the Allies, calling the beachhead "the largest self-supporting prisoner-of-war camp in the world."

In Rome the partisans continued to come out of hiding to launch hit-and-run attacks with deadly effect before melting back to their hideouts. The failure to locate them had finally produced a response from the one man the Resistance both hated and feared.

General Karl Wolff, appointed by Hitler as the SS *Polizeiführer* for Italy, had remained in post after the cancelation of the plot to kidnap the pope. But the führer had instructed Wolff to destroy the Rome Resistance. He had sent five hundred SS troops to the city in late February. The three companies—the 9th, 10th, and 11th—were drawn from the newly formed SS *Polizei*-Regiment Bozen. The 9th was deployed to the south of the city; the 10th was sent to Castelli Romani, the hills outside Rome from where the partisans launched attacks on German road traffic.

The 11th company was still at the stage of being trained in crowd control, house-to-house search tactics, and how to crush an uprising. They had been given an additional task by *Stadtkommandant* Mälzer. Every afternoon they were to march through the city center singing SS songs. In their uniforms, steel helmets, jackboots, hand grenades hooked to their ammunition belts, and rifles on their shoulders, Mälzer intended them to show a presence of Nazi power.

Since the goose-stepping parades started, the military council of the Resistance had sent spies to study their route from the time they crossed the Piazza del Popolo and on down the Via del Babuino, chanting as they marched, their voices blending with the tramp of their boots. They swung past the Spanish Steps toward the office of *Il Messaggero,* whose staff stood in the windows awed by the intimidating sight. Ahead lay an underpass through one of the Seven Hills of Rome.

Before reaching the tunnel, a makeshift air-raid shelter during the night, the parade would turn into Via Rasella. The street was narrow and the soldiers were forced to march in closer file as their voices echoed off the old buildings. At the top of the street the column reformed, once more five abreast, to march down one of Rome's main avenues, Via Quattro Fontane, to the Interior Ministry where they were barracked. The parade of 156 soldiers took the same route every day.

For three weeks the two spies—Carla Capponi, a laboratory technician and Rosario Bentivegna, a medical student—had shadowed them. The troops had always entered Via Rasella at 2 P.M.

Both students had a common contempt for the privileged background from which they came. Carla, a striking twenty-four-year-old was the daughter of a mixed marriage family; her mother was Jewish, and claimed Virginia Woolf as a relative. Carla had lived a comfortable, sheltered life in a large apartment across from Mussolini's office on Piazza Venezia and had grown up listening to the duce fulminating to the crowd below.

Rosario was the slim son of a wealthy family who owned property across Rome, some of which had been destroyed by Allied bombs. His diplomat father had hoped he would have followed him into the foreign service. Instead Rosario had chosen medicine—"to save lives, not to find diplomatic excuses for why they died in the cause of Fascism," he once said. Like many students they had been drawn to the Resistance for its promise to sweep away the inequity of Fascism. But first they had to remove the Nazi occupiers.

In the weeks following the ghetto roundup, they had proven themselves. Bentivegna had killed a Fascist policeman who had been one of Dannecker's *carabinieri* squad; Carla had shot dead a German soldier. She would recall, "I dropped my gun into my handbag and ran from the scene, weeping." Now on that March day she was ready to kill again.

On the afternoon of Wednesday, March 22, the leaders of the military council made their separate ways to a building near the Coliseum. They had all read the story *Il Messaggero* had published that the Germans were planning to withdraw from Rome. Since the newspaper was regarded as a Fascist mouthpiece the report created understandable excitement over its suggestion they were leaving because they wanted to save Rome from further destruction by Allied bombings. Sister Luke, however, was more doubtful. In her diary she posed a question: Could it possibly be true?

For Bishop Hudal the story was another opportunity to support the idea that the Germans were prepared to turn Rome into an "open city" and leave it without a battle. In Hudal's view that would give an opportunity for the world to see that it was the Allies who were destroying the history of Christian civilization and Western culture with their ruthless bombing. Hudal had decided that a retreat from Rome should be seen as proof of German concern and humanity.

The Resistance leaders met to hopefully hasten the German departure by giving the go-ahead to launch the largest operation the Resistance had carried out. It would come on the most important day in the *Era Fascista* calendar which celebrated that occasion in 1919, twenty-five years ago, when Mussolini had founded the Fascist movement. All week the news-papers and Radio Rome had devoted time and space to the coming cele-brations. There would be a morning church service in Piazza Venezia which all "good Fascists" should attend followed by an afternoon parade through the city.

But even as the military council met, another meeting was under way in the Villa Wolkonsky. Dollmann had used his influence with General Wolff to have Moellhausen reinstated as the ambassador in the German embassy. The grateful thanks of the diplomat had been waved aside by Dollmann saying that a display of Fascist pomp and ceremony was unac-ceptable while the people of Rome were going hungry and being bombed every day. He recommended that the ambassador should cancel the cele-brations. Moellhausen hesitated. The last time he had made a decision on his own it had nearly cost him his post. He said he would call a meeting with Kappler and Mälzer. The gestapo chief said the celebrations were a matter for the Fascists to police themselves. The *Stadtkommandant* said he would allow the religious service but cancel the parade and allow only the celebrations to take place in the Ministry of Corporations.

For Mälzer there must be no parade which would distract from the daily march of his SS troops past the building and on toward Via Rasella.

In a basement in an apartment block on Via Marco Aurelio, a short walk from the Coliseum, Giulio Cortini and his wife, Laura, set about their work. They were the bomb makers of the Resistance. In their secret world they were the most respected of its last remaining explosives experts. A month ago a colleague—like Giulio, a graduate university physicist—had been one of nine partisans executed in the yard at Fort Bravetta. Kappler had stood beside the firing squad after inviting each of the condemned men to save their lives by betraying other members of the Resistance. Each remained silent.

Like the alchemists of old, Giulio and Laura worked by experience and instinct and their language was rich with words which brought death: "deflagration," "oxidizer," "depressant point." They knew the exact quantity of explosives needed to blow up a fuel truck, an armored car, a roadside command post; the right fuse to select the amount of TNT needed for a pipe bomb.

Having been briefed on the target, they had walked the length of Via Rasella; arm in arm they looked like any other young couple out on a stroll before the curfew. They had noticed the municipal refuge cart parked on the street. It solved the problem of where to place the bomb. Grenades would be thrown from Via del Boccaccio and Via dei Giardini, both little more than alleys on either side of Via Rasella.

Walking to their hideout Giulio and Laura began to discuss the composition of the bomb they would make.

During the night the couple first tamped twelve kilograms of TNT into a cast-iron casing which was then placed in a sack and covered with a further six kilograms of explosives. A fifty-second fuse was then placed on top of the mix. Finally six more kilograms of TNT were used to make pipe bombs, which were packed in shopping bags.

The bomb makers had completed their work by midnight.

Dawn on March 23 promised a sunny day and Radio Rome predicted the temperature would be in the mid-seventies. Tittmann felt it could be the start of another long, hot summer in Santa Marta.

The only hope now was that the distant rumble of gunfire from the direction of Anzio heralded the Allies would arrive soon. At night he and Osborne had stood on the flat roof of their home and watched the tiny pinpoints of light in the sky from antiaircraft guns shooting at German planes. But it was Allied aircraft which concerned Tittmann.

That morning he expected yet another protest from Maglione. Despite its roof being painted yellow and white—the Vatican colors—and marked with the words VATICAN CITY, a food truck had been machine-gunned by an American fighter which resulted in the death of its driver.

Tittmann had once more tried to explain to the secretary of state that it was "virtually impossible for Allied warplanes attacking road transport to distinguish particular markings on motor transports."

Maglione had sent for Montini and told him to take Tittmann up to the roof of St. Peter's to view several Vatican trucks parked in the basilica's square. Montini had pointed out that their recognition marks were clearly visible. Tittmann had responded that aircraft pilots flying at four hundred miles an hour would not have time to recognize the markings. The future pope had silently led the way down from the roof.

That morning a similar refuse cart which Giulio and Laura had seen in Via Rasella was left outside the apartment building on Via Marco Aurelio. Shortly afterward Rosario Bentivegna arrived dressed in the blue uniform and cap of a street cleaner. The porter emerged with Giulio carrying the sack between them and carefully placed it in the rubbish cart. It consisted of two silver-colored iron containers to hold refuse supported on a four-wheel chassis. Rosario set off, the cart rumbling over the cobblestones. The porter and the bomb makers went back into the building. All they could do now was to wait.

At midday on that Wednesday Celeste di Porto walked up the Via della Conciliazione toward St. Peter's. The broad avenue was filled with men and women like her, dressed in black. They were going into the basilica to pray for the life of a young priest, Giuseppe Morosini, who had been arrested by the gestapo and accused of trafficking in arms and spying for the

Allies. He was being held in Regina Coeli prison. A plea made for clemency by the pope had so far gone unanswered.

The raven-haired teenager had not come to pray for his life but to help spring a trap which would lead to the arrest of O'Flaherty. Kappler had identified him as the organizer of the network which had helped Allied soldiers and Jews to hide. The gestapo chief had told Celeste there was a thirty thousand lire reward if she could entice O'Flaherty to step outside the Vatican boundary.

She was to approach him where he usually stood at midday Mass on the steps of the basilica. She must wear a crucifix and explain she was the daughter of an impoverished widow who was sheltering an Allied soldier, a devout Catholic, who was now dying and needed a priest to administer the last rites. The soldier had told her that the only priest in Rome he knew was Father O'Flaherty who he had met in a prison camp. Would he come with her to give the soldier the Sacrament of Extreme Unction? Once she had brought him over the white-line boundary a gestapo snatch squad would arrest him.

Twice Celeste had come to the square and each time O'Flaherty had not been there.

She could not know that the pope had ordered O'Flaherty to limit his appearances in public after news of the plan to capture him reached the Vatican.

Later, there would be claims he was an Allied spy. Another allegation was that O'Flaherty had passed information to the Germans. Despite the absence of any documentation the story gained momentum in postwar Britain, Ireland, and Italy. In London *The Times* wrote a story headlined: SAVIOUR OR STOOGE?

More certain is that on that Wednesday in Rome O'Flaherty was at work organizing more shelter for Allied soldiers and Jews.

Overnight Carla Capponi had cut her long red hair and dyed it black to disguise herself. By one o'clock she had passed other members of the attack team, and was carrying the bags with the pipe bombs. Eight partisans, veterans of street attacks, would be waiting in the two side alleys ready to throw the pipe bombs after Rosario's bomb exploded. Two more partisans would be positioned to provide covering fire while Rosario and the others fled to the underground tunnel.

As he came closer to Via Rasella Carla caught up with him and dumped her bags in the cart. They would be collected by the partisans in the alley shortly before the attack. By then Carla had taken up her own position outside the offices of *Il Messaggero*. To signal the approaching soldiers she would fold a copy of the newspaper she had bought. It would be a sign for the partisan standing on the corner of Via Rasella to signal Rosario it was time to light the bomb's fifty-second fuse.

He parked his refuse cart halfway down Via Rasella and began to sweep the cobbles with a street broom. He looked at his watch: 2:15 P.M. The soldiers were late. Perhaps they had been caught up in the crowds going to the Fascist celebrations at the nearby Ministry of Corporations auditorium. Maybe the parade had been cancelled. Then what would he do with the bomb? He couldn't leave it here, but where could he take it? He felt hot and sticky in his uniform. He checked the time: 2:30 P.M. He began to count the seconds, to experience the length of a minute. He began to count again. He had learned that watch time went slowly: A minute could seem like an hour when he waited to attack a target. His watch showed it was 2:40.

Carla finally heard the approaching sound of marching men, the pounding of their boots on the cobbles almost drowning out the rhythm of the singing voices. The parade swept past her on the way to Via Rasella. The waiting partisan at the corner of the street raised his cap. It was the signal.

At the top end of the street a truck had arrived and was starting to unload goods with the help of the building's doorman. Rosario shouted for them to run as a bomb was about to explode. They left the goods and truck and ran into the building as he lit the fuse.

The marching column turned into Via Rasella, singing, Rosario remembered, "not in the language of Goethe but of Hitler." From inside the sack came the first smell of acrid smoke and the splutter of the fuse. He ran back up the street into the safety of Via Quattro Fontane, a main road. There was a massive explosion and a violent wind. The abandoned truck was turned over and the goods sent whirling into the air. Window glass showered down and front doors were ripped off their hinges.

There were bodies everywhere, killed instantly or dying. The pipe bombs hurled from the alleys had decimated those not caught in the initial blast which had created a huge crater and massive holes in walls. Cobblestones were flying through the air. Incredibly some of the soldiers had staggered to their feet and were firing up at the buildings before collapsing from shrapnel wounds. Two civilians lay among the dead, a thirteen-year-old boy and a middle-aged man, who had come out to watch the march pass. The 11th SS company of the Bozen regiment was left in dismembered pieces in pools of blood. The attack had taken only a minute on Rosario's watch. Along with him and Carla all the partisans escaped.

The explosion was heard across Rome and reached the Vatican. In the Apostolic Palace people rushed to the windows and looked up into the cloudless sky for any sign of a bomber. The sky was empty and the air raid siren had not sounded. On the roof of Santa Marta, Osborne and May took turns with the minister's binoculars to try and identify where the explosion had occurred and both agreed it seemed to have happened in the area where the Fascists were celebrating the anniversary of their foundation.

Two hundred yards from Via Rasella the platform guests in the auditorium were rushing in their cars to the scene of the explosion. Among them were Dollmann and Moellhausen. Police had already arrived with soldiers, who were laying out the corpses. *Stadtkommandant* Mälzer who had been lunching with Kappler in the Excelsior arrived with two trucks of SS troopers who immediately began to smash their way into houses to drag out occupants and line them up against walls.

Dollmann later recalled: "Mälzer was demented, he kept shouting: 'Revenge! Revenge for my poor *Kameraden!*' People lined up against the walls were screaming in terror. One woman was hanging half out of the window, shot by a burst of submachine gunfire. Mälzer was running up and down the street screaming and weeping like a madman."

Moellhausen tried to calm him as Mälzer raved he was going to blow up every house in the street. The ambassador calmly told him that would turn the entire city against them.

Kappler, who had silently followed the exchanges took Mälzer aside. The *Stadtkommandant* looked at him, his face flushed, eyes darting from the row of corpses to the terrified people lined up against the walls. "They must all be shot! Every one of them," Mälzer shouted. Kappler understood the wild, uncontrolled emotional madness that fed Mälzer's rage, fuelled by the amount of liquor he had consumed at lunch. But the gestapo chief had learned that only cold logic solved any issue.

To shoot the probably innocent people of Via Rasella would most likely result in a full-scale war exploding in the streets of Rome and Mälzer did not have the resources to control an enraged city which Kappler had come to suspect was already secretly armed. The Romans would also have the Allied soldiers to help them. With the troops Wolff had sent cut to a third and his own gestapo only a small force, and despite the assurance from Pietro Caruso that his men would fire on the population, Kappler believed an uprising would succeed.

Yet he knew there *had* to be a reprisal to satisfy Mälzer's bloodlust. People must die—and the gestapo had a word for it: *Todeskandidaten*, "candidates for death." Regina Coeli prison, Fort Bravetta, and the cells of Kappler's headquarters on Via Tasso all had their cells full of people who were either awaiting trial before a German military court or had already been condemned to death. They included Jews who had escaped the roundup before being caught. They would serve his plan.

Kappler believed executing the prisoners would not provoke an uprising and told the *Stadtkommandant* the Romans would understand the need for a firm hand against criminals. The gestapo chief led Mälzer away from the carnage on Via Rasella to his car and drove him to Kappler's headquarters.

After they had left, Moellhausen ordered Caruso to release the civilians lined up against the walls and allow them back into their homes. The ambassador then drove Dollmann to the German embassy. They agreed there would be reprisals but Dollmann suggested these could be contained if the Vatican could be involved. He told the ambassador he would tell Bishop Hudal what had happened and propose that before the bodies were returned to Germany there should be a suitable religious service in the nearest basilica to Via Rasella, St. John Lateran. The pope, in his capacity as the bishop of Rome, and Kesselring could take the opportunity to call for peace and appeal for the Resistance to halt their attacks.

Hudal had welcomed the idea and said he would convey it to Father Pfeiffer, the pope's liaison with the German high command. No record remains if he did.

By early evening, attempts by Maglione to discover what had happened were still unsuccessful. Parish priests in the area of the explosion were being kept well back by troops. There were rumors that it had been an attempt to attack an ammunition depot or that a weapons carrier bound for the front had blown up.

Sister Luke's route home to her convent took her close enough to Via Rasella to learn that thirty-two soldiers had been killed and another twenty badly injured; almost everyone in the parade had been hit. In her diary the nun wrote: "No one knows what the consequences of this will be nor what horrible reprisals will follow."

Meanwhile, Mälzer had been busy trying to obtain backing for the reprisals he wanted. He had called Kesselring's headquarters to be told he was at the front. However when the field marshal's chief of operations heard what happened he immediately telephoned Hitler's headquarters in East Prussia. Thirty minutes later the call was returned. Hitler had ordered that for every dead soldier thirty Italians were to be shot.

Kappler then spoke to General Wolff and said the figure was guaranteed to cause an uprising. He proposed that the number be reduced to ten reprisals for every death. Within an hour Wolff had called back; he had spoken to the führer and the figure was agreed upon. Hitler had demanded that the executions must be completed within twenty-four hours.

Throughout the night of March 23–24 Kappler and his assistant, SS *Hauptsturmführer* Erich Priebke had checked what Priebke later called "every possible source for enough prisoners." In the small hours he was told the number of dead soldiers had increased to thirty-three and they would therefore need to find three hundred and thirty men, as Kappler put it, "worthy of death."

During the night Moellhausen had found him seated at his desk, check-ing the number of names on his list. The ambassador would recall:

"I told him that if I was in his place my conscience would tremble. He told me that for every name he added to his list he would think three times."

The number was finally made up of 258 political prisoners and seventy-seven Jews. Several had been betrayed by Celeste di Porto, some only re-cently, after escaping the ghetto roundup. One name on Kappler's list replaced that of Celeste's brother who was being held on a charge of bur-glary. She persuaded Kappler to set him free.

The political prisoners included lawyers, doctors, and accountants. While some were members of the Resistance, none had taken part in pre-paring and carrying out the Via Rasella attack. Among them were four Italians already condemned to death and seventeen serving long sentences. The political group also included Italian soldiers who were awaiting trial for refusing to join the German army. Prisoners from other jails in Rome would make up the number; there were no records against their names of what crimes they had committed. The Jews were simply listed as *"Jude."*

The list of 335 hostages who needed to die was finalized by dawn on Thursday.

After breakfast Kappler sat down and drafted the rules for the executions. Since the majority of the killing squad consisted of sixty-two NCOs and of-ficers who had never killed before, he ordered several cases of cognac to be taken to the execution site to calm their nerves. They would all be told that they must regard the executions as "a symbolic necessity." The killings would take place in groups of five. One shot would be fired into the back of the head of each kneeling prisoner. Pistols would be provided for those who did not normally carry one. Anyone who refused to perform his duty would be shot. They would take place at the Ardeatine Caves on the Appian Way, close to where legend claims the apostle Peter saw a vision of Jesus. The killings were under the command of Captain Karl Hass, a short man with a skin rash and a squint. SS *Hauptsturmführer* Priebke would keep a record to ensure the numbers killed corresponded with Kappler's list.

By early Thursday morning the pope knew the full extent of the Via Ra-sella bombing. Prince Filippo Doria Pamphilj had called Father Leiber with the information which had been provided by Ivanoe Bonomi, the head of the military council. The pope told his secretary he wanted an im-mediate meeting with Maglione and Count Dalla Torre, the editor of *L'Osservatore Romano.*

Both arrived with further news that the reprisal was to take place that day. The secretary of state's attempt to contact Ambassador Weizsäcker to ask him to intervene in the executions had failed; both Kesselring and Wolff had said they could not go against Hitler's order. Father Pfei-ffer had been unable to make contact with General Mälzer, who had been a boyhood schoolmate. Bishop Hudal insisted he had been unable to reach Dollmann. The experienced secretary of state said it all pointed to a serious situation in which no one wanted the Holy See to become involved.

The pope had turned to the editor and told him that he wanted a *"Carita Civile"* published in the paper that afternoon. It was an editorial, rarely used, and always published on the front page. It would be under-stood by readers as representing the view of the pope.

At dictation speed Dalla Torre took down the pope's words and rushed back to the office.

We recall that on other occasions we have addressed ourselves to the grave times through which the country is passing. Now in these anxious hours we turn spe-cifically to Rome.

Our appeal is made to the honest heart of the people, who have so admirably demonstrated their spirit of sacrifice and profound sense of dignity. Do not with violent urges shatter this attitude, which is so worthy of the virtues of our people. Every ill-considered act would have no other result than to end by injuring many innocent people, already too tired by anguish and privation.

All those on whom it is incumbent to maintain public order have the task of as-suring that it is not disturbed by any attitude whatsoever that might in itself be used as the reason for reactions that would give rise to an indefinable series of painful conflicts; those who can and know how to effectively influence the minds of the citizenry, above all the clergy, have the high mission of persuasion, pacifi-cation, and giving comfort . . .

Dalla Torre was told to make sure that the pope's *"Carita Civile"* was delivered to the German high command as soon as the paper was off the press.

When the first truck arrived in midafternoon at the caves a number of the executioners were drunk when they led the doomed prisoners into the caves. Among them was Father Pappagallo in his robes and sandals. When he was ordered to kneel he went to his death calling out, "Father bless us."

By the end of the first hour those about to die found they had to kneel before the bodies of those already killed. Despite the alcohol they continued to consume some of the Germans were still horrified by the slaughter. An officer who refused to shoot was forced at gunpoint to do so by Hass. Some of the victims' heads were blown off, their brains splattering the cave walls. It was eight o'clock that Thursday evening when the last of the prisoners were shot. It was well within the twenty-four-hour limit set by Hitler.

Kappler, who had attended the final killings, ordered the bodies to be piled in meter-high heaps and gave the order for the waiting *Wehrmacht* engineers to seal the caves with explosives to hide the atrocity.

Mälzer issued a communiqué on the Fascist news wire service:

> On the afternoon of March 23, 1944, criminal elements executed a bomb attack against a column of German police in transit through Via Rasella. As the result of this ambush, thirty-two men of the German police were killed and several wounded.
>
> The vile ambush was carried out by *communist-badogliani*. An investigation is still under way to clarify the extent to which this criminal act is attributable to Anglo-American incitement.
>
> The German command has decided to terminate the activities of these villainous bandits. No one will be allowed to sabotage with impunity the newly affirmed Italo-German cooperation. The German command has therefore ordered that for every murdered German ten *communist-badogliani* criminals be shot. This order has already been executed.

Erich Priebke and Karl Hass, who had jointly commanded the executions at the caves, later admitted to each shooting two prisoners.

In the chaos of postwar Europe, Priebke was able to obtain a false passport to travel to live in Argentina; there would be claims the document was provided by the ODESSA organization which Bishop Hudal had set up. In 1996, after being exposed by an American television program, Priebke was extradited to Italy. A first trial refused to convict him because the judge said, "the accused was only following orders." A second trial sentenced him to fifteen years but the sentence was reduced by ten years based on a long-standing amnesty enacted by the Italian government. In the end he served six months.

Hass had lived in Switzerland before he faced trial in 1966 after being extradited to Italy. Convicted, he was sentenced to ten years and eight months imprisonment, but the term was suspended and he did not serve any jail time.

Celeste di Porto—the girl who used to push an old-clothes cart with her father and ended up as a moll for the Black Panther leader—left Rome, knowing she was a hunted woman by the Resistance. When Rome was liberated her father walked into a police station and asked to be arrested to atone for his daughter's crimes and save the family's honor. He was sent away and he and his wife took their cart and walked off into the countryside and were never heard of again. On Italy's liberation Celeste was recognized in a Naples brothel where she was working by a Jewish veteran of the Italian army. She was arrested and brought to Rome. She was put on trial in 1945 and sentenced to twelve years. She was released after seven years under an amnesty and became a Roman Catholic. In 1981 she died.

But she was not forgotten. Still scratched on the wall of a cell in Regina Coeli prison on that Friday of March 24, 1944 are the words: "If I never see my family again, it is the fault of Celeste di Porto. Avenge me."

17

AFTERMATH

Stadtkommandant Mälzer's wire-service announcement had ended up in the office of Vatican Radio and *L'Osservatore Romano* as well as Rome's daily newspapers. Time and again, the editor of *Il Messaggero,* Bruno Spampanato, cast his eyes back to the phrases "thirty-two killed," "for every murdered German, ten Communist criminals shot," and "order already been executed."

Here was a story that warranted not only the entire front page but a "special" edition. But Spampanato decided he would wait to see what, if any comment, came from *L'Osservatore Romano.* A similar decision was taken by other Fascist newspaper editors.

The wire-service message continued to shock Count Dalla Torre. He had spoken to Padre Nasalli Rocca, the prisoners' confessor at Regina Coeli prison, who said several of the wardens had confirmed to him that the jail had been emptied of all its prisoners.

"Hundreds of the pope's fellow Romans—Catholics and Jews—over which he exercised a duty of pastoral care—had been murdered," Rocca recalled being told.

After speaking with Dalla Torre the priest sought an urgent audience with the pope. "The Holy Father was alone and when I related what I heard in the prison, he raised both his hands, burying his head in a gesture of astonishment and pain, and he cried, 'What are you telling me? It cannot be!' It was clear to me that he knew nothing about what had happened."

He invited Rocca to accompany him to his private chapel to pray for the souls of the dead. It would be the first of several such prayers Pius was to offer. Afterward he asked the priest to return to the prison and obtain as much evidence as he could: names of the executed prisoners, the crimes for which they were imprisoned, and, above all, where the executions had taken place.

On the day of the Ardeatine executions the number of Jews sheltering in the Vatican had risen to 477. Another 4,238 had found refuge in monasteries and convents in Rome. Years later at the trial of Adolf Eichmann in Jerusalem, Israel's attorney general, Gideon Hausner, stated that once the pope had known of the Ardeatine slaughter he continued to do all he could to help the Jews.

At noon on Saturday, March 25, Carla Capponi stood outside the offices of *Il Messaggero,* her black hair dye washed out and back to its fair color, waiting for the day's edition to be posted behind the glass frames which allowed readers to have a free read. Rosario was with her, one of the growing crowd.

On the front page was Mälzer's communiqué. Carla stood rooted in the spot, transfixed by every word. A lifetime later, after she had married Rosario, became an Italian member of Parliament, and received Italy's highest decoration, the *Medaglia d'oro* for military valor, she could recall every word of her reaction to what she read.

"It was as if the entire city had fallen on us, crushing us in an agony so much worse than the long wait leading up to it. There was the communiqué and then nothing else. No comment, no explanation of the way or where they had been executed. Not a word about whom they had killed. Were the men chosen from those in prison or chosen from the roundups of the days just before our attack? No names, not even what kind of people they were, chosen for what I knew at once not to have been an execution but totally a massacre."

Rosario's first reaction was to take revenge.

"To kill, to show them that the Resistance was intact, was more resolute than ever. Now I understand in a way I had never known before, how beastly an enemy we faced."

The couple walked away through the gathering reading the message, many already in tears, others shouting where were the bodies. Some who went to police headquarters were directed to gestapo headquarters on Via Tasso. Ordered away, they went to Mälzer's headquarters on Corso d'Italia. They found it surrounded by SS troops ready to deal with any Resistance attack.

Soon, through word of mouth, the names of the dead began to emerge. A warden at Regina Coeli had compiled a list and smuggled it out to people waiting outside the prison. The last days of March passed in tension. The names of the dead were now known throughout the city and its grief-stricken people had placed bunches of flowers on every street. Radio Rome had warned that a repeat of Via Rasella would lead to even more severe reprisals.

On Sunday, April 2, the start of Italian summertime, the pope was told that his latest appeal to Field Marshal Kesselring to spare the life of the young priest, Giuseppe Morosini, had failed. He was to be executed that morning, guilty of helping the partisans.

When he had been told his death was only hours away the priest asked Padre Rocca if he would hear his confession and arrange for him to celebrate Mass in the prison chapel. The prison governor had telephoned the Vatican to ask if it wished to have someone present and the pope ordered Monsignor Traglia, the Holy See's vice-regent to Rome, to attend the Mass and to remain with Morosini until the end. They sat together in the van that drove to Fort Bravetta. Only when they were in the execution yard did the prison guard remove the priest's handcuffs.

Traglia recalled: "He asked me to thank the Holy Father for his efforts on his behalf and to say that he offered his life for him. Before being blindfolded he kissed his crucifix, blessed the platoon of soldiers who were to shoot him, and publicly forgave the man who had betrayed him. Possibly because the executioners were overcome by his quiet heroism he was not killed by their volley and fell to the ground, wounded but conscious. He begged for the Sacrament of Extreme Unction which I administered at once. The platoon commanding officer then shot him at the base of the skull with his revolver."

Through April into May the mood, like the weather, changed in Rome. On a sunny Good Friday O'Flaherty learned that two of the network helpers had been arrested and were being held in Regina Coeli. On Easter Sunday Mälzer ordered a band concert to be given outside his headquarters. Among the large crowds who gathered was Sister Luke who noted: "There is no doubt they are born musicians. If only they would stick to music instead of making war."

In mid-April special prayers the pope had ordered for the repose of the souls of the victims in Ardeatine Caves continued to be made in every basilica and church in the city. On Friday, April 21, the sirens once more wailed across the city but no bombs fell to add to the number of 2,437 buildings already damaged or destroyed in air raids.

Within the Resistance a split developed over the Via Rasella operation. Some felt the price it had cost was too high. Others argued it was important a follow-up operation should be launched. The proposed target would be the truck carrying the change of guards to Regina Coeli. The attack was abandoned by the military council because of the risk of killing civilians. Nonetheless individual partisans continued to choose targets-of-opportunity, killing a policeman and a patrolling soldier.

The Germans drew comfort from the phone-tapping unit based in the central telephone exchange. For the first time Romans started to criticize the Resistance; the monitors passed on every word which could be used against the partisans for Fascist newspapers to publish.

Vatican relations with the German high command further soured when Secretary of State Maglione complained about the Germans painting some of their trucks and vans in Vatican colors to avoid being attacked by Allied aircraft. The protest was ignored by Mälzer. Food shortages continually increased. There were claims that flour was adulterated. The pope decided to send a fleet of heavy trucks with trailers into Umbria and Tuscany to purchase food. When the trucks returned they drove into the

Vatican, and under the control of nuns and priests, supplies were brought to convents, monasteries, and hospitals. Essential drugs had come with the food to treat some of the K-Syndrome "patients" in the *Fatebenefratelli* and those in other hospitals.

Increasingly those arrested by the Gestapo no longer had the doubtful chance of a trial before a military court. Instead they were tortured in Kappler's headquarters. Those "required to speak at all cost" were brought to a separate room, where ropes hung from the ceiling. Victims were kept there until they confessed and were either strangled or hanged. Kappler had also created his network of V-Men—*Vertrauens-Mann*—a "person of trust": someone already in a position of authority: a school teacher, university lecturer, or a businessman in a position to spy and report on their community in return for food or other privileges.

Every morning at dawn in the closing days of May, D'Arcy Osborne, John May, and Sam Derry made their way through the Vatican gardens to their vantage point on its walls to peer out across the expanse of country visible in every direction. The sounds of battle were drawing closer.

"Give it a couple of weeks and our people will be here," Derry said.

To the north of the city they could see the first German columns retreating north.

On June 1, Vatican Radio announced that the Allies had said once they arrived they were going to prioritize bringing food into Rome.

That evening Sam Derry and John May met with O'Flaherty to discuss the escapees and Jewish refugees. Their concern was that they might emerge from hiding and either make a run to link up with advancing Allies or join the Resistance. O'Flaherty said he would send an order to be passed down the network for everyone to remain in their hiding places.

Zolli, the chief rabbi, had become a familiar figure in the Vatican, joining the other Jews in the dining halls Pius had ordered to be set up for the Jews. Zolli would lead them in prayers and afterward conduct discussions.

In the evening he would update his diary. After meeting the pope, Zolli wrote, "People will blame him for the world's silence in the face of Nazi crimes. The truth is that he has ensured that the Vatican will always help the Jews and we should be grateful for that. I know that many priests have died in concentration camps for following his request to keep the Jews safe."

For Zolli his time in the Vatican had "quenched my physical hunger with spiritual nourishment." In those months of sanctuary, the rabbi had formed his own opinion of the pope, calling him "my pastor who has seen the abyss of misfortune toward which mankind is advancing."

Beyond the walls of the Vatican the people Zolli had abandoned waited in hope that soon they would be pulled back from the abyss.

On that Friday morning, June 4, against the background of guns booming ever closer, the pope received the cardinals who had come to present him with their good wishes on his name day. He told them that he intended to broadcast to the world and invited them to stay and listen. Seated before a microphone in his study Pius proclaimed over Vatican Radio, "Whoever raises his hand against Rome will be guilty of matricide before the civilized world and the eternal judgement of God."

That evening Pascalina was among others in the Apostolic Palace who had stood on its terrace to look at the city. "It was red as if blood has been poured over it. The gunfire was no longer like distant thunder. It was noise like no other," she would observe.

In the past weeks she had noticed the pope had come to look thinner and more fragile and she had become even more the sentinel nun who kept people away as much as possible so he could try and rest.

She cooked and served his meals and sat at his table while his tame canary flew around the dining room. She noticed that chilblains on his hands appeared to be worse and she reminded him to rub in the cream his doctor had prescribed. His hiccupping had also returned; nowadays the attack came more frequently. She wondered if stress was the cause. More than once she had confided to her diary if only they could go to Castel Gandolfo as they did every summer, but the war had made it too dangerous to make the journey. She was determined that once the Allies arrived she would insist he must go to the retreat and breathe in the clean air not the acrid stench that drifted in from Rome.

On a Saturday evening Ernst von Weizsäcker had driven through the dangerous streets to the Vatican to keep an appointment he had made with Maglione. He wanted to apply for asylum for his wife and staff under the Lateran Treaty.

The secretary of state explained there was no accommodation available until the Allied diplomats left. Maglione suggested that the solution would be for Weizsäcker to return to Berlin. The usually calm ambassador had flinched. He knew that his secret mission to try and involve the pope in Admiral Canaris's plot to oust Hitler had already failed and it would only be a matter of time before his role was discovered and he would face a certain death. Mälzer could be ordered to have him shot.

Weizsäcker had pleaded that there must be room, given all the Jewish refugees who had been given shelter. Maglione's response had ended the argument. Weizsäcker must understand that the Jews would only feel secure when the Allies arrived. Once they took over the city, he would ensure their diplomats would leave Santa Marta. Then, of course Weizsäcker would be given asylum along with other Axis diplomats accredited to the Holy See.

The ambassador thanked him and drove to the German military hospital in the city suburbs where Marianna, his tall, elegant wife, was helping nuns soothe many of the wounded young German soldiers. Their doctors had left with the last of the ambulances to join the endless convoys of trucks, cars, and ox-drawn carts carrying equally scared soldiers who had retreated ahead of the advancing U.S. Fifth Army of General Mark Clark.

At the hospital Weizsäcker began to work alongside his wife to attend to the casualties.

At midnight on that Saturday Kappler was in his headquarters with a handful of prisoners in the cells. He was still undecided regarding what to do with them. The previous day he had sent his wife, Leonore, and their son out of Rome in a staff car. His mistress Helen Brouwer had insisted she would remain with him. However, Mälzer had ordered that all SS women were to leave Rome and she was among them in a truck which had left Rome that Saturday afternoon.

Kappler had decided to sleep in his office. In the early hours he was jerked out of sleep to find himself staring at the rifle barrels of one of the British scouting teams which had made its way up the Appian Way into the city. Via Tasso was on their list of targets. They found the prisoners in the basement and frog-marched Kappler down to the cells and ordered him to open them. Then before the prisoners could attack the gestapo chief they marched him to their truck and threw him in. He would be the first of the German high command to be captured.

Early on Sunday morning, June 4, Pascalina was among those awakened in the Apostolic Palace by the sound of a solitary bomber flying low over the Vatican and on across the city. From its open bomb doors showered paper, settling everywhere including St. Peter's Square. She hurried down to the piazza to join others picking up the leaflets. Pascalina collected a handful and returned to the papal apartment. After distributing them to the domestic staff she brought a copy to the pope. Together they read:

"Citizens of Rome. This is not the time for demonstrations. Obey these directions and go on with your regular work. Rome is yours! Your job is to save the city. Ours is to destroy the enemy."

There followed a list of instructions. Barriers and obstructions from the streets were to be removed. The presence of enemy mines and war materials were to be reported to Allied patrols. Railways and all public transport services along with telephone and telegraph offices, broadcasting stations, and other lines of communications were to be protected.

"It is vital for the Allies that the troops should pass through Rome without hindrance, in order to complete the destruction of the German army which is retreating northward."

By early afternoon, almost to the hour when 270 days before the Germans had occupied the city, Rome was in the hands of American and British forces of General Clark's Fifth Army.

On June 8, 1944, the massive doors of the ghetto opened for the first time since they had closed on the eve of the roundup. That evening there would be a service to celebrate freedom for the congregants. But over a thousand would not return from Auschwitz, never again to worship in their temple.

Foa, Almansi, Rosina, and her brother, Settimio, were among those who emerged from hiding. Foa's first duty had been to go to the basement with Almansi to retrieve the precious gold plates and cups from the tank of holy water which fed the temple's ritual baths. Rosina went around turning on the synagogue lights before going to the empty library, and beginning to dust the shelves that had been emptied. Settimio set out to find which members of the *giunta*, the temple's council, had survived.

In the streets of the ghetto, as elsewhere across the city, troops were carrying flowers in the barrels of their guns and the netting over their helmets. Crowds cheered at every passing tank and jeep. No one could remember such laughter since the beginning of the war.

Houses began to be reoccupied as their owners returned. With them they brought a mood of a score to settle about the roundup and Ardeatine massacre. A number of men formed a group and marched to Regina Coeli demanding to be let in to deal with Fascists and Germans being held there. Allied military police told the group that innocent people would be set free but all others must undergo interrogation. Elsewhere other groups were also searching for collaborators.

Jews began to leave the Vatican, carrying their bags and suitcases with which they had entered. Across the city hundreds of other convents, monasteries, and other shelters were opening their doors for their guests to leave.

Among them were Chief Rabbi Zolli and his family. They had been brought from the Vatican in a car driven by Father Weber to the Palatine house where they discussed the rabbi's plans. Zolli said he intended to return to his role as chief rabbi of Rome, but needed time to decide.

Zolli did not attend the synagogue celebration that evening.

His absence created anger and bitterness. Martin Stern, an American correspondent for *The New York Times* interviewed Foa who said, "This man deserted his people in the time of their need. He is no longer our

rabbi." The diligent Stern had tracked down Zolli who justified his decision to go into hiding. "Foa knows that my name was on the top of the
gestapo list to be liquidated. Dead, what good could I have been to
my people?"

In his address to a crowded synagogue Foa said not only had Zolli abandoned the faithful, but he had failed to safeguard the sacred objects and
cultural treasures of the synagogue. "He has only been concerned with his
personal safety but has yet to visit the ghetto, let alone to inquire about his
surviving congregants," he said.

General Clark had appointed Colonel Charles Poletti as Allied regional
commissioner for Rome with Captain Maurice Neufeld, a Jew, as his adju-
tant with "special responsibility for Rome's Jews."

Zolli had met with the two officers. In his robe and hat he cut an imposing figure and, already aware of the attacks launched against him by Foa,
wasted no time in defending himself, saying how sad he was that there remained within the community "a little clique of Fascist Jews led by Foa."

He had concluded with the words, "I am an old sick man. But I would
die for my community." Neufeld would remember how Zolli had looked
at the two officers, close to tears.

Poletti had turned to Neufeld and asked what should be done. He suggested that the ghetto *giunta* should be dismissed and an election held to
elect new members. All known Fascists should be barred from serving
and Foa should be told that Zolli was to remain in post.

The rabbi expressed his satisfaction. He had one further request. He
required his salary to be paid by the community to cover his absence
in hiding.

Poletti told Neufeld to attend to the matter, "so that their rabbi leaves
here completely satisfied."

News that Zolli was to remain as their chief rabbi, led to an increasing
internecine feud between him and the community.

On the Day of Atonement, the holiest of Jewish holidays, Zolli had a
mystical vision during the religious service.

"I felt so far withdrawn from the ritual that I let others recite the
prayers. I was conscious of neither joy nor sorrow. I was divided of thought

and feeling. My heart lay as dead in my breast. And just then I saw with my mind's eyes a meadow sweeping upward, with bright grass but with no flowers. In this meadow I saw Jesus Christ clad in a white mantle and behind his head the blue sky. I experienced the greatest interior peace."

Zolli decided he had been called to take Catholic instruction while he was chief rabbi, presiding over divorce cases and weddings and funerals. On February 1, 1945—his salary while in hiding finally secured—he resigned. Sixteen days later he received the sacrament of baptism in the basilica of St. Mary of the Angels and became a Catholic. He changed his given name from "Israel" to "Eugenio," the Christian name of Pope Pius XII. The ceremony was done with much publicity.

The pale hollow-cheeked convert emerged from the church to tell a waiting reporter: "I continue to maintain unchanged all my love for the people of Israel; and in my sorrow for the lot that has befallen them. I shall never stop loving the Jews. I did not abandon the Jews by becoming a Catholic."

Zolli took up his new post at the Pontifical Biblical Institute as a librarian.

His conversion caused outrage in Jewish religious circles. Overnight, the once venerated, learned rabbi became a heretic. The synagogue of Rome proclaimed a fast of atonement for Zolli's defection, and mourned him as dead, while at the same time they denounced him as a *meshumad*—an apostate, one struck by God—and excommunicated him.

The order of excommunication demanded that, "Hereby all are warned against holding conversation with him either by word of mouth or by writing. No one is allowed to do him any service; no one may live under the same roof with him; no one may come within four cubits' length of him; and no one may read any document dictated by him or written by his hand."

Early in 1956 Zolli contracted bronchopneumonia and was admitted to the hospital. On Friday, March 2, he received Holy Communion and drifted into a coma and died. He was seventy-five years old.

Monsignor O'Flaherty had been told to return to his duties in the Holy Office. But he found his reputation had preceded him. Before the armistice thousands of Italian prisoners of war captured by the British in North

Africa were sent to prison camps on the South African veldt. They had become virtually forgotten. However with the liberation of Rome their relatives came to the Vatican seeking its help. They were directed to O'Flaherty.

Priests in South Africa received his orders to visit the camps and compile lists of the prisoners and their state of health. He arranged food parcels and letters to be sent through the Red Cross.

He then borrowed Osborne's car—the first time it had been driven since the minister had brought it into the Vatican—and drove to see General Harold Alexander, the Allied commander of Italy and asked him to arrange for the Italian POWs to be brought home as quickly as possible. Within weeks they were on their way by ship from Cape Town.

O'Flaherty wanted Alexander to resolve another problem: the transfer of Jewish refugees who now wanted to leave Rome to go to their homeland.

Alexander pointed out that Palestine was under British mandate and Jewish immigration was strictly controlled. O'Flaherty replied he would arrange for them to have Vatican travel documents. A bemused Alexander shook his head. "What, make them into Catholics?" The monsignor's booming laugh filled the general's office. "If needs be, by God, then yes!"

Alexander had promised he would see what could be done. But it was an undertaking he could not keep—stopped from doing so by British policy.

Infuriated by the British government's refusal to allow the pope's Jews permission to travel to their homeland, O'Flaherty had once more gone into action. He had approached Delasem, the restarted committee for aid to Jewish refugees. Powerful Jewish organizations in the United States were contacted. Funds were transferred to Europe to buy ships. Haganah, the Jewish underground army, found crews to man them. Finally when all was in place, priests and nuns led them along secret routes which had saved so many Allied lives to the boats waiting off the Italian coast to carry refugees to Palestine.

"Quotidie morior"—"Every day I die a little" had become the pope's increasingly frequent lament when he and Sister Pascalina were alone in the papal

apartment. He was now in his seventieth year and the war had taken its toll. With the coming of peace the demands on the papacy had increased as he focused on the urgent need to rebuild Europe while at the same time he had to deal with church affairs.

Sister Pascalina had noticed changes in his work habit. While he still held audiences and consistories, she saw that he displayed hesitation over decisions he had to take on Vatican affairs. The first whispers had started to surface in the media. "His papacy seems to have lost its intellectual virility and any sense of pastoral mission, any desire is fading to come to grips with the problems of the real world. He and his church are settling into childish, devoting dotage," wrote one critic.

Sister Pascalina could see that it was growing harder for her to keep the pope in touch with all the Vatican politicking. Still a powerful, practical pragmatist with an almost fanatical devotion to the pope, she ensured which orders of business, temporal or spiritual, would receive papal priority. Though she was still referred to as *la papessa* it was no longer with affection, but with caustic derision.

In November, 1944, Osborne became the last Allied diplomat to move out of the Vatican. His apartment in Santa Marta had been assigned to Weizsäcker and his wife; they would remain inside the Vatican until he returned to Germany to find the Americans were to put him on trial at Nuremberg. He was sentenced to seven years. By then Osborne had bought an apartment overlooking a fashionable area of the Tiber and he and O'Flaherty would play golf and reminisce about their wartime experiences as they walked the course.

In London, Sir Anthony Eden had paid tribute to Osborne for his years in Rome as "service under conditions which are unique in the history of diplomatic service."

Upon his retirement Osborne chose not to return to England and became involved in running a boys' club in Rome which fed one thousand members and paid for the education of three hundred. It was part of what he called, "my Rome fever to help the less fortunate." His health was failing, he had diabetes and heart trouble—and May was no longer there to make sure he took his tablets. His manservant had returned to London and, in the words of Sam Derry, "disappeared off the radar." Derry himself had done much the same, having been recruited into MI6 where he had an adventurous career during the Cold War.

In 1973 Osborne assumed the title of the duke of Leeds, in his seventieth year and the twelfth to hold the title. A year later he died on March 24, and was buried in Rome's Protestant cemetery. Among the huge crowd were representatives of England's Queen Elizabeth and the Queen Mother. Also there were members of the Boys Town of Italy which Monsignor Carroll-Abbing had founded in 1944 and became one of the most successful ventures in the reclaiming of boys—and later girls—from the ravages of war. The pope sent Father Leiber to represent the Holy See.

In his cell in Regina Coeli prison, *Obersturmbanführer* Herbert Kappler waited anxiously. Stripped of his rank and his SS uniform exchanged for drab prison garb, he was listed on the prison roll as a war criminal awaiting trial by an Italian tribunal. He was charged with having "a major responsibility in the Ardeatine Cave massacre" and of "extorting fifty kilograms of gold from the Jews of Rome." On both accounts he was accused of making "considerable patrimonial damages to the Jewish community of Rome."

After his capture by the Allied patrol he had been sent to Dachau for interrogation by American intelligence officers and then brought to a British interrogation center in Naples. Finally he had been handed over to the Italian administration in Rome.

He had already given evidence for the prosecution at the trial of *Stadtkommandant* Mälzer in Rome and later in Venice to testify against Field Marshal Kesselring. Both prisoners had argued that Kappler had told them the victims of the Ardeatine shootings were already under sentence of death for crimes against the German military code. Both Mälzer and Kesselring were condemned to die before a firing squad. Weeks later the sentences were commuted to life imprisonment. Mälzer died in a British military prison in March 1952. In that year Kesselring was released and returned to live in Germany, no doubt comforted that General Clark had written in his memoirs that Kesselring had fought a "hard but clean war." In Italy there were demonstrations against his release.

Since November 1946 Kappler had been held in Regina Coeli awaiting his own trial, spending his days writing letters to a variety of people whom he hoped would help him. Among them was Monsignor O'Flaherty. Already he had twice visited Kappler.

At first Kappler had spoken to him of his life in Stuttgart and how he had been recruited into the *Abwehr* and trained as a spy in Canaris's organization, and first came to Rome in 1939 to work in the German embassy and spy on the Mussolini regime. He insisted he despised Fascism. But Rome and its people he "loved as my second fatherland."

All this O'Flaherty had heard without comment. But gradually the talk had turned to religion. Kappler had no formal faith. Prison visiting time had been too short to explore further his beliefs and Kappler had told O'Flaherty that on his next visit he wished to discuss something "important."

Throughout that cold November afternoon he heard sounds of guards walking down the corridor and stopping at other cells to take a prisoner to meet a visitor. Finally one evening footsteps stopped outside his cell and a key turned in the lock. O'Flaherty entered.

When Kappler had first asked to see him O'Flaherty was astonished. Why would the man who had tried to have him killed want a meeting? Was it to confess his crimes? Then he should ask to see the prison chaplain. But finally O'Flaherty had gone to see the gestapo chief.

On his previous visits Kappler had described his work as "part of the reality of war." He had insisted he had opposed the plan for the deportation of the ghetto Jews and he insisted "my role in the Ardeatine Cave massacre was small. The orders came directly from Germany." He had continued to justify himself, outlining what would be his defense when he came to trial. But first he wanted to be baptized into the Catholic Church. If he was to be convicted and faced death for his crimes, he wanted to do so as a Christian in the grace of God. That was the "important" matter.

That evening, escorted by a warden, they had gone to the prison chapel where Kappler was baptized by Padre Rocca. Since then Kappler had attended Mass in the chapel every day while his trial dates continued to be postponed.

Finally in July 1948, Kappler was sentenced to life imprisonment for extorting the gold. On the second count of being present at the Ardeatine massacre he was sentenced to a further fifteen years. It was the severest penalty under the postwar Italian constitution. The prosecution team had included Ugo Foa, who had regained his position in the state judiciary system.

Kappler's first wife had divorced him while he was serving his sentence. In 1975 he was diagnosed with terminal cancer and moved to a hospital in Rome. There he met and married Anneliese, a nurse who had carried on a lengthy correspondence with Kappler before they had married in the hospital chapel. Appeals by both his wife and the West German government to release him were rejected by Italian authorities. Because of Kappler's deteriorating condition and his wife's nursing skills, she had been allowed almost unlimited access to him. On a visit in August 1977, she smuggled him out of the hospital and drove them to West Germany. The Italians demanded Kappler be returned, but the German government authorities refused to extradite him due to his ill health. He died on February 9, 1978 at home in Soltau at the age of seventy.

In June 1949 Koch was brought before the Italian High Court of Justice, sitting at the University of Rome to judge Fascist war crimes. He was found guilty of high crimes against the Resistance and handing over numerous Jews to the Germans to be deported. He was sentenced to death by firing squad.

In the hours before his execution he had written a letter of apology to the pope for his violation of the basilica of St. Paul's. That afternoon he knelt before the firing squad while the prison priest heard his confession. "I feel the weight of the tears of many others for what I have done and ask for forgiveness." The priest administered the last rites. Koch rose to his feet and stood before the firing squad and refused the proffered blindfold. Seventeen bullets penetrated his body. In a few days he would have been twenty-seven.

In 1960 the Vatican discussed with Monsignor O'Flaherty an appointment as a papal nuncio to Tanzania. But illness was already attacking his body after a stroke. That year he retired from the Holy See and returned to live in Ireland. He died on October 30, 1963. A year later a grove of trees, sent from Rome, was planted in Ireland's national park in Killarney in his memory.

Bishop Alois Hudal was asked to resign from the German college in 1952 after the pope became aware of the full extent of his help to Nazi war criminals to escape justice and live their lives in foreign countries, mostly South America. They included Franz Stangl, the *Kommandant* of Treblinka and Sobibor; Gustav Wagner, deputy commander of Sobibor; Klaus Barbie; and Adolf Eichmann. Hudal had provided them—and hundreds more Nazis—with false papers and arranged for many to have Vatican passports posing as priests. In his memoirs, *Römische Tagebücher: Lebensbeichte eines alten Bischofs* (*Diaries of Rome: The Confession of Life of an Old Bishop*), he boasted that "over thirty thousand so-called war criminals made their way to freedom and I thank God that He allowed me to help them escape."

Barred from the Vatican, Hudal lived out his years in his sumptuous residence in Grottaferrata near Rome. There would be persistant rumors that the money to pay for his lifestyle came from Nazi supporters. He devoted his days to writing bitter attacks on the pope and the Vatican for failing to recognize that "a bargain between National Socialism and Christianity is the only way into the future." He died in 1962 and is buried in Rome's Campo Santo Teutonico cemetery. His grave is never without flowers. Who provides them has remained a mystery. Within Nazi circles he would continue to be called "Our Scarlet Pimpernel."

At the end of the war in 1945 Settimia Spizzichino came home on September 11. She was the only woman of the seventeen ghetto survivors of the October roundup. Her weight loss was the result of the experiments Dr. Mengele had performed on her and she would forever bear the scars. On the day of her liberation she had been found sheltering under a pile of bodies. She was twenty-four years old. On her arm was tattooed the number 67210 corresponding to the number on her admission paper to Auschwitz.

The train which carried her back into Italy was marginally only more bearable than the one which had deported her along with her mother and sisters, and over a thousand other ghetto Jews to Auschwitz. The train had been met north of Rome by an "assistance committee." Each man was given a packet of razor blades and a bar of soap. Settimia received only the soap. After a wash in the railway station toilets they continued their journey to Rome.

Settimia returned to her home on Via della Reginella to find it had been completely plundered. The thieves had even taken the family photograph which had hung in the kitchen. She didn't cry; she had long forgotten how to. For days she had remained alone in the house, sitting on the floor; the furniture had been removed. Outside she could hear the sounds of the ghetto.

In her mind the stolen months of her life were too painful to talk about to people who called to bring food, to offer to replace the furniture, to do anything for this young woman who had returned from the dead. One day another knock came. Standing there was her father, Mose. It was a moment that no words would convey, that neither wanted to share with anyone else. All she would ever say was that "the emotion we both felt can never be felt by any outsider."

In the weeks to come she would increasingly find life in postwar Rome difficult. There were new faces in the ghetto. Some nodded and hurried on; many avoided her. The other survivors told her it was the same for them. "We were a reminder of how many had not come back. People didn't want to hear. It was as if we should not have come back," Settimia would say.

She began to plan what she must do. "Memory is my duty," she told one of the survivors. She said that every year there must be a commemoration. "I made a promise to God. I didn't know whether to curse Him or pray to Him. I prayed. I said, Lord save me; save me to do what I must do when I am back."

Settimia and the other survivors suffered various physiological or psychological impairments; in her case it was crippling headaches and a nervous stutter.

In 1968, under a bilateral agreement between Italy and West Germany, a "global indemnity" of ten million dollars was given to the Italian government "in settlement forever." The sum was to be divided among 17,700 persons: 3,899 survivors of the Nazi camps and nearly 14,000 relatives of deportees who died there. The one-time payment, in Settimia's name, came to $564. The blue numbers scarred on her forearm—the brand mark of Auschwitz—and her eyes carried the memory of what had happened to her.

In 1955 Settimia revisited Auschwitz accompanied by a documentary film crew. She stood underneath the arch with its words ARBEIT MACHT FREI and spoke: "I again feel my fears and anguish. These emotions cannot be described or filmed. Those are things that no book or screen can ever portray. I will never forgive."

In 1995 she had told another BBC documentary: "I came back from Auschwitz on my own. I lost my mother, two sisters, one brother, and my niece. Pius XII could have warned us about what was going to happen. We might have escaped from Rome and joined the partisans. He played right into the Germans' hands. It all happened right under his nose. But he was an anti-Semitic pope, a pro-German pope. He didn't take a single risk. And when they say the pope is like Jesus Christ, it is not true. He did not save a single child. Nothing."

In August 2000 she died in Rome at the age of seventy-nine.

She would carry to her grave the memory of a near neighbor who increasingly stood before the world accused of not doing enough to save the Jews—Pope Pius XII.

EPILOGUE

CONFLICT

On November 20, 1945 the pope had received in audience eighty representatives freed from various concentration camps in the Third Reich who had come to thank him for his help in saving Jewish lives. He told them he was sure they had held firm in their humanity and steadfastly clung to their values in the cruel circumstances in which they were held in that world of darkness and despair. When he delivered his blessing some believed they saw behind his glasses his eyes close to tears.

It was the first of many moving and eloquent tributes which Pius XII would receive in the postwar years. Across the Diaspora various examples were cited in the Jewish press and in synagogues of the Vatican's efforts to save the Jews.

The Jewish World Congress donated twenty thousand dollars to Vatican charities "in recognition of the work of the Holy See in rescuing Jews from Nazi persecution." Other Jewish relief agencies in Canada, Australia, and South Africa also made donations. Thousands of messages had come from all over the world from other religious communities.

While ensuring everyone received a suitable response—many prepared by Sister Luke and her assistants for him to sign—Pius had to fit into his busy day delegations from all over the world who also wanted to thank him. They represented not only Catholics but other religions. There were also the wartime leaders to meet. Winston Churchill had been accompanied by Harold Macmillan, a future prime minister of Britain but in 1945 the Allies' chief political officer in Italy. He had found Pius "a saintly man, rather worried, obviously selfless and holy with a birdlike mind that flitted from one point to another."

Cardinal Secretary of State Maglione's recent death had led to the pope's decision to take on his duties. It was one that had concerned Maglione's two assistants, Montini and Tardini. The pope told them: "I don't need colleagues, but people who will obey." To Tardini Pius had become "alone in his work, alone in his struggle."

The postwar years continued to be busy for Pius. To Catholics he was the dauntless champion of mankind's spiritual glory. To non-Catholics he was a statesman, a world leader who had sought to prevent World War Two through personal intervention, a man who had fought against Communism, its purges and wholescale arrests of priests and nuns, and imprisonment of their cardinals behind the Iron Curtain. Despite that, the Catholic Church had grown by 1954 to 496 million the largest church in the world. It had been achieved through his writings which promised reform in Catholic teaching and make it more relevant and accessible to the faithful.

Catholic scholars and ecclesiastics agreed that his most significant theological decision had been in 1950 when he proclaimed the dogma of the Virgin Mary's bodily ascension to Heaven. It was the climax to the jubilee Holy Year ceremony in St. Peter's Square before half a million pilgrims from all over the world.

It was followed by the encyclical *Humani Generis* in which Pius made clear that he had no objection to further research into Darwin's theory of evolution which had been denounced by other churchmen, but also insisted that "souls are immediately created by God."

The first serious illness of his pontificate came after the exhausting ceremonies of the consistory in January, 1953. For two months he was virtually bedridden in his apartment with a chest infection. Even then as he began to recover he found time to write and read. His doctors were delighted with his stamina and, they decided, he was fully recovered and able to study the affairs of the various congregations, tribunals, and offices on such matters as heresy, priestly formation, and the activities of the church around the world.

He also announced his position on several problems of the time. He called for an international penal code to punish war criminals and those who had been able to flee their homelands to escape justice. He reiterated the church's ban on birth control and urged doctors and especially psychiatrists to respect their patient's personality. In that year's Christmas message he called for a united Europe.

Early in 1954 he fell ill again, this time with a severe attack of gastritis. The acute stage of the illness was accompanied by hiccups—forcing him to cancel all audiences until March of that year when he stood at his bedroom window and blessed the huge crowd gathered below.

That summer he suffered a recurrence of his gastritis at his summer residence at Castel Gandolfo. He returned to the Vatican, thinner and paler. Thousands of pilgrims stood for hours every day in St. Peter's Square to wave toward his closed window—a further sign that he had become more loved as no other pope before him. By December 1954, he had received more than ten million persons in mass audiences during his pontificate.

There was talk in the secretariat of state that in the New Year he would like to go to the Middle East to see if he could lift the shadow of war between the Arab states and Israel. Any such talk ended with the news on Vatican Radio on December 2, 1954. It reported that the pope was once more seriously ill. For days a team of five doctors had struggled to save his life, feeding him intravenously. He improved sufficiently to be X-rayed to reveal he was suffering from gastritis and hernia of the esophagus. Vatican Radio announced that at the peak of his illness Pius had seen "the sweet person of Jesus Christ at his bedside."

Illness now became a constant companion for the pope. Each time his doctors managed to save him. But they conceded among themselves it was a miracle that he lived, once more becoming strong enough to address the world's problems. More than once he spoke of his admiration for the fifty million communicants behind the Iron Curtain.

On Monday October 6, 1958, he suffered a stroke which left him paralyzed and weak and he received the last rites. The following day he suffered a second stroke. Vatican Radio announced there was little hope of recovery. That afternoon the station reported the pope had suffered a grave cardiopulmonary collapse. Just before sundown the radio's medical bulletin announced that Pius had developed pneumonia and his doctors were in attendance with oxygen and blood plasma.

That night the head of the medical team, Professor Antonio Gasbarrini, told the group gathered at the bedside that death was near. They began to recite prayers for the dying. A choking, rasping sound came from the unconscious pope.

Sister Pascalina gently wiped his lips with water during the prayers. At one point she took the crucifix, which had been resting on the pope's chest and put it to his mouth.

At 3:52 A.M. on Thursday, October 8, Professor Gasbarrini placed a stethoscope to the pontiff's chest, felt the pulse, and turned to the others and said: *"È morto"*—he is dead.

Monsignor Tardini repeated the words: *"È morto."* He then recited the inspiring *Magnificat*.

> *My soul doth magnify the Lord*
> *My spirit doth rejoice in Him.*
> All present filed slowly past the pope's deathbed out of the room.

The church bells of Rome tolled the start of nine days of official mourning. By midday the cardinals had elected Benedetto Masella as camerlengo to organize the funeral and set in motion the ancient ritual of conclave to elect a successor to the eighty-two-year-old Pius who Vatican Radio was calling the "Pope of Peace" during a reign which had lasted nineteen years, seven months, and seven days. Messages of condolence began to come from political and religious leaders around the world.

Only Moscow expressed no sorrow. For hours Moscow Radio did not even mention the pope's death. The Soviet Union had jammed news bulletins about his condition.

More than two million mourners would process through St. Peter's Basilica where the pope lay upon the high altar under Michelangelo's great dome. Guardia Palatina watched over the catafalque. Beside it were the three coffins in which the corpse would be placed.

Television cameras, the first to be allowed to film a papal funeral, discreetly moved their focus from the body as it was placed in the first coffin. The face was covered with a silk square, and the body wrapped in a crimson shroud. The coffin was placed in the second casket. The funeral eulogy was placed in a brass tube along with a purse containing gold, silver, and bronze coins which had been minted during his pontificate. The second coffin was sealed with silk ribbons and placed in a case of lead. Finally the third casket of elm was secured with golden nails and the huge weight of the triple coffin was wheeled past the high altar and lowered on pulleys into the grotto below. It came to rest twenty feet from the tomb of Saint Peter.

That night Sister Pascalina entered in her diary, "The world is on the eve of a new era. Let us not forget all His Holiness has done to help so many people."

She died in 1983 and is buried in the Vatican cemetery. Among those who attended her funeral was Cardinal Ratzinger, the future Pope Benedict XVI. She was eighty-two years old.

On an autumn afternoon in October, 1958, Golda Meir, the state of Israel's foreign minister, stood at the lectern in the United Nations Assembly in New York. Over the past decade she had addressed the delegates many times. But never had she spoken on an issue she feared would divide her own people.

But Golda Meir was determined to deliver her eulogy. In her plain black dress, unrelieved by a broach, bracelet, or necklace, she looked like a woman mourning for the six million victims of the Holocaust. Yet when she spoke there was a certainty in her voice.

"When fearful martyrdom came to our people in the decade of Nazi terror, the words of Pope Pius XII were raised for the victims. The life of our times was enriched by a voice speaking out with great moral truths above the tumult of daily conflict. We mourn a great servant of peace."

———

From Moscow came the first attack on Pius. *Pravda* published a series of bizarre articles that Pius didn't just "accept Hitler but agreed with him about everything; that the pope had secretly worked with Mussolini."

The defamation and evisceration was under way. His praise was brushed aside as articles began to appear in Europe and the United States linking him to racial hatred and Vatican nefariousness toward the Jews. It was no longer enough to attack him for his alleged wartime attitude—"the pope who remained silent during the Holocaust." He stood accused of hating all Jews. Centuries of suffering and humility inflicted on Jews were used to support attacks on Pius in newspapers, radio, and television. Questions came with repetitive speed. Why had the pope not warned the Jews that mass extermination was about to happen? Why had he not published an encyclical during the war condemning the Holocaust? Why had he stayed neutral? The tsunami of questions threatened to drown out the voices of those who tried to defend Pius. Often well crafted to provoke anger and indignation the articles lacked one item: truth. Instead half-truths and misrepresentations were trundled out. Who can doubt that in Moscow Stalin smiled.

That first wave of attacks set in motion an avalanche of other revisionists to tramp their own pathways through the life and war of Pius XII. It climaxed, at least momentarily, with the production of Rolf Hochhuth's play, *The Deputy,* with its portrait of a financially greedy pontiff who was silent about the Holocaust. Then came John Cornwell's *Hitler's Pope,* a book with a title guaranteed to make the pope's critics salivate. Soon other titles appeared with the pope, Hitler, the Vatican, and the Nazis linked on their covers. Along the way Pius was singled out as "merely the puppet of his German housekeeper," Sister Pascalina.

Such attacks are an outrage against history. There is also about them a sameness: that Pius led an institutionally anti-Semitic church; that he suffered from a pathological fear of Communism; that he paid little attention to the murder of six million Jews. Those who tried to answer the smears spent endless time trying to refute the claims and in some cases made a dent in the attacks. But they went on. In London Peter Stanford, a one-time editor of a Catholic publication, was given space in *The Sunday Times,* to describe Pius as a "war criminal." As far as attacks went it was par for the course in its lack of evidence.

Yet evidence already existed to totally refute the claims. They are available in Pius's own words in which he expresses his very forceful attacks on anti-Semitism, Hitler, Nazis, and the Holocaust—effectively destroying the charge he was "silent." The evidence has been assembled by the distinguished Catholic historian, William Doino, Jr. It is both a remarkable document and one that any critic of Pope Pius XII should read before launching yet another attack on Pius.

Those who continue to do so insist they are motivated by a search for the truth. Yet Pinchas Lapide, a former Israeli diplomat, declared in his book, *Three Popes and the Jews* that the church under Pius "was instrumental in saving at least 700,000, but probably as many as 860,000 Jews from certain death at Nazi hands."

It is a claim not one of the pope's attackers have yet been able to demolish. Michael Tagliacozzo, indisputably the leading authority on Roman Jews during the Holocaust has a folder on his desk entitled "Calumnies against Pius XII. Without him many of our own would not be alive."

Richard Breitman, one of four historians authorized to study U.S. World War Two espionage files confirmed that "the secret documents prove the extent to which Hitler distrusted the Holy See because it hid Jews."

A study of those secret German intercepts by U.S. and British code breakers provide evidence which further gainsay other allegations against Pope Pius XII.

Some of his critics say they write because they want to make sure the Jews and the Holocaust are never forgotten. They forget that in 1943, Chaim Weizmann, who would become Israel's first president, wrote that "the Holy See is lending its powerful help wherever it can, to mitigate the fate of my persecuted coreligionists." In 1944, the chief rabbi of Jerusalem, Isaac Herzog, sent a message to the pope: "The people of Israel will never forget what His Holiness and his illustrious delegates, inspired by the eternal principles of religion which are the foundations of genuine civilization, are doing for our unfortunate brothers and sisters at the most tragic hour in our history."

Moshe Sharett, Israel's second prime minister, met with the pope in 1952. He told him "my first duty is to thank you, and through you the Catholic Church, on behalf of the Jewish public for all they have done in various countries to rescue Jews."

None of them would ever have called Pius "silent." In attacking him now, his critics show an ill-informed, devious, and self-serving attitude—that does no more than abuse the memory of the Holocaust. The pope was not "Hitler's pope" but very likely the closest the Jews had come to having a papal voice in the Vatican when it mattered most.

On December 19, 2009 Pope Benedict XVI authorized the Congregation for the Causes of the Saints that Pope Pius XII should be declared "venerable," the first of three steps before canonization. Both Jewish and Catholic scholars asked Benedict to delay a church investigation to conclude that Pius "lived a life of exemplary holiness and heroic virtue." They wanted further time for World War Two archives to be studied. The scholars said fully accessible archives only go up to 1939. They were told that sixteen million files cover the period relating to the wartime.

Benedict had been first asked to process the cause of Pius XII in 2007 but had put the process on hold for a "period of reflection." Father Peter Gumpel, a German Jesuit priest and a Vatican historian who has to date spent twenty years supporting Pius's cause for sainthood said he was "delighted by the decision for reflection as it would enable the accusation that Pius was anti-Semitic or anti-Judaic to be dismissed as absolutely nonsense."

In 2001, Aharon Lopez, who had just retired from his position as Israel's ambassador to the Holy See said, "Justice however, should not only be done, it must be seen to be done. Hundreds of thousands of Holocaust survivors are alive. They are entitled to have all their questions on Pius XII and the church's behavior answered. It is the least one could expect from the Vatican, an important component of the international community. The beatification of Pope Pius XII is a traumatic test case. Even more so as the Vatican speaks about expiation and atonement and its desire to contribute to the correction of the terrible moral evil done to the Jewish people."

SOURCES

The Vatican has a seventy-five-year rule of secrecy to protect its release of sensitive documents. While sustained pressure has helped to make the Holy See publish a selection of those relating to its decisions in World War Two, it may not be until 2020 that the remainder of the wartime documentation will appear. Until then they will remain in their repository in the *L'Archivio Segreto Vaticano,* arguably the most secret archive in the world.

Those wartime files—a sizeable library of papers—will finally end the controversy that Pius was "Hitler's pope" and silence the argument that he is not worthy to become a saint of the Roman Catholic Church. To his opponents he is no more than a man of faith as the 262nd successor to St. Peter. For them remains the question: Did he really speak out against the Holocaust and genuinely help to save the Jews? Those who do now reluctantly concede he did try, say it was still not enough to justify him being made a saint.

Searching for an answer to their opposition and whether it is justified, motivated me to write this book.

Having written three books on the Vatican—*Pontiff* (1983) and *The Year of Armageddon* (1984) with Max Morgan-Witts, together with *Desire and Denial: Celibacy and the Church* (1986), I knew there were men and women, nuns and priests, within the Vatican walls who would be ready to once more help me. Even so the Vatican is an institution baffling in its complexity and in many ways still mysterious. What would make their answers valuable in unpicking the controversy surrounding Pius XII was that they were "insiders." One worked in the Holy Office; another worked in the secretariat of state, the Vatican Foreign Office; others worked in various congregations and tribunals. Some asked for their contributions to go unacknowledged and probably spoke for several others when they said they were not seeking recognition, only the satisfaction of knowing they had tried to help in explaining the role of Pius during World War Two—especially the network the pope set up to help Jews of the Rome ghetto and the escaped Allied prisoners of war who were hiding in the city. I saw then how the theme of the book and its title could work.

Among those who helped me was Sister Margherita Marchione. She is a Fulbright Scholar, holds a Ph.D from Columbia University, and is a member of the Religious Teachers Filippini, one of the most respected of the church's teaching orders. She is also a passionate supporter for the beatification of Pope Pius. In all her books she makes no secret of her support, insisting that not only have his many critics defamed Pius but there is ample evidence to prove he did help the Jews during World War Two. She is one of the few scholars who has been given permission to research his wartime record in the Secret Archives. She made material available to me, along with many of the original photographs which appear in this book.

She urged me to rekindle my relationship with the writings of Father Robert A. Graham, an expert on Holy See diplomacy during World War Two. He is a prime source on Nazi espionage against the Vatican. His insights provided an element of the Vatican at war which went deeper than the material he had shared with me in *Pontiff*. He was one of four Jesuit scholars who edited *Acts and Documents of the Holy See,* an essential guide to the war years in the Vatican. His death in 1997 is a loss to historians of the intelligence world. But I have tried to ensure that his knowledge is a reminder of the moods and attitudes in wartime Rome.

In her usual generous way of opening doors Sister Margherita arranged for me to contact William Doino, Jr., a Vaticanologist whose studies of the reign of Pius XII had already made him a respected authority. From his California office came a steady flow of e-mails culminating in his own eighty-thousand-word essay which lay out all the aspects of the controversy surrounding the role of Pius in relation to the Holocaust.

The focus of his argument is that the pope had not remained "silent" and was not "Hitler's pope." He listed documents and articles I had not heard of before, among them: Yossi Klein Halevi's "Catholicism Is Our Friend" in the *Jerusalem Post*; "Dabru Emet: A Jewish Statement of Christians and Christianity," signed by 170 Jewish scholars, which repudiated attempts to blame the Holocaust on Christianity.

He directed me to the Sisters of Our Lady of Sion in Rome who foster a Catholic-Jewish alliance. He suggested Web sites to look at, and yet more books to read. His help was a master class in coming to understand that Pius had not remained "silent," let alone had been "Hitler's pope." The more I read, and the more my wife, Edith, discovered with her tireless Internet research and her linguistic skills, the more it became clear that the evidence supported the answers I was seeking: Pius had condemned anti-Semitism, racism, and genocide, before, during, and after the Holocaust.

Father David Jaeger, at the Vatican secretariat of state, an authority on Jewish-Christian relations, enabled me to understand aspects of the relationship between Pius and the Jews of the ghetto.

Father Giancarlo Centioni who, at the age of ninety-seven in 2010 would recall how, as a member of the Pallottine fathers, he had worked alongside Father Anton Weber to help Jews escape from Europe. He revealed that "money and passports were received in the name of and paid for by Pius XII. I had at least twelve German priests working with me."

In Ireland, Deirdre Waldron's campaign to have Hugh O'Flaherty recognized by Yad Vashem in their list of "Righteous Among the Nations" has continued for him to join 23,788 from forty-five countries who have received the honorific used by the State of Israel to describe non-Jews who risked their lives during the Holocaust to save Jews.

Marco Cavallarin, together with his cousin, Luciana Tedesco, provided between them the first detailed accounts of Dr. Vittorio Sacerdoti and Professor Giovanni Borromeo and the *Fatebenefratelli*.

Cesare Sacerdoti, a former publisher, provided his own account of his life in Italy in 1943 after the roundup. His notes are a moving insight into a life shared by many ghetto families who were hidden by the church.

Rosina Sorani's diary provided a powerful insight into what she called "Chronicles of Infamy," her day-by-day account of her life in wartime Rome.

A number of personal interviews were conducted by either myself or the research team. But I would like to convey my thanks to all those who were approached so frequently and at some length and who always answered questions patiently, even though they must have sometimes reopened painful memories.

SELECT BIBLIOGRAPHY

Alvarez, David and Graham, Robert A. *Nothing Sacred: Nazi Espionage Against the Vatican, 1939–1945*. Routledge, London 1997.

Ascarelli, A. *Le Fosse Ardeatine*. Canesi, Bologna 1965.

Bassett, Richard. *Hitler's Spy Chief: The Wilhelm Canaris Mystery*. Weidenfeld & Nicolson, London 2005.

Blet, Pierre et al. (Eds.) *Actes et du Saint Siège relatifs à la Seconde Guerre Mondiale*. 11 vols. Vatican City 1965–81.

Bottum, Joseph and Dalin, David G. *The Pius War: Responses to the Critics of Pius XII*, Lexington Books; Lanham, Maryland 2004.

Breitman, Richard et al. *U.S. Intelligence and the Nazis*. Cambridge University Press 2005.

Brown, Anthony Cave. *Bodyguard of Lies*. Harper & Row, New York 1975.

Carroll-Abbing, Monsignor J. Patrick. *But for the Grace of God*. Secker & Warburg, London 1966.

Chadwick, Owen. *Britain and the Vatican during the Second World War*. Cambridge University Press, Cambridge 1987.

Ciano, G. *Ciano's Hidden Diary, 1937–1938*. E.P. Dutton & Co., New York 1953.

Cornwell, John. *Hitler's Pope: The Secret History of Pius XII*. Viking Press, New York 1999.

Dalin, Rabbi David G. *The Myth of Hitler's Pope: How Pope Pius XII Rescued Jews from the Nazis.*Regency Publishing, Inc.; Washington, DC 2005.

Dalla Torre, G. *Memorie.* Verona 1967.

Debenedetti, Giacomo. *October 16, 1943: Eight Jews.* University of Notre Dame Press; Notre Dame, Indiana 2001.

Derry, Sam I. *The Rome Escape Line.* Harrap 1960.

Dollman, Eugenio. *Roma Nazista.* Longanesi & Co., Milano 1949.

Falconi, Carlo. *The Silence of Pius XII.* Faber and Faber, London 1970.

Fleming, Brian. *The Vatican Pimpernel: The Wartime Exploits of Monsignor Hugh O'Flaherty.* The Collins Press, Cork 2008

Foot, M. R. D. and Langley J. M. *MI9: Escape and Evasion 1939–1945.* The Bodley Head, London 1979.

Gallagher, J. P. *Scarlet Pimpernel of the Vatican.* Fontana, London 1967.

Gallergher, Charles R. *Vatican Secret Diplomacy: Joseph Hurley and Pope Pius XII.* Yale University Press 2008

Graham, Robert A. *Pius XII's Defense of Jews and Others: 1944–1945.* Catholic League For Religious and Civil Rights, Milwaukee. 1962.

Ibid. *Vatican Diplomacy: A Study of Church and State on the International Plane.* Princeton University Press, Princeton 1959.

Gregorovius, Ferdinand. *The Ghetto and the Jews of Rome.* Schocken Books, New York 1966.

Hochhuth, Rolf. *The Deputy.* Grove Press, New York 1967.

Hudal, Alois. *Die Grundlagen des Nationalsozialismus: Eine Ideengeschichtliche Unter-suchung.* Johannes Gunther Verlag, Leipzig 1937.

Immermann, Joshua D. (Edited by Yoshiva University.) *Jews in Italy Under Fascist and Nazi Rule, 1922–1945.* Cambridge University Press, New York 2009.

Katz, Robert. *Black Sabbath: A Journey Through a Crime Against Humanity.* Arthur Barker Ltd., London 1969.

Ibid. *Death in Rome.* Duke of Cornwall's Light Infantry (Regimental History Committee), 1967.

Ibid. *Fatal Silence: The Pope, the Resistance and the German Occupation of Rome.* Weidenfeld & Nicolson, London 2003.

Knopp, Guido. *Hitler's Holocaust.* Sutton Publishing, Stroud 2001.

Kurzman, Dan. *The Race for Rome.* Doubleday & Co., New York 1975.

Lamb, Richard. *War in Italy 1943–1945. A Brutal Story.* St. Martin's Press, New York 1994.

Lapide, Pinchas E. *The Last Three Popes and the Jews.* Souvenir Press, London 1967.

Lehnert, Pascalina. *Ich Durfte Ihm Dienen : Erinnerungen and Papst Pius XII.* Naumann, Würzburg 1983.

Marchione, Sister Margherita. *Did Pope Pius XII Help the Jews?* Paulist Press, New York 2007.

Ibid *Shepherd of Souls: A Pictorial Life of Pope XII.* Paulist Press International, New York 2002.

Ibid. *Yours Is a Precious Witness: Memoirs of Jews and Catholics in Wartime Italy.* Paulist Press, New York 1997.

Milano, A. *Il Ghetto di Roma.* Staderni, Rome 1964.

Morley, John F. *Vatican Diplomacy and the Jews during the Holocaust 1939–1943.* Ktav Publishing House, New York 1980.

Portelli, Alessandro. *The Order Has Been Carried Out: History, Memory, and Meaning of a Nazi Massacre in Rome.* Palgrave Macmillan, New York 2007.

Rhodes, Anthony. *The Vatican in the Age of the Dictators 1922–1945.* Hodder & Stoughton, London 1973.

Roth, C. *The History of the Jews of Italy.* Jewish Publication Society, Philadelphia 1946.

Rychlak, Ronald J. *Hitler, the War, and the Pope.* Our Sunday Visitor, Huntington 2000.

Scivener, Jane. *Inside Rome with the Germans.* The Macmillan Co., New York 1945.

Sorani, Settimio. *Che Cosa Chiediamo al Nuovo Consiglio.* Tipografia Del Senato, Rome 1945.

Tagliacozzo, Michael. *"La Comunita" di Roma Sotto L'incubo della Svastica—La Grande Razzia del Ottobre 1943 in Gli Ebrei in Italia Durante il Fascism* a cura di Guido Valabrega Quaderni del Centro di Documentazione Ebraica Contemporanea Sezione Italiana, Milano 1963.

Tedesco, Luciana. *Ragazzi Nella Shoa.* Paoline, Milan 2010.

Tittmann, Harold H., Jr. (Edited by Harold H. Tittmann III.) *Inside the Vatican of Pius XII: The Memoir of an American Diplomat During World War II.* Doubleday, New York 2004.

Trachtenberg, Joshua. *The Devil and the Jews: The Medieval Conception of the Jew and its Relation to Modern Antisemitism.* Yale University Press, New Haven 1943.

Trevellyan, Raleigh. *Rome '44: The Battle for the Eternal City*. The Viking Press, New York 1981.

Waagenaar, Sam. *The Pope's Jews*. Alcove Press, London 1974.

Walker, Stephen. *Hide & Seek: The Irish Priest in the Vatican who Defied the Nazi Command*. Harper Collins, London 2011.

Weizsäcker, Ernst von. *Memories of Ernst von Weizsäcker*. Victor Gollancz, London 1951.

Zolli, E. *Before the Dawn*. Ignatius Press, San Francisco 2008.

Zucotti, Susan. *The Italian and the Holocaust: Persecution, Rescue and Survival*. Basic Books, Inc. Publishers, New York 1987.

Ibid. *Under His Very Windows*. Yale University Press, New Haven 2000.

INDEX